LAND AND FRESH-WATER MAMMALS OF THE UNGAVA PENINSULA

To
  Herbert L. Stoddard
     with the sincere regards of
        Francis Harper
September 17, 1961

Land and Fresh-water Mammals of the Ungava Peninsula

BY
FRANCIS HARPER

Biological investigations in this region in 1953 were supported by the Arctic Institute of North America (through contractual arrangements with the Office of Naval Research) and by the Research and Development Division, Office of The Surgeon General, Department of the Army. The results are being prepared for publication under a grant from the National Science Foundation.

Reproduction in whole or in part is permitted for any purpose of the United States Government.

UNIVERSITY OF KANSAS
LAWRENCE · KANSAS

University of Kansas
Museum of Natural History

EDITOR: E. RAYMOND HALL

Miscellaneous Publication No. 27, pp. 1–178, 8 pls., 3 figs., 45 maps.

Published August 11, 1961

Means for publication were supplied by the National Science Foundation

PRINTED
IN
U.S.A.
THE ALLEN PRESS
Lawrence, Kansas
1961

CONTENTS

	Page
INTRODUCTION	9
Previous investigations	9
Investigations in 1953	11
Physiography and vegetation	15
Climate, faunal distribution, and life-zones	15
Comparative abundance of species	21
French and Montagnais names of mammals	23
Names of plants	23
Summation of distributional records	25
Explanation of maps	26
Conservation	27
Nomenclature	29
Measurements and weights	29
Color terms	29
Acknowledgments	29
ACCOUNTS OF SPECIES	31
PLATES 1–8 _following_	128
DISTRIBUTIONAL MAPS—4–45	145
A SYSTEMATIC LIST OF MAMMALIAN ECTOPARASITES, WITH HOST RECORDS, FROM THE UNGAVA PENINSULA	152
LITERATURE CITED	156
INDEX	171

INTRODUCTION

The general paucity of information hitherto available concerning the distribution of mammals over the greater part of the interior of the Ungava Peninsula has made it a particularly inviting field for study. I was anxious to investigate life histories and ecological relations before they had been appreciably affected by the mining and other industrial developments that have inaugurated a new era in the vast interior wilds. By 1954 the Quebec North Shore and Labrador Railway had reached Knob Lake and had begun to transport iron ore to the port of Seven Islands, 360 miles to the southward on the Gulf of St. Lawrence. It was a rare privilege to be able to spend a season on that biological frontier while natural conditions prevailed for the most part.

The present report deals with the land and fresh-water mammals of the peninsula. A few in the latter category occur also—in fact, predominantly—in salt water; these are *Delphinapterus leucas*, *Thalarctos maritimus*, and *Phoca vitulina concolor*.

A total of approximately 49 species, with some 29 additional subspecies, have been recorded. Some of these were not observed or collected by myself, but are included on the basis of records in the literature or of unpublished information obtained from friends and acquaintances.

Previous investigations

The records of mammalogical observations in the interior of the Ungava Peninsula go back at least as far as 1792, when André Michaux, the French botanist, traveling by way of Lake St. John, penetrated as far as Lake Mistassini and the upper waters of Rupert River. His journal, published in 1889, makes brief references to nine species of mammals occurring between Lakes St. John and Mistassini. William Mendry in 1828? and Nicol Finlayson in 1830 crossed from Richmond Gulf on Hudson Bay to the lower Koksoak River by way of the Larch River; and their journals (in the Hudson's Bay Company's Archives) contain a few notes on mammals. John McLean was probably the first white man to make a traverse of the main part of the peninsula—from Fort Chimo to Northwest River in 1839; and on this journey he discovered Grand Falls on the Hamilton River. His notes (1849; 1932) refer occasionally to game and fur-bearing mammals.

While maintaining headquarters at Fort Chimo from 1882 to 1884, Lucien M. Turner went inland at least as far as The Forks (junction of the Kaniapiskau and Larch rivers). He was one of the most accomplished and versatile naturalists who have studied the regional fauna. Several of his papers are cited in the appended bibliography; but some of his finest work is still in manuscript form. Notable among his collected material at the United States National Museum are a skin or two and about a dozen skulls (with antlers) of Cabot's or the Labrador Barren Ground Caribou.

In the 1880's and 1890's A. P. Low, of the Geological Survey of Canada, made a remarkable series of geological reconnaissances along many of the rivers and lakes of the region. He maintained an active interest in the fauna and included notes thereon in the several papers cited in the bibliography. His annotated list of the mammals (1896:313–321) has remained the chief single source of information on the species of the far interior, although the specific locality records that it presents are comparatively few in number.

Napoleon A. Comeau bore the distinction of being one of the few resident naturalists in the peninsula. His headquarters were at Godbout, where he was visited by Dr. C. Hart Merriam. The several editions of his *Life and Sport on the North Shore of the Lower St. Lawrence and Gulf* (1909; 1923; 1954) constitute a mine of information on the local mammals, birds, and fishes.

In 1903 Leonidas Hubbard, Jr., and Dillon Wallace made a canoe journey from Northwest River by way of Grand Lake, Susan River, and a series of small lakes almost to Michikamau Lake, when they were forced to turn back. Hubbard succumbed on the return journey. Two years later Mrs. Hubbard, with several canoemen, reached Michikamau Lake by way of the Naskaupi River and then descended the George River to its mouth on Ungava Bay—a remarkable feat for one without previous experience in the interior wilderness. She was followed over much the same route, a little later in the season, by Wallace. Notes on various mammals observed (particularly Caribou) are included in publications by Mrs. Hubbard (1906; 1908) and by Wallace (1906; 1907).

H. Hesketh Prichard, a British sportsman, traveled across the eastern Barren Grounds in 1910 from the Atlantic Coast to Indian House Lake. His volume (1911) contains useful information on Wolves, Bears, and Caribou. After successive trips in the same general area, William B. Cabot (1912a) produced a Labrador classic, with an outstanding essay on the recurring peak populations of mice in the Barrens. His book is also notable for its glimpses of Barren Ground Caribou and for its insight into the way of life of the Naskapi during the years before the dearth of Caribou drove them to the coast.

T. H. Manning, in addition to extensive travels along the coasts of Hudson and James bays, has made brief sojourns in the interior at such widely separated points as Bienville, Minto, Mushalagan, Panchia, and Sawbill lakes. His records of mammal distribution appear chiefly in a paper of 1947. J. Kenneth Doutt (1939; 1942; 1954) has made various trips in the interior (especially to Lower Seal Lake and along the Hamilton River) as well as along the coasts. Some of his results appear in papers of 1942 and 1954. Austin W. Cameron and his associates have investigated and reported (1950; 1951) upon the mammals of the Lake St. John and Lake Mistassini areas. During the summer of 1949 Carl R. Eklund (1957) made notes on eight species of mammals in the northwestern part of the peninsula, from the Koksoak and Larch rivers northward. Dale J. Osborn spent the seasons of 1951 and 1952 investigating mammals in the Knob Lake area and elsewhere in the interior.

Outram Bangs and Rudolph M. Anderson have published extensively on the mammals of the region, but have based their work on the collections of others. Bangs was particularly active from 1896 to 1900, and Anderson from 1934 to 1948, as indicated in the "Literature Cited" in the present report; they have described and named a large proportion of the mammals peculiar to the Ungava Peninsula.

This slight review is restricted mainly to work done in the interior of the peninsula. For references to several additional investigations, covering various coastal areas, see pages 25–26. Also, for information on certain investigations made in the interior subsequent to 1953, see Banfield (1957) and Banfield and Tener (1958).

Investigations in 1953

My own itinerary during this season was as follows: May 20 to 22, Quebec to Seven Islands, by steamer; May 22 to June 2, Seven Islands and vicinity; June 3, Seven Islands to Knob Lake; June 3 to July 1, Knob Lake and vicinity, including a trip to Al's Lake and return on June 22; July 1 to 22, Attikamagen Lake; July 22 to August 2, Lac Aulneau; August 2 to 9, Knob Lake; August 9 to 18, Mollie T. Lake and vicinity (including Sunny Mountain); August 18 to 21, Leroy Lake; August 21 to 22, Knob Lake; August 22 to September 8, and September 18 to 21, Mile 224 Airstrip and vicinity; September 8 to 18, Carol Lake and vicinity (including Lorraine Mountain, September 11); September 21 to October 8, Knob Lake and vicinity; October 8 to 9, Knob Lake to Seven Islands, via Mile 224 Airstrip; October 9 to 13, Seven Islands and vicinity; October 13, Seven Islands to Rimouski,

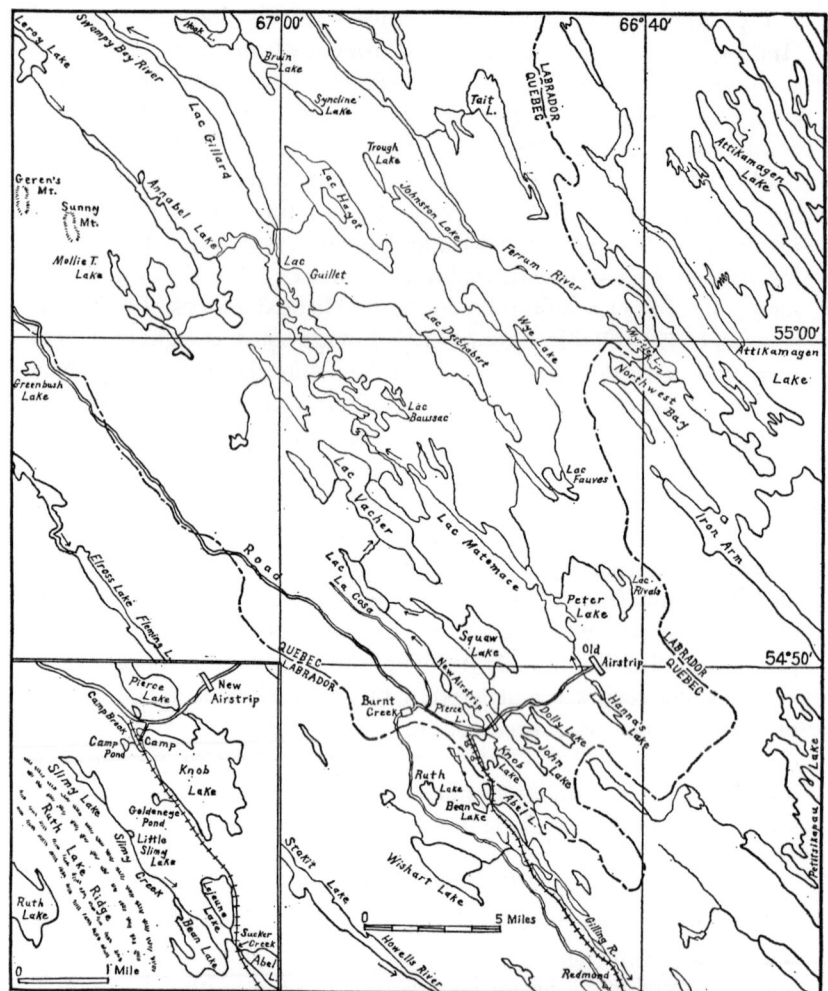

Map 1.—The Knob Lake area, Labrador and Quebec. (Redrawn from the Boundary Lake, Tait Lake, Elross Lake, Knob Lake, and Stakit Lake sheets of the National Topographic Series.)

by steamer. All major travel, from June 3 to October 9, was by plane.

A very rough estimate of the proportionate amount of time spent on various branches of biology while I was in the field might be made as follows: mammals, 40 per cent; birds, 30; plants, 18; insects, 5; fishes, 3; ethnology, 3; amphibians, 1.

The present report includes personal observations along the St. Lawrence from Rimouski to Seven Islands and vicinity, and in the interior from Ashuanipi Lake north to Lac Aulneau. Notes derived from other persons, and offered here, extend over a considerably wider area within the bounds of the peninsula. The following list shows the latitude, longitude, and at least the approximate altitude of the interior localities from which records of mammals were obtained. Most of these appear on maps in the National Topographic Series of the Canada Department of Mines and Technical Surveys, but by no means are all the less important localities named thereon. For the Knob Lake area I have prepared a sketch map (map 1), on which various minor features (such as Camp Brook, Goldeneye Pond, Sucker Creek, and Ruth Lake Ridge) are supplied with personally bestowed and wholly unofficial names, in order to pinpoint the places where certain observations were made.

LABRADOR

	Latitude	Longitude	Altitude (feet)
Abel Lake	54°46' N.	66°47' W.	1,624
Ashuanipi Lake, N. end	53°00' N.	66°15' W.	1,750
Ashuanipi River, 2 mi. below Ashuanipi Lake	53°02' N.	66°15' W.	1,740
Astray Lake	54°32' N.	66°28' W.	1,514
Atikonak River (middle)	53°00' N.	64°42' W.	1,575
Attikamagen Lake, Iron Arm, NW. end	54°56' N.	66°39' W.	1,536
Attikamagen Lake, Northwest Bay	54°59' N.	66°41' W.	1,536
Bean Lake	54°46' N.	66°49' W.	1,645
Bosh Lake	54°06' N.	66°02' W.	1,900
Carol Lake	53°04' N.	66°58' W.	2,000
Chaulk Lake	53°00' N.	64°15' W.	1,600
Comeback Lake	54°43' N.	65°56' W.	1,575
Deception Lake	52°07' N.	65°42' W.	2,200
Dodette Lake	54°33' N.	66°04' W.	1,575
Dyke Lake (middle)	54°30' N.	66°18' W.	1,510
Elross Lake	54°52' N.	67°09' W.	1,636
Evening Lake	53°35' N.	66°15' W.	1,600
Gabbro Lake	53°35' N.	65°15' W.	1,550
Gilling River (mouth)	54°39' N.	66°38' W.	1,510
Grand Falls	53°35' N.	64°17' W.	1,400
Greenbush Lake	54°59' N.	67°14' W.	1,990
Guy's River	54°43' N.	66°19' W.	1,520
Howell's River (mouth)	54°35' N.	66°40' W.	1,510
Huguette Lake	52°54' N.	67°07' W.	2,300
Jackson Lake	52°58' N.	67°17' W.	2,100
Julienne Lake	53°11' N.	66°46' W.	1,700

	Latitude	Longitude	Altitude (feet)
Kasheshibaw Lake	54°14′ N.	63°11′ W.	1,500
Little Slimy Lake	54°47′ N.	66°50′ W.	1,760
Long Lake	52°52′ N.	66°59′ W.	1,900
Lorraine Mountain	53°06′ N.	66°57′ W.	2,955
Mackenzie Lake	54°10′ N.	63°17′ W.	1,460
Menihek Lake (middle)	54°10′ N.	66°32′ W.	1,562
Michikamau Lake (middle)	54°10′ N.	64°00′ W.	1,470
Mile 224 Airstrip	53°02′ N.	66°15′ W.	1,790
Molson Lake	53°23′ N.	66°18′ W.	1,620
Neal Lake	52°57′ N.	67°10′ W.	2,300
Nip Lake	52°50′ N.	67°10′ W.	2,300
Ossokmanuan Lake (middle)	53°26′ N.	65°00′ W.	1,550
Panchia Lake	53°10′ N.	64°40′ W.	1,570
Redmond Lake	54°40′ N.	66°41′ W.	1,640
Reid Lake	53°05′ N.	67°05′ W.	2,200
Ruth Lake Ridge	54°47′ N.	66°50′ W.	2,273
Sandgirt Lake	53°55′ N.	65°15′ W.	1,470
Sawyer Lake	54°26′ N.	65°58′ W.	1,600
Seahorse Lake	52°13′ N.	65°48′ W.	1,950
Seal Lake (on Naskaupi River)	54°23′ N.	61°45′ W.	925
Shabogamo Lake	53°15′ N.	66°32′ W.	1,700
Slimy Creek	54°47′ N.	66°49′ W.	1,750
Slimy Lake	54°47′ N.	66°50′ W.	1,770
Sucker Creek	54°46′ N.	66°48′ W.	1,630
Sudbury Lake	52°54′ N.	67°16′ W.	2,200
Sylvia Lake	54°06′ N.	66°02′ W.	1,900
Wabush Lake (middle)	53°01′ N.	66°52′ W.	1,710
Whiteman Lake	53°10′ N.	66°14′ W.	1,675

Quebec

	Latitude	Longitude	Altitude (feet)
Al's Lake	55°17′ N.	67°13′ W.	1,500
Burnt Creek	54°49′ N.	66°53′ W.	1,900
Camp Brook	54°48′ N.	66°50′ W.	1,650
Camp Pond	54°48′ N.	66°50′ W.	1,800
Dillon Lake	55°06′ N.	65°41′ W.	1,475
Dolly Ridge	54°49′ N.	66°45′ W.	1,900
Donald Lake	55°14′ N.	66°21′ W.	1,775
Eric Lake	51°55′ N.	65°40′ W.	1,980
Forks, The	57°40′ N.	69°30′ W.	75
Fort McKenzie	56°50′ N.	68°57′ W.	250
Gad Lake	50°44′ N.	65°17′ W.	1,400
Geren's Mountain	55°05′ N.	67°15′ W.	2,821
Goldeneye Pond	54°47′ N.	66°49′ W.	1,775
Harris Lake	55°07′ N.	67°26′ W.	1,730
Helluva Lake	55°18′ N.	67°34′ W.	2,200
Indian House Lake (middle)	56°15′ N.	64°44′ W.	890
John Lake	54°48′ N.	66°47′ W.	1,647
Knob Lake	54°48′ N.	66°49′ W.	1,645
Lac Allard	50°32′ N.	63°31′ W.	400
Lac Aulneau. (Thus on the Fort McKenzie sheet of the National Topographic Series of maps. Known among the mining personnel as Lake Marymac.)	57°01′ N.	68°38′ W.	510
Lac Boisvert	49°57′ N.	72°15′ W.	600
Lac Bringadin	54°50′ N.	67°43′ W.	1,900
Lac Cramolet	55°50′ N.	67°35′ W.	1,100
Lac Effiat	56°00′ N.	67°26′ W.	1,000

	Latitude	Longitude	Altitude (feet)
Lac La Cosa	54°52' N.	66°55' W.	1,590
Lac Le Fer	55°20' N.	67°20' W.	1,350
Lac Hayot	55°04' N.	66°56' W.	1,590
Lac Montagni	55°11' N.	66°00' W.	1,825
Lac de Morhiban	51°50' N.	62°53' W.	1,720
Lac Ochiltrie	52°35' N.	73°15' W.	1,400
Lac Romanet	56°17' N.	67°45' W.	1,000
Lake Paterson	49°55' N.	72°05' W.	600
Lake Wapanikskan, N. end	57°04' N.	68°51' W.	720
Leaf Lake	58°40' N.	70°00' W.	0
Lepage Lake	56°55' N.	68°33' W.	600
Leroy Lake	55°08' N.	67°14' W.	1,590
Magpie Lake (middle)	51°00' N.	64°40' W.	500
Manitou Lake (middle)	50°53' N.	65°17' W.	520
Mary Jo Lake	54°49' N.	66°48' W.	1,630
Mollie T. Lake	55°02' N.	67°09' W.	1,625
Nachikapau Lake	56°40' N.	68°15' W.	560
Nemiscau River (headwaters)	52°00' N.	75°00' W.	500
Opiscoteo Lake	53°15' N.	67°58' W.	1,950
Otelnuk Lake	56°10' N.	68°12' W.	890
Retty Lake	55°15' N.	66°08' W.	1,875
Rivière de Pas (jct. with George River)	55°53' N.	64°46' W.	950
Scott Lake	55°11' N.	67°24' W.	1,775
Squaw Lake	54°50' N.	66°50' W.	1,616
Star Lakes	54°51' N.	66°57' W.	1,775
Sunny Mountain	55°03' N.	67°12' W.	2,700
Syncline Lake	55°07' N.	66°58' W.	1,690
Trough Lake	55°05' N.	66°55' W.	1,625
Wacouno Lake	51°35' N.	65°43' W.	1,883
Wakuach Lake	55°35' N.	67°35' W.	1,250
Wye Lake	55°00' N.	66°46' W.	1,698

Physiography and vegetation

These features of the interior of the peninsula have been discussed hitherto by a number of authors, including Macoun (1886), Low (1896), Hustich (1949; 1951a; 1951b), Hare (1950; 1952; 1959), Bartram (1954), Abbe (1955), Dix (1956), Löve, Kucyniak, and Johnston (1958), and Harper (1958). Reference to these papers may be substituted for repetition or elaboration here.

Climate, Faunal Distribution, and Life-zones

The generally recognized amelioration of climate during the past twoscore years or more has resulted in a fairly pronounced shift northward of certain elements in the fauna of the Ungava Peninsula (Harper, MS). This phenomenon has been noticed particularly among birds and fishes, and to a lesser extent among terrestrial mammals since these in general are less mobile than birds and marine fishes. The most striking case among mammals is probably that of the Moose (see account of that species).

Temperature conditions and faunal distribution during the past several decades seem to require a reappraisal of the extent, and a revision of the boundaries, of the time-honored Merriam (1898) life-zones in the Ungava Peninsula, as I have pointed out in the manuscript just referred to. I have suggested maintaining the boundary between the Arctic and the Hudsonian life-zones at the tree-limit, while recognizing that the present temperature along this boundary during the six hottest weeks of summer is from three to five degrees higher than it was in Merriam's time (say 53° to 55° instead of 50° F.). At the same time I have suggested shifting the boundary between the Hudsonian and the Canadian life-zones northward to approximately latitude 52° over the greater part of its east–west extent. On earlier versions (1958:maps 1, 3–26) of the present map 2, I continued this boundary (and the main part of the Canadian Life-zone) eastward to about the St. Augustin River only, at the same time representing an outlier of that life-zone as occupying the lower Hamilton Basin.

The recent remarkable photo-reconnaissance surveys of vegetation types of the Ungava Peninsula by Hare and Taylor (1956) and Hare (1959) have contributed significantly to an understanding of life-zone limits in the region as a whole, and in particular have enabled me to suggest (tentatively) such an extension of the Canadian Life-zone in the southeastern part of the peninsula as to join up the main part of that life-zone with its former outlier in the Hamilton Basin.

Hare (1959:map 1) has drawn a line between predominant closed-crown forests on the south and predominant lichen woodlands on the north; and I have adopted this as the boundary between the Canadian and the Hudsonian life-zones on the present map 2. In this revised version (as well as the earlier versions) there is no evident conflict with Merriam's temperature criterion (57.2° F.) for the dividing-line between these two life-zones, although admittedly there is a decided dearth of temperature data along this boundary in the whole Ungava Peninsula.

The principal modification of the present map 2 from the above-mentioned ones of 1958 consists in tentatively allocating a large area in the southeast to the Canadian Life-zone. This area is indicated by Hare (1959:33, fig. 5, and overlay to map 1) as "southeastern poor forests." On page 39 he describes it as "scrub forest, short in growth and thin in density. It is nevertheless closed-crown forest according to the present classification, since the forest floor is invisible; one must therefore include it in the forest sub-zone. Much of this area is very wet." There is distinct need both of ground surveys of the biota and of temperature records in this area. In respect to both biota and

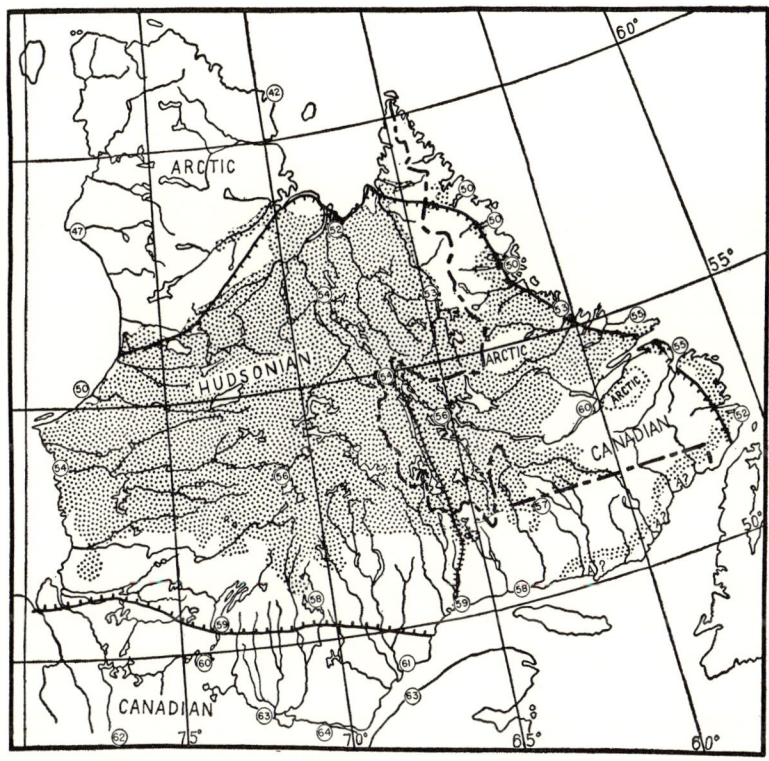

Hudsonian Life-zone according to present delimitation.

Hudsonian Life-zone (*fide* Merriam et al., 1910).

Labrador-Quebec boundary.

Circled numerals indicate the approximate averages of daily mean temperature during the six hottest weeks of summer at various meteorological stations.

Map 2.—Life-zones of the Ungava Peninsula. (Basic outline of map constructed, with permission of the Geological Survey of Canada, from Map 1045A, Geological Map of Canada, 1955.)

climate it may be more or less intermediate between the Canadian and the Hudsonian life-zones.

Hare (1959:map 1) represents a coastal strip in the southeast as composed predominantly of tundra. It is almost unbroken from Sand-

TABLE 1.—ZONAL DISTRIBUTION OF SPECIES OF TERRESTRIAL MAMMALS IN THE UNGAVA PENINSULA (PRESENCE INDICATED BY "x"; ABSENCE BY "-.")

Mammal	Canadian Life-zone	Hudsonian Life-zone	Arctic Life-zone
Sorex cinereus subspp.	x	x	x
Sorex arcticus arcticus	x	-	-
Sorex palustris subspp.	x	x	-
Microsorex hoyi subspp.	x	x	-
Blarina brevicauda talpoides	x	-	-
Condylura cristata cristata	x	x	-
Myotis lucifugus lucifugus	x	x	-
Myotis keenii septentrionalis	x	-	-
Lepus arcticus subspp. (summer)	-	-	x
Lepus americanus americanus	x	x	-
Marmota monax subspp.	x	x	x
Tamias striatus quebecensis	x	-	-
Tamiasciurus hudsonicus subspp.	x	x	-
Glaucomys sabrinus subspp.	x	x	-
Castor canadensis subspp.	x	x	-
Peromyscus maniculatus subspp.	x	x	x
Dicrostonyx hudsonius	-	-	x
Synaptomys cooperi cooperi	x	-	-
Synaptomys borealis subspp.	x	x	x
Clethrionomys gapperi subspp.	x	x	x
Phenacomys ungava subspp.	x	x	x
Microtus pennsylvanicus subspp.	x	x	x
Microtus chrotorrhinus subspp.	x	x	-
Ondatra zibethicus subspp.	x	x	x
Rattus norvegicus	x	x	-
Mus musculus domesticus	x	-	-
Zapus hudsonius subspp.	x	x	-
Napaeozapus insignis subspp.	x	x	-
Erethizon dorsatum dorsatum	x	x	x
Canis lupus subspp.	x	x	x
Alopex lagopus ungava	x	x	x
Vulpes fulva bangsi	x	x	x
Euarctos americanus americanus	x	x	x
Thalarctos maritimus	x	x	x
Martes americana subspp.	x	x	-
Martes pennanti pennanti	x	-	-
Mustela erminea richardsonii	x	x	x
Mustela rixosa rixosa	x	x	x
Mustela vison subspp.	x	x	-
Gulo luscus luscus	x	x	x
Mephitis mephitis mephitis	x	-	-
Lutra canadensis subspp.	x	x	x
Lynx canadensis canadensis	x	x	-
Alces alces americana	x	x	-
Rangifer caboti (mid-summer)	-	x	x
Rangifer caribou caribou	x	x	x
Total number of species present	43	36	22

wich Bay southward to the Strait of Belle Isle, and thence southwestward to about longitude 63°; it also appears in several small detached areas as far west as longitude 67°. It is true that Arctic conditions are approached or at least simulated in many such treeless areas. Furthermore, a few typically Arctic birds, such as the Willow Ptarmigan, the Northern Horned Lark, and the American Pipit, breed along the more easterly parts of the North Shore of the Gulf. On the other hand, still more birds, whose affinities are with the Hudsonian or even the Canadian Life-zone, occur on the same part of the coast (in scattered forested areas), while such typical Arctic mammals as the Newfoundland Hare, the Labrador Varying Lemming, and (normally) the Ungava Arctic Fox are absent. Finally, it is rather doubtful whether Merriam's criterion for the southern limit of the Arctic Life-zone would apply to any part of the North Shore west of the Strait of Belle Isle. (This criterion in former years was a mean daily temperature of 50° during the six hottest weeks of summer; now it would be about 53°.) To indicate the problematical status of this stretch of coastal tundra as part of the true Arctic Life-zone, I have inserted "A?" in three places on it; I have also placed an adjoining narrow strip of the Hudsonian Life-zone a few miles inland, to serve as a transition from the Canadian Life-zone still farther inland.

There are two isolated areas that Hare (1959:map 1) is no doubt justified in classifying as tundra. One is situated between Michikamau Lake and the east coast; the other (composed of the Mealy Mountains), just south of Lake Melville. I have indicated these on map 2 by superimposing the word "ARCTIC."

Maps 3–45 of the present report, showing the distribution of mammalian species and subspecies, were prepared before Hare's work became available and thus represent my earlier concept of the extent of the three life-zones in the peninsula.

Among the 46 terrestrial mammals of the Ungava Peninsula, listed in table 1, about 43 have summer breeding ranges in the Canadian Life-zone, 36 in the Hudsonian Life-zone, and perhaps 22 in the Arctic Life-zone.

Nineteen species appear to be common to all three zones:

Sorex cinereus —— Masked Shrew
Marmota monax —— Woodchuck
Peromyscus maniculatus —— White-footed Mouse
Synaptomys borealis —— Lemming Mouse
Clethrionomys gapperi —— Red-backed Mouse
Phenacomys ungava —— Spruce Mouse
Microtus pennsylvanicus —— Meadow Mouse
Ondatra zibethicus —— Muskrat

Erethizon dorsatum	Canada Porcupine
Canis lupus	Wolf
Alopex lagopus	Arctic Fox
Vulpes fulva	Red Fox
Euarctos americanus	American Black Bear
Thalarctos maritimus	Polar Bear
Mustela erminea	Short-tailed Weasel
Mustela rixosa	Least Weasel
Gulo luscus	Wolverine
Lutra canadensis	Otter
Rangifer caribou	Woodland Caribou

Rangifer caribou is included here on the basis of its occurrence in Arctic-Alpine areas within the confines of the Hudsonian Life-zone; but it evidently does not reach the main Arctic Life-zone. *Alopex* and *Thalarctos* are of merely occasional occurrence in the Canadian Life-zone. Some of the foregoing, such as *Marmota, Peromyscus, Clethrionomys, Microtus, Ondatra, Erethizon,* and *Lutra,* probably do not range *throughout* the Arctic Life-zone to the northwestern extermity of the peninsula. The anomalous distribution of *Peromyscus* does not seem to include the greater part of the interior.

There are 16 species that occupy both the Canadian and the Hudsonian life-zones, but do not appear to enter the Arctic Life-zone. (The members of this group may be readily ascertained from table 1.) Some of them (*Condylura, Myotis lucifugus, Glaucomys, Napaeozapus,* and *Alces*) occur in the more southerly parts of the Hudsonian Life-zone, but probably do not range throughout that life-zone.

A striking feature of this tabulation is the exceedingly slight difference that it reveals between the mammalian faunas of the Canadian and the Hudsonian life-zones. This difference is considerably less evident than that between the avifaunas of the two life-zones. Among the mammals of the Canadian Life-zone, only the following do not appear to range into the Hudsonian Life-zone:

Sorex arcticus arcticus	Saddle-backed Shrew
Blarina brevicauda talpoides	Gapper's Short-tailed Shrew
Myotis keenii septentrionalis	Acadian Bat
Tamias striatus quebecensis	Quebec Chipmunk
Peromyscus maniculatus plumbeus	North Shore White-footed Mouse
Peromyscus maniculatus gracilis	Le Conte's White-footed Mouse
Synaptomys cooperi cooperi	Cooper's Lemming Mouse
Clethrionomys gapperi gapperi	Ontario Red-backed Mouse
Microtus pennsylvanicus pennsylvanicus	Pennsylvania Meadow Mouse
Mus musculus domesticus	House Mouse
Martes pennanti pennanti	Eastern Fisher
Mephitis mephitis mephitis	Northeastern Striped Skunk

Among the mammals wintering in the Hudsonian Life-zone, apparently the only kinds that do not penetrate the Canadian Life-zone are *Lepus arcticus* and *Rangifer caboti.*

Taking only the normal summer or breeding ranges into consideration, we find that only three of the 22 species of the Arctic Life-zone are almost restricted to it:

Lepus arcticus subspp. ─── Arctic Hare
Dicrostonyx hudsonius ─── Labrador Varying Lemming
Alopex lagopus ungava ─── Ungava Arctic Fox

Probably *Dicrostonyx*, even in summer, ranges very slightly into the upper edge of the Hudsonian Life-zone. Of the other two species, the Arctic Fox occasionally wanders southward in winter into the forested regions, and the Arctic Hare may do so to some slight extent.

Nearly half (21) of the 46 species are represented in the peninsula by more than one subspecies. In some species the division into subspecies seems to be a zonal one (on a more or less south–north basis); examples are *Peromyscus maniculatus plumbeus*, *Clethrionomys gapperi gapperi*, and *Microtus pennsylvanicus pennsylvanicus*, which, in the peninsula, are apparently confined to the Canadian Life-zone. In other species subspecific differences seem to have evolved in the damp east-coast region, with the result that the division into subspecies is evidently more on an east–west basis than on a life-zone basis.

Most of the east-coast subspecies have their type localities between Hamilton Inlet and the Strait of Belle Isle, where the mean annual total precipitation ranges from about 30 to 45 inches, compared with about 20 to 35 inches in the central and southern interior (*cf.* Thomas, 1953: chart 5-1). Subspecies in this group are:

Sorex cinereus miscix ─── Labrador Masked Shrew
Sorex palustris labradorensis ─── Labrador Water Shrew
Marmota monax ignava ─── Labrador Woodchuck
Synaptomys borealis medioximus ─── Labrador Lemming Mouse
Clethrionomys gapperi proteus ─── Labrador Red-backed Mouse
Phenacomys ungava crassus ─── Labrador Spruce Mouse
Microtus pennsylvanicus enixus ─── Hamilton Inlet Meadow Mouse
Microtus chrotorrhinus ravus ─── Labrador Rock Vole
Ondatra zibethicus aquilonius ─── Labrador Muskrat
Zapus hudsonius ladas ─── Labrador Meadow Jumping Mouse
Vulpes fulva bangsi ─── Labrador Red Fox

The apparently greater prevalence of fog on the coast than in the interior (*cf.* Tanner, 1947, 1:316–323) would mean a greater difference in humidity than that indicated merely by the precipitation data. Higher humidity in the coastal areas may have been a factor in the evolution of some of the darker subspecies.

Comparative Abundance of Species

It may be useful to attempt a very rough estimate of the comparative abundance of the various species of mammals in the interior of the peninsula. This estimate is based primarily upon personal collections and observations and on reports received from others—all pertaining to the year 1953. At best it represents nothing more than a mere approximation to actual conditions. Variation in size and secretiveness of the animals, and the frequent uncertainty in identifying tracks, scats, nests, or other signs of the species, are some of the factors that render accurate estimates difficult. How to translate reports of "many," "few," or "common" into even approximate numerals is an especially vexatious problem.

With this explanation of its shortcomings, I venture to present the following list. It is divided into three taxonomic categories, in each of which I have attempted to arrange the species in the order of estimated abundance (the most numerous ones being placed first). The numeral immediately following the name of a species is intended to indicate the total number of individuals of that species that were collected, observed, or reported. The following number (in parentheses) indicates the number of complete specimens (skin and skull) that were collected and preserved; at least this part of the information may be considered accurate.

The number of individuals observed or reported is not the final criterion of comparative abundance. In some cases I have taken the liberty of arranging the species in what I believe to be a truer sequence of frequency than that suggested by the accompanying numerals.

Insectivora, Chiroptera, Lagomorpha, and Rodentia

Clethrionomys gapperi subspp.	Red-backed Mouse	137	(37)
Microtus pennsylvanicus subspp.	Meadow Mouse	101	(16)
Tamiasciurus hudsonicus subspp.	Red Squirrel	82	(3)
Lepus americanus americanus	American Varying Hare	50	(2)
Erethizon dorsatum dorsatum	Eastern Canada Porcupine	30	(2)
Phenacomys ungava subspp.	Spruce Mouse	5	(4)
Ondatra zibethicus subspp.	Muskrat	14	(1)
Dicrostonyx hudsonius	Labrador Varying Lemming	14	(2)
Myotis lucifugus lucifugus	Little Brown Bat	10	(2)
Castor canadensis subspp.	Beaver	8	(0)
Marmota monax subspp.	Woodchuck	10	(0)
Glaucomys sabrinus subspp.	Flying Squirrel	7	(1)
Synaptomys borealis medioximus	Labrador Lemming Mouse	3	(3)
Peromyscus maniculatus plumbeus	North Shore White-footed Mouse	2	(0)
Sorex palustris turneri	Turner's Water Shrew	1	(0)
Microsorex hoyi alnorum	Alder Pygmy Shrew	1	(1)

Carnivora

Mustela erminea richardsonii	Richardson's Short-tailed Weasel	29	(0)
Mustela vison subspp.	Mink	42	(1)
Vulpes fulva bangsi	Labrador Red Fox	27	(0)
Lutra canadensis chimo	Ungava Otter	10	(0)
Lynx canadensis canadensis	Canada Lynx	8	(0)
Euarctos americanus americanus	American Black Bear	21	(1)
Martes americana americana	Eastern American Marten	16	(0)

Mustela rixosa rixosa	Least Weasel	1	(0)
Canis lupus subspp.	Wolf	26	(0)
	Artiodactyla		
Rangifer caboti	Cabot's Caribou	4	(0)
Rangifer caribou caribou	Eastern Woodland Caribou	73	(0)
Alces alces americana	Eastern Moose	2	(0)

The above-indicated sequence of numerical status among the Carnivora is in full accord with the wild fur returns in the Province of Quebec for ~~the~~ 1950–51 (Cowan, 1955:169).

French and Montagnais Names of Mammals

The account of each mammal includes, besides the technical and English names, the French and the Montagnais Indian names as far as I have ascertained them. A few of the French vernacular names were picked up in the field, but the majority are derived from Anderson (1947). Some of the subspecies have distinctive French names (which are bookish rather than vernacular). The Montagnais names, on the other hand, do not extend below the category of species; to avoid repetition, they are inserted just once (generally in the heading of the first form of the species treated).

The greater part of the Montagnais names were very obligingly supplied by Francis McKenzie and his father, Sebastien McKenzie, in their own printed script. Père J. E. Beaudet, O. M. I., of the Pensionnat Indien Notre-Dame, near Seven Islands, most kindly checked these names and in addition furnished still others out of his special knowledge of the Montagnais language. A very large proportion of the Montagnais names of mammals bear a recognizable resemblance, on the one hand, to those used by the Naskapi of the Davis Inlet band (Strong, 1930) and, on the other hand, to those in use among the Crees (Seton, 1929). I am much indebted to Jean P. Labrecque, of the RCAF, for conducting in English and French my conversations with Francis McKenzie.

Only about half of the mammals here discussed are provided with names in Lemoine's *Dictionnaire Français-Montagnais* (1901). While the Montagnais names in the Seven Islands dialect bear a marked similarity to those in Lemoine, in no case are those in one list quite identical with those in the other. Perhaps the most evident difference is that the letter *o* in some of the Seven Islands words is replaced with the letter *u* in Lemoine.

Names of Plants

Of the plants recorded on other pages of this report, some are mentioned by their technical names, and some by their common names.

The former may be more comprehensible and convenient in some cases, and the latter in other cases. A factor to be considered is whether or not the reader is an experienced botanist. To provide for the needs of all classes of readers, the following list, which includes both technical and common names, is provided.

Mosses

Sphagnum spp.	Sphagnum moss
Pleurozium schreberi	A moss
Hypnum crista-castrensis	Feather moss
Hylocomium pyrenaicum	A moss
Polytrichum sp.	Hair-cap moss

Lichens

Cladonia rangiferina	Caribou lichen
Cladonia alpestris	Caribou lichen
Cladonia gracilis	Caribou lichen
Parmelia centrifuga	
Alectoria implexa	
Alectoria ochroleuca	
Usnea	

Vascular plants

Equisetum sylvaticum	Wood horsetail
Abies balsamea	Balsam fir
Picea glauca	White spruce
Picea mariana	Black spruce
Larix laricina	Tamarack
Pinus banksiana	Jack pine
Deschampsia flexuosa	Common hairgrass
Calamagrostis canadensis	Blue-joint grass
Hierochloë odorata	Sweet grass
Carex spp.	Sedge
Clintonia borealis	Yellow Clintonia
Smilacina trifolia	Three-leaved Solomon's seal
Streptopus sp.	Twisted-stalk
Habenaria dilatata	Leafy white orchis
Salix vestita	A willow
Salix planifolia	A willow
Myrica gale	Sweet gale
Betula papyrifera	Canoe birch
Betula glandulosa	Dwarf birch
Alnus crispa	Mountain alder
Oxyria digyna	Mountain sorrel
Polygonum viviparum	Alpine bistort
Coptis groenlandica	Goldthread
Mitella nuda	Miterwort
Ribes glandulosum	Skunk currant
Potentilla fruticosa	Shrubby cinquefoil
Dryas integrifolia	Dryas
Rubus chamaemorus	Baked-apple berry
Rubus idaeus var. strigosus	Raspberry
Sanguisorba canadensis	Canadian burnet
Empetrum nigrum	Black crowberry
Viola spp.	Violet
Epilobium angustifolium	Fireweed
Cornus canadensis	Bunchberry
Ledum groenlandicum	Common Labrador tea

Ledum decumbens	Narrow-leaved Labrador tea
Kalmia angustifolia	Sheep laurel
Chamaedaphne calyculata	Leather-leaf
Gaultheria hispidula	Creeping snowberry
Arctostaphylos uva-ursi	Common bearberry
Vaccinium uliginosum	Bog bilberry
Vaccinium angustifolium	Low sweet blueberry
Vaccinium vitis-idaea var. *minus*	Mountain cranberry
Trientalis borealis	Star-flower
Menyanthes trifoliata	Buckbean
Linnaea borealis var. *americana*	Twinflower
Viburnum edule	Mooseberry
Solidago sp.	Goldenrod
Petasites palmatus	Sweet coltsfoot
Taraxacum sp.	Dandelion

The plant materials that I collected have been determined by specialists as follows: mosses, by Edwin B. Bartram (1954); lichens, by W. L. Dix (1956); and vascular plants, by A. E. Porsild.

Summation of Distributional Records

In order to arrive at a better understanding of the significance of the records secured in 1953 in the zoologically unexplored parts of the interior, it seemed essential to assemble previous distributional records of mammals from the peninsula as a whole. This has meant primarily a search through the published literature. The results are presented in the final paragraphs of the accounts of the various species.

Previous mammalogical investigations, beginning with those of Cartwright in the 1770's and 1780's, have been conducted mainly in the more accessible coastal areas. Consequently the distribution of the species along the eastern and southern coasts, in particular, has already become fairly well known. In summing up the records, therefore, I have not felt it necessary to present them in much detail for the coastal areas. On the other hand, it has seemed well worth while to supply moderately full particulars of the rather meager records from the interior.

It appears that so far there have been only two attempts to compile a special distributional list of the mammals of the Ungava Peninsula. The first was by Low (1896:313–321), and it is especially valuable for its records from the interior, although it is not wholly accurate nor complete. It strangely omits what is probably the most abundant mammal of the entire region—the Red-backed Mouse. The second list was brought out by Bangs in 1898, with a condensed revision in 1912. It was devoted primarily to the east coast, and it is naturally far out of date.

A majority of the various faunal lists for *parts* of the peninsula do not present any detailed summation of previous locality records for those parts; for example, Strong (1930) for the Davis Inlet area; Anderson (1934) for the more northerly areas and (1939; 1940) for the Province of Quebec; Weaver (1940) for the North Shore of the Gulf; Manning (1947) for the east side of Hudson Bay and several localities in the more southerly interior; Cameron and Orkin (1950) for the Lake St. John area; and Doutt (1954) for the east side of Hudson Bay. On the other hand, Eidmann (1935), besides reviewing the status and distribution of the mammals of the greater part of the peninsula, presents range maps of eight species; these, however, are constructed in part on a hypothetical basis. C. F. Jackson (1938) discusses previous records for the North Shore of the Gulf; and Cameron and Morris (1951) do likewise for the area about Lakes Mistassini and Albanel.

The southwestern limits of the peninsula were placed by Bell (1895:335) at a line extending from the mouth of Rupert River to Lake St. John; by Low (1896:19) at a line "extending in a direction nearly east from the south end of James Bay near latitude 51°, to the Gulf of St. Lawrence near Seven Islands in latitude 50°"; and by Townsend and Allen (1907:279–280) at the line indicated by Low. According to Speck (1931:573), the boundary extends "from the mouth of the Saguenay river to the mouth of the Nottaway river." In essential agreement with the views of Bell and Speck, I might venture to propose a slightly more explicit boundary, extending upstream from the mouth of the Nottaway, through its tributary rivers, the Waswanipi, the Chibougamau, and the Obatogamau, to Obatogamau Lake (49°32' N., 74°30' W.); thence across the divide to the headwaters of the Ashuapmuchuan River, down that stream to Lake St. John, and thence down the Saguenay to the St. Lawrence. This boundary is indicated by a broken line on map 3.

Islands lying off the west coast of the peninsula, in Hudson and James bays, while belonging politically to the District of Keewatin, are included in the present report.

Explanation of Maps

Distributional maps (Nos. 3–45) are provided for all the mammals except the six kinds (*Sorex arcticus arcticus, Blarina brevicauda talpoides, Myotis keenii septentrionalis, Rattus norvegicus, Mus musculus domesticus*, and the Labrador Grizzly) for which definite locality records are extremely few or even wanting. The original plan of showing the distribution of merely the species has been modified so as to indicate the far more uncertain ranges of the subspecies. In the present state of our knowledge, this can scarcely be done with a desirable degree of confidence or exactness; yet I have made the attempt. Revisions will be required as biological investigations are pushed in the out-of-the-way spots of the peninsula, and especially in the interior wilds.

In this provisional effort I have ventured to correlate the ranges (as far as seemed feasible) with life-zones (*cf.* map 2), forest regions (*cf.* Rowe, 1959), geological formations, watersheds, or snowfall. For example, Rowe's map shows the environs of Lake St. John as an isolated portion of the Great Lakes – St. Lawrence Forest Region, surrounded by Boreal Forest. Adjacent to the lake are lowlands, on which marine clays and sands of considerable depth have been deposited. Beyond the lowlands is a rolling and partly mountainous terrain of crystalline rocks—part of the great Canadian Shield, which extends far to the north and includes the Lake Mistassini area. Besides the differences in soil, geological formation, and forest covering between the Lake St. John and the Lake Mistassini areas, there is a difference in climate—a daily mean July temperature of 64° at St. Félicien (close to Lake St. John) and of 58° at Mistassini Post (Addendum to Volume 1 of Climatic Summaries for Selected Meteorological Stations in Canada, published by Meteorological Division, Department of Transport, 1954).

This state of affairs may account for the occurrence of certain subspecies about Lake St. John that are different from those about Lakes Mistassini and Albanel, although both areas are included in the Canadian Life-zone. Examples may be found in the genera *Microsorex* (perhaps), *Tamiasciurus, Peromyscus, Napaeozapus,* and *Lutra* (see maps 5, 12, 15, 25, and 40).

The letters (*a, b, c,* etc.) on the maps, designating the ranges of the subspecies, are generally placed as near as feasible to the respective type localities (provided these are within the limits of the Ungava Peninsula).

On the use of a dotted band to represent the gradual transition from one life-zone to another, see Harper (1958:26).

Conservation

When the Naskapi were forced, several decades ago, to withdraw from certain portions of the interior of the peninsula by reason of the dearth of Labrador Barren Ground Caribou, the fur-bearing mammals of the deserted areas may be said to have obtained a new lease of life. These areas were chiefly along the George River and probably in the country between Petitsikapau, Attikamagen, and Michikamau lakes in the south and the Koksoak River in the north. Reoccupation of the territory by other trappers has been a slow process, and apparently it is not yet completed.

Those kinsmen of the Naskapi, the Montagnais, with summer homes on the North Shore of the St. Lawrence, have apparently been accustomed for long years to occupy winter trapping-grounds as far north as Petitsikapau and Attikamagen lakes (*cf.* Speck, 1931; 1935). But the journey from the coast was a long and very arduous one, and it was undertaken perhaps by comparatively few families. Before the building of the railway from Seven Islands to Knob Lake, Wakuach Lake (lat. 55°35′ N.) may have been one of their northernmost outposts. The railway reached the north end of Ashuanipi Lake in 1953, and the terminus at Knob Lake in 1954. From the winter of 1953 on, with the new advantage of railway travel into the interior, a larger number of Montagnais than in previous years were expected to penetrate the wilds for winter trapping. Quite possibly they are now also pushing northward into former Naskapi territory that will be new to them. Furthermore, during the early 1950's a certain proportion of the increasing white population, drawn into the interior by the mining developments, had begun to undertake trapping. The establishment of settlements along the railway, with the influx of hundreds of more or less permanent residents, can scarcely fail to have an adverse effect upon the wild life. There will evidently be a hitherto unprecedented pressure upon the game and fur-bearing animals of the region. The original native proprietors of these wilds will find themselves obliged to forego the virtual monopoly that they have enjoyed for so long a time, unless restrictions are placed upon the operations of white trappers and hunters. According to a recent report from Fred Farah (*in litt.*, August 5, 1960), the Montagnais have been justly granted exclusive hunting rights on their ancestral grounds. By 1957, Montagnais from the Seven Islands area and Naskapi from the Chimo area, totaling about 300 persons, had relocated at John Lake, near Knob Lake, for local employment in mining and related industries (Ross, 1957); this inevitably means a vast change in their primitive culture. Although this group of natives will be less dependent than previously upon hunting, fishing, and trapping as a means of livelihood, the increase in their numbers in the interior will probably prevent any diminution in the total pressure upon the wild life.

Even before the completion of the railway, field parties of white men, engaged during the summer in various kinds of exploratory work, secured a few Woodland Caribou, thereby reducing the population of this particularly important (and none too numerous) food animal of the Montagnais. In years gone by a considerable number of the natives have starved to death on their trapping grounds.

Trapping and hunting along the lower and middle courses of the Hamilton River have hitherto been carried on chiefly by men (largely of mixed blood) from the Northwest River area (*cf.* Merrick, 1933). Their operations may not be affected greatly or immediately by the coming of the railway to the upper Hamilton River basin (Ashuanipi and Menihek lakes area).

The statistics of wild fur production in Quebec (Cowan, 1955) indicate that the Marten and the Wolverine are the fur-bearers that have suffered the most serious depletion. In fact, the latter seems to be on the verge of extinction in the peninsula. Drastic measures may be required to save this extremely interesting (though somewhat obnoxious) mammal from its impending fate.

Nomenclature

The nomenclature and sequence of the species are in general accord with Miller and Kellogg (1955).

Measurements and Weights

For considerations of space, the following brief terms are used: LENGTH = total length from tip of snout to end of tail vertebrae (the measurement of embryos is made from crown to rump); TAIL = distance from its base to end of the vertebrae; FOOT = hind foot, from heel to tip of longest claw; EAR = distance from crown (not the notch) to fleshy tip of the ear (not including the projecting hairs); WEIGHTS of the smaller species are expressed in grams, and of the larger species, in pounds.

Color Terms

Capitalized color terms are those of Ridgway (1912).

Acknowledgments

At the beginning of this paper acknowledgment has been made of the generous support provided for the investigations in the Ungava Peninsula. The several organizations concerned—the Arctic Institute of North America, the Office of Naval Research, the Office of The Surgeon General of the Army, and the National Science Foundation—have my very warm appreciation and gratitude for affording the opportunities I have enjoyed in this fascinating region.

I am particularly indebted to A. E. Moss, chief geologist of the Iron Ore Company of Canada, and to many others among the personnel of that and affiliated companies, for the exceptional hospitality of their base camps and field parties, which very greatly facilitated my work. In this connection I must mention Richard Geren, R. D. Macdonald, H. E. Neal, and the following leaders or members of various field parties: Robert Girardin, James Murdoch, Gilbert Simard,

J. L. Véronneau, Robert Slipp, and Peter Almond. In addition to their hospitality, they provided much useful information on the mammalian fauna of the region. Among others who furnished very welcome information and assistance were D. O. Macdonald, F. D. Foster, R. Gordon Racey, A. E. Boerner, Arthur C. Newton, and Fred Farah; also a number of very obliging Montagnais friends—Sebastien, Francis, and Ben McKenzie, Georges Michel, Willé and Kom Pinette, and Jérôme and Joseph Georges St. Onge. The names of still other helpful informants appear here and there in the following pages.

The Quebec Department of Game and Fish (through the late Charles Frémont) and the Newfoundland Department of Mines and Resources very kindly granted the essential collecting permits.

A number of specialists on external and internal parasites of mammals have placed me under great obligation by determining material and enabling me to present the records here. The fleas (Siphonaptera) were determined by Robert Traub, Lt. Col., MSC, of the Army Medical Service Graduate School; the sucking lice (Anoplura), chiefly by C. F. W. Muesebeck, but in part by Phyllis T. Johnson, both of the Entomology Research Branch, United States Department of Agriculture; the mites (Acarina), chiefly by E. W. Baker, of the same organization, but in part (*Hirstionyssus* and *Ichoronyssus*) by R. W. Strandtmann, of Texas Technological College, Lubbock, Texas; and the internal parasites, by Aaron Goldberg, of the Animal Disease and Parasite Research Branch, United States Department of Agriculture.

Charles O. Handley, Jr., of the United States National Museum, has my warm thanks for critically examining this report in manuscript; also for checking, and in some cases modifying, my preliminary determinations of the specimens brought from the field. His comments thereon, as quoted in the following pages, are subscribed with his initials. His own field experience in the peninsula, and his special knowledge of the taxonomy of the mammals of that region, have made his contributions particularly useful and welcome.

Ralph S. Palmer, of the New York State Museum, also has kindly read the manuscript and given me valuable criticisms and suggestions.

The manuscript has also had the benefit of E. Raymond Hall's penetrating scrutiny, in both zoological and editorial spheres.

The basic outline of maps 2–45 was redrawn, with permission of the Geological Survey of Canada, from Map 1045A, Geological Map of Canada (1955).

For generous permission to reproduce photographs of various mammals (Cabot's and Woodland Caribou, Black and Polar Bears, and Timber Wolf), I am most particularly indebted to J. M. Harrison, D. A. Déry, Viger Plamondon, Robert Darveau, J. L. Véronneau, Pierre Côté, and Roland C. Clement.

The major part of the mammal specimens have been presented to the United States National Museum, and the remainder to the National Museum of Canada, in grateful recognition of various courtesies and assistance.

It is fitting that I should also express my particular appreciation for the privilege of utilizing the excellent library facilities of the following institutions: Academy of Natural Sciences of Philadelphia, American Philosophical Society, Historical Society of Pennsylvania, Free Library of Philadelphia, United States National Museum, University of North Carolina, National Museum of Canada, Ottawa Public Library, Library of Parliament, Ottawa, and McGill University.

Accounts of Species

Sorex cinereus cinereus Kerr
Common Masked Shrew; Musaraigne commune (Fr.); Tsinistoapokoshish (M.). (Map 3.)

J. L. Véronneau (*in litt.*, April 30, 1954) observed two shrews (possibly *S. c. cinereus*) that came into his tent at night at Lac Boisvert in the Mistassibi River area. This was in January, 1954, when the temperature was –46°. They kept coming from the mess-tent to his tent. Hildebrand (1949) describes similar winter invasions of tents in the Fort Chimo area.

Map 3.—Distribution of *Sorex cinereus* in the Ungava Peninsula: a, *Sorex cinereus miscix*; b, *S. c. cinereus*.

This subspecies is recorded from George River post, Fort Chimo, Lake Mendry, south of Leaf Bay, Lower Seal Lake, and Richmond Gulf south to Godbout and Lakes St. John and Albanel (H. H. T. Jackson, 1928:40; Anderson, 1939:55; Cameron and Orkin, 1950:98; Cameron and Morris, 1951:123; Bateman, 1953:4; Doutt, 1954:237; Hall and Kelson, 1959, 1:26, map 12). The area of intergradation with *S. c. miscix* is uncertain.

In four months of field work in the central interior, where the land was overrun with *Clethrionomys* and *Microtus*, I did not find a single *Sorex*.

Sorex cinereus miscix Bangs
Labrador Masked Shrew; Musaraigne du Labrador (Fr.). (Map 3.)

Three adults (two females and a male) of this shrew were taken in the vicinity of Seven Islands, May 24 and 29 and June 1. The first and the last were in mossy woods that included spruce, balsam, jack pine, *Cornus canadensis*, *Ribes glandulosum*, Labrador tea, mountain cranberry, *Clintonia borealis*, *Linnaea*, and *Cladonia*. The female of May 29 was in a thicket of *Myrica gale* and alder in a wet meadow bordering the bay; other near-by plants included raspberry, *Hierochloë odorata*, and *Viola*. The male had testes 4.5×2.75 mm.; lateral glands were slightly evident, and there was little odor; the hide was unprime. The females contained no embryos, but the mammary glands were much developed, and three pairs of mammae were evident (fig. 1); the hides were prime. In the first female there was scarcely any odor, and in the other a moderate odor. The male and the two females measured, respectively: length, 102, 108, 110; tail, 45, 49, 43; foot, 12, 12, 11.5; ear, 5, 5, 5; weight, 5.1, 5.6, 6.3 g. In length, tail, and weight these specimens considerably exceed a series of *S. c. cinereus* from southwestern Keewatin (*cf.* Harper, 1956:12); *miscix* is evidently a much more robust animal.

The specimens of May 29 and June 1 yielded three fleas—one male and two females of *Corrodopsylla c. curvata*; the former also had two mites (*Haemogamasus alaskensis*).

Sebastien McKenzie calls this shrew a "bad bugger," because it damages Martens and other animals in his traps (in the central part of the peninsula, perhaps chiefly in the Hamilton Basin). Sometimes he finds it inside the body of the fur-bearer, and he sees its tunnels in the snow. The Naskapi name (tcéen-is-tóo-yap-óok-a-dgish) cited by Strong (1930:9) bears a recognizable resemblance to the Montagnais name given above, as spelled by Sebastien McKenzie.

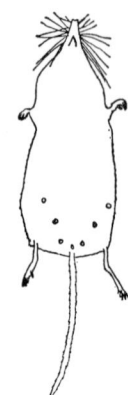

Fig. 1.—*Sorex cinereus miscix*, mastology (× ½). Adult female, No. 1275. Seven Islands, Quebec. May 29, 1953.

The range of *S. c. miscix* extends along the east coast from Okak southward and along the south coast as far west as Seven Islands (H. H. T. Jackson, 1928:50; C. F. Jackson, 1938:431; Weaver, 1940:418; Anderson, 1947:14; Hall and Kelson, 1959, 1:27, map 12).

"Jackson (1928:51) refers to *miscix* as a poorly marked subspecies, larger, paler, and grayer than *cinereus*. The Seven Islands specimens agree with abundant comparative material from Hamilton Inlet in size and coloration." (C. O. H., Jr.)

Sorex arcticus arcticus Kerr
Arctic Saddle-backed Shrew; Musaraigne ensellée (Fr.).

From the Ungava Peninsula C. F. Jackson (1938:431) recorded three specimens (under the name of *S. a. laricorum*) from the Moisie River near its mouth. These form the basis for subsequent mention of occurrence (as *S. a. arcticus*) in Saguenay County (Anderson, 1939:56, and 1947:16; Miller and Kellogg, 1955:15; Hall and Kelson, 1959, 1:43, map 22).

Sorex palustris labradorensis Burt
Labrador Water-shrew; Musaraigne d'eau du Labrador (Fr.).
(Map 4.)

Published records of *labradorensis* are from Red Bay (Burt, 1938: 1), Cartwright, and Astray Lake (Johnson, 1951:110). See also Hall and Kelson (1959, 1:39, map 19).

Sorex palustris turneri Johnson
Turner's Water-shrew; Musaraigne d'eau de Turner (Fr.). (Map 4.)

Gilbert Simard, J. L. Véronneau, and Henry Larouche described to me a shrew that they had observed in late September on Swampy Bay River at its entrance into Lac Le Fer. It was almost black above and gray (or perhaps partially white) below; there was a darker area where its eyes should be; it had a pointed snout, about ¾ of an inch in length; it had a long tail, and hind legs quite a bit longer than the front legs. There was also mention of "webbing" of the hind feet—presumably the fringe of stiff hairs on both margins. Thus it was evidently some form of *Sorex palustris*; and it is assigned provisionally to the subspecies *turneri*, whose coloration it seems to fit better than that of *labradorensis*.

The place of observation was a dry area in large timber, about 50 feet from the river and 15 or 20 feet above it. The vegetation included spruce, alder, birch, Labrador tea, *Cornus canadensis*, moss, and caribou lichen. The shrew was seen a number of times in the mess-tent, and it went into a hole beneath a near-by spruce. When Véronneau made a mouselike squeak, the shrew would reappear at the entrance to the hole and seize a piece of meat held out to it on a stick. In feeding, it sat up on its haunches like a squirrel, with its tail coiled beneath it. Although captured several times, the shrew managed to escape, and so could not be brought to me by my friends, to whom I am greatly indebted for these unusual observations.

Specimen material of this subspecies has been recorded only from the type locality at Fort Chimo (Johnson, 1951:110).

Sorex palustris gloveralleni Jackson
Acadian Water-shrew; Musaraigne d'eau des Maritimes (Fr.).
(Map 4.)

S. p. gloveralleni has been recorded from St. Charles Point and Seal River (C. F. Jackson, 1938:431) and from Godbout (Johnson, 1951: 111). Earlier reports from Godbout (H. H. T. Jackson, 1928:181; Anderson, 1939:57) had been assigned to *albibarbis*.

Sorex palustris albibarbis (Cope)
White-lipped Water-shrew; Musaraigne à moustaches blanches (Fr.). (Map 4.)

This subspecies ranges northeastward to St. Félicien, on the west side of Lake St. John (Cameron and Orkin, 1950:98) and to Mistassini Post (Cameron and Morris, 1951:124). See also Hall and Kelson (1959, 1:38, map 19).

Microsorex hoyi alnorum (Preble)
Alder Pygmy Shrew; Musaraigne pygmée des aunes (Fr.). (Map 5.)

The only shrew I found in the interior (and the first *Microsorex* I ever collected) entered a live-trap on July 21 at the Northwest Bay of Attikamagen Lake. The trap had been set between 4 and 5 p. m., and it was sprung by dusk. The place was a fairly open bog, grown with moss, sedge, white spruce, dwarf birch, sweet gale, *Habenaria dilatata*, and *Equisetum*. The specimen is an adult female: length, 91; tail, 35.5; foot, 12; ear, 5; weight, 3.2 g. There were no embryos; lateral glands were evident internally; and the hide was prime. The measurements and weight are very close to those of a series of *Sorex c. cinereus* from southwestern Keewatin (*cf.* Harper, 1956:12). In length of tail and foot the specimen is nearer to *M. h. alnorum* than to *M. h. intervectus*. In color it is almost indistinguishable from *Sorex cinereus miscix*. "Compared with the type of *intervectus*, this specimen is larger in most dimensions and has a deeper braincase, in these respects agreeing closely with the type of *alnorum*. It is tentatively referred to the latter subspecies, although it is grayer in summer pelage than any other specimen of *Microsorex* examined." (C. O. H., Jr.)

Although *alnorum* is known definitely only from central Manitoba and northwestern Ontario (Anderson, 1947:22), H. H. T. Jackson (1928:208) suggests the possibility that it may range "northeastwardly into Quebec." The Fort Chimo specimen that the latter refers somewhat doubtfully to *intervectus* is here considered tentatively as *alnorum*.

Microsorex hoyi intervectus Jackson
Northern Pygmy Shrew; Musaraigne pygmée du Nord (Fr.).
(Map 5.)

The subspecies *intervectus* has been recorded from Hopedale (G. M. Allen, 1920) and Godbout (H. H. T. Jackson, 1928:206; Hall and

Kelson, 1959, 1:50, map 28); also from St. Charles Point (C. F. Jackson, 1938:432). Hall and Kelson's map indicates a range extending to the northernmost parts of the peninsula; but this is evidently not a Barren Ground animal.

Blarina brevicauda talpoides (Gapper)
Gapper's Short-tailed Shrew; Musaraigne à queue courte (Fr.).

The inclusion of this species in the fauna of the Ungava Peninsula rests upon a single specimen taken at St. Méthode, on the west bank of the lower Mistassini River (Cameron and Orkin, 1950:98). These authors also report 10 other specimens from Val Jalbert and St. Félicien on the west side of Lake St. John (and thus barely outside of the peninsular limits). See also Hall and Kelson (1959, 1:55, map 29).

Condylura cristata cristata (Linnaeus)
Star-nosed Mole; Taupe au nez étoilé (Fr.). (Map 6.)

A huge mound of this species, with a tunnel beneath it, was found on May 28 among *Myrica gale* in a wet meadow bordering the bay at Seven Islands.

R. Gordon Racey reported many Star-nosed Moles seen in the spring, and one on September 5, at Mile 213 of the railway, on the east side of Ashuanipi Lake. Charles Grace reported the species about August 1 at Mile 232, near the south end of Whiteman Lake.

There are records on the east coast from Rigolet southward (Bangs, 1912:468; H. H. T. Jackson, 1915:86; Hall and Kelson, 1959, 1:75, map 42); on the south coast from Godbout eastward (H. H. T. Jackson, 1915:86; Eidmann, 1935:41; C. F. Jackson, 1938:431); in the west from Little Whale River (Banfield, 1960b:1) and East Main River (H. H. T. Jackson, 1915:86); and in the interior from Lakes St. John and Mistassini (Cameron and Orkin, 1950:97; Cameron and Morris, 1951:123). The northern limit of the range, as known to date, extends across the peninsula from Rigolet to Whiteman Lake and Little Whale River.

Myotis lucifugus lucifugus (Le Conte)
Little Brown Bat; Chauve-souris brune (Fr.). (Map 7.)

Through the kindness of M. T. Burke, John Macko, and Fred Farah I received two of these bats, found on August 31 and September 2 in the same woodpile at a camp at the north end of Ashuanipi Lake. Both were immature males: length, 92, 92; tail, 39, 40.5; foot, 11, 9.5; ear, 14, 13; tragus, 7, 7; forearm, 38, 38; testes, 1.5×1, 2.5×1.25;

weight, 7.8, 7.6 g. Their hides were prime. The first specimen yielded some mites (*Ichoronyssus britannicus* and *Laelaps alaskensis*) and two male and three female fleas (*Myodopsylla insignis*); the second yielded numerous mites from ears and wings (*Spinturnix* sp., *Ichoronyssus britannicus*, and *Laelaps* sp.).

Ross McFarland reported a bat over the near-by Ashuanipi River one evening in August; R. Gordon Racey saw two on September 5 over the same part of this river; Jack Craig reported bats as seen frequently at Menihek Lake in the summer of 1952; Lloyd Hogan found one in a pail of water at Fort McKenzie in 1950; and A. E. Boerner saw them frequently at Gad Lake in 1953. It is not at all certain, however, that all—or even any—of these were *M. l. lucifugus*, although no other bat has been found so generally in the peninsula.

This species has been recorded more or less definitely on the east coast north to Makkovik (Miller and Allen, 1928:43; Hall and Kelson, 1959, 1:161, map 118) and perhaps to Davis Inlet (Strong, 1930:9); on the south coast at Godbout (Bangs, 1898*b*:497) and Trout Lake (sight record only—Eidmann, 1935:43); on the west coast at Rupert House (Miller and Allen, 1928:43; Hall and Kelson, 1959, 1:161, map 118); and in the interior at Lake St. John (Cameron and Orkin, 1950: 99) and perhaps at Lakes Mistassini and Albanel (sight records— Cameron and Morris, 1951:124)

Myotis keenii septentrionalis (Trouessart)
Acadian Bat; Chauve-souris de Trouessart (Fr.).

This bat has been recorded at two points along the North Shore: Natashquan and Godbout (Stearns, 1883:116; Miller, 1897*b*:75; Miller and Allen, 1928:105; Hall and Kelson, 1959, 1:168, map 124). The vernacular name Acadian Bat was proposed by me (1928:15).

Lepus arcticus labradorius Miller
Labrador Arctic Hare; Lièvre arctique (Fr.). (Map 8.)

During 20 years' residence at Fort McKenzie, Sebastien McKenzie met with the Arctic Hare only once—at a point apparently to the westward and perhaps at a considerable distance. It may be migratory to some extent.

The present subspecies ranges over the Barrens of the northern part of the peninsula, south to Great Whale River in the west and to Davis Inlet in the east (Payne, 1887:73; Miller, 1899:39; Nelson, 1909:61, fig. 7; Wheeler, 1930:456; Hantzsch, 1932:9; A. H. Howell, 1936:322, fig. 1; Hall, 1951*a*:179, fig. 45; Burt, 1958; Hall and Kelson, 1959, 1:

279, map 190). Nearly all of the records are coastal, but Low (1896: 321) reports a few of the animals at Michikamau Lake.

Lepus arcticus bangsii Rhoads
Newfoundland Arctic Hare; Lièvre de Terre-Neuve (Fr.). (Map 8.)

The range of the Newfoundland Hare extends along the east Labrador coast from Hopedale and Makkovik (Allen and Copeland, 1924:11; A. H. Howell, 1936:324) southward to Hamilton Inlet, Isthmus Bay, Stony Island, and Fox Harbour (Cartwright, 1792:3: *passim*; Bangs, 1897:237; A. H. Howell, 1936:324, fig. 1).

The occurrence of this identical subspecies in both Newfoundland and Labrador may bespeak its successful crossing of the Strait of Belle Isle on occasions when these waters have been frozen over.

Lepus americanus americanus Erxleben
American Varying Hare; American Snowshoe Rabbit; Lièvre d'Amérique (Fr.); Oaposh (M.). (Map 9.)

The year 1953 was by no means one of rabbit abundance; I saw no more than half a dozen in the wild in the entire season. Yet pellets or gnawings were common enough in most of the localities visited, including Seven Islands and Knob, Slimy, Attikamagen, and Ashuanipi lakes. Snowshoes seemed more numerous in the green timber about Attikamagen Lake than in the burnt area about Knob Lake.

On July 6 an adult male came hopping along on a hillside above the Iron Arm, grown with white spruce, dwarf birch, Labrador tea, *Vaccinium uliginosum*, and *Cladonia alpestris*. Data for it were: length, 444; tail (after skinning), 37; foot, 141; ear, 88; weight, approximately 2.75 lb.; testes, 47×12; iris pale brownish; hide prime. These measurements do not correspond closely to those given by Nelson (1909:86) for "Keewatin" (=Manitoba) and Saskatchewan specimens. The underfur of the venter is white to the base; that of the dorsum, pale plumbeous.

On July 7 a Snowshoe Rabbit appeared in our camp area on the Iron Arm, and permitted an approach within about 20 feet as I filmed it. Later in the day perhaps the same animal came within a rod of the mess-tent, where it kept thrusting its nose deep into the moss (*Pleurozium schreberi*), till its eyes were almost out of sight. Presently I saw there some slender roots or rhizomes that it may have been seeking.

Several baby Snowshoes were captured about Ashuanipi Lake, where William Thomson, Jr., endeavored to rear one of them by hand, feeding it mainly on evaporated milk with a medicine dropper (pl. 3, fig. 1). One of its interesting habits was "washing" its face with its forepaws. After barely a week in captivity, it succumbed on August 28. It was then quite emaciated, probably owing to lack of natural food, and it weighed only 88 g.; length, 176; tail (after skinning), 20.5; foot, 52; ear, 34; testes, 5×3. Its hide was generally unprime.

"These specimens are white-footed and as gray on the dorsum as typical *L. a. americanus* (Oxford House, Manitoba; Indian Head, Saskatchewan; and Fort Chipewyan, Alberta). The hind foot of the adult is longer than those of most Manitoba and Saskatchewan specimens examined, but it agrees in this respect with examples collected 50 miles north of Edmonton and at Fort McMurray, Alberta." (C. O. H., Jr.)

At Carol Lake a large Snowshoe Rabbit leaped away among spruces on September 11, and one about two-thirds grown was flushed from beneath a spruce on September 17.

During the season of 1952 Arthur C. Newton saw no Rabbits in the Fort McKenzie area, though the local Indians had skins. The following year Robert Slipp had seen none at Lac Aulneau or thereabouts up to July 31. In June, 1953, Hugh Smith spoke of seeing scarcely any about Knob Lake. At Attikamagen Lake James Murdoch had seen only one up to July 19, 1953. Near Mile 224 Airstrip, on September 6, William Schrøpfer reported two running in front of his car before daybreak, one of them for several hundred yards.

Leopold Gelinas reported a Rabbit coming into a tent at night at Julienne Lake, and one staying about camp for a week at Shabogamo Lake. Four young captured there were kept in a tent, but were free to come and go at any time. They were furnished with water, cabbage, and carrots. Garth D. Jackson saw Rabbits at Huguette, Nip, Sudbury, and Jackson lakes. Many were reported at Eric Lake (Willé Pinette) and at Gad Lake (A. E. Boerner). Philip Loth spoke of a "herd" of about 60 crossing Lac de Morhiban in the winter (about February) of 1952. During the winter of 1953–54 there were very few about Lake Paterson, according to J. L. Véronneau (*in litt.*, April 5, 1954). In January, 1955, Mr. Véronneau (*in litt.*, June 26, 1955) found the species abundant about the headwaters of the Nemiscau River. The local Indians were eating many of the Rabbits and making garments for young children out of the fur.

The foregoing records indicate, in general, considerably larger numbers in the more southerly areas (lat. 51°–53°) than in the more northerly areas, with a marked scarcity in 1952 and 1953 in latitude 57°.

This species occurs more or less throughout the wooded regions of the Ungava Peninsula: south coast (Stearns, 1883:115; Cabot, 1920: 315; Comeau, 1923:17; Eidmann, 1935:57, fig. 8; C. F. Jackson, 1938: 434); east coast, north to Hamilton Inlet (Cartwright, 1792: *passim*; Bangs, 1898a:78; Nelson, 1909:87, fig. 8; Hall and Kelson, 1959, 1:273, map 189); in the north, at The Forks and Fort Chimo (Turner, 1888b: 83; Nelson, 1909:87; Hall, 1951a:174; Hall and Kelson, 1959, 1:273, map 189); on the west coast north to latitude 56° (Hall, 1951a:174); in the interior—Lake Mistassini (Low, 1890:20); throughout (including Nichicun Lake), and visited about once in five years by a devastating throat disease (Low, 1896:100,321); Natashquan River (Townsend, 1913:176); lower Naskaupi River and near Windbound Lake (Mrs. Hubbard, 1908:31,107); inland from Davis Inlet (Strong, 1930:1); Hamilton River basin (Merrick, 1933:20,112,142,350); Mushalagan Lake (Manning, 1947:83); near Otish Mountains (Pomerleau, 1950: 14); Lake St. John (Cameron and Orkin, 1950:101); Lakes Mistassini and Albanel (Cameron and Morris, 1951:125); (Lower) Seal Lake (Doutt, 1954:245).

Marmota monax canadensis (Erxleben)
Canadian Woodchuck; Marmotte du Canada (Fr.); Otshek (M.).
(Map 10.)

This subspecies is predominantly an inhabitant of the Canadian Life-zone, although in western Canada it pushes through the Hudsonian Life-zone as far as York Factory (Preble, 1902:47) and Amery, Manitoba (Harper, 1956:16). In Quebec, Hall and Kelson (1959, 1:321, map 211) extend the range northeastward approximately to the East Main, Temiscamie, and Saguenay rivers—and thus not beyond the boundary of the Canadian Life-zone. In the dearth of essential material for determining the area of intergradation, we may provisionally consider that the present subspecies continues eastward to, or nearly to, the limits of that zone, while *ignava* occupies the Hudsonian Life-zone.

On May 31, along the shore of the Gulf about 4 miles east of Seven Islands, I noticed a Woodchuck's burrow beneath a clump of alders in some balsam woods; there was a trail leading to another den 9–10 feet away. In 1957 Roland C. Clement (*in litt.*, August 8) saw Woodchucks at Miles 15 and 22 of the Quebec North Shore and Labrador Railway and had a report of others at Mile 13.

The following records from the literature may also be attributed to *canadensis*: between Lakes St. John and Mistassini (Michaux, 1889:

83); Mingan (Stearns, 1883:115); Romaine River, and between Lake St. John and East Main River (Low, 1896:320); Matamek area (Eidmann, 1935:46, fig. 2); Lake St. John area (Cameron and Orkin, 1950:102); Temiscamie River (Cameron and Morris, 1951:126).

Marmota monax ignava (Bangs)
Labrador Woodchuck; Marmotte du Labrador (Fr.). (Map 10.)

The following reports from various interior localities seem to represent extensions of the known range of the species, as known hitherto. Joe Laporte reported a "Ground Hog" passing the mess-tent in our camp area at the northwestern end of the Iron Arm, Attikamagen Lake, on the evening of July 11. J. L. Véronneau saw one of the animals and its burrow near Squaw Lake in early July. Cyrille Dufresne spoke of seeing a Woodchuck and its burrows on August 20 on a steep, rocky slope at Trough Lake. Norman Delmage reported observing three between Knob and Menihek lakes and one at Slimy Lake. Several persons reported a Woodchuck as seen on several occasions in the summer of 1953 at the north end of Ashuanipi Lake, and one was secured in this vicinity by Kom Pinette. Robert Slipp noticed a "Ground Hog" and its trails, and heard it whistle, on July 5, 1953, at a lake 1.5 miles southeast of Lac Aulneau. The spot was among bushes and grass on a steep cliff with a southern exposure, above the timber-line and about 400 feet above the lake. In 1945 Richard Geren saw single animals at Lac Cramolet and Lac Effiat. James Murdoch secured one in 1951 on Atikonak River, between Ossokmanuan and Panchia lakes.

Reports of Woodchucks about "the head of Hamilton Inlet" or Northwest River (Low, 1896:320; Strong, 1930:8) remain to be subspecifically allocated, since this locality is in an extension of the Canadian Life-zone. Will they prove to be *canadensis*, which occupies the main Canadian Life-zone, or *ignava*, which presumably ranges through the Hudsonian Life-zone?

The previously published records, presented below, were all from coastal areas, and all except the first were attributed to *ignava* on first publication. A report by Spencer (1889:78) appears to apply to the Fort George area on James Bay (not Ungava Bay, as cited by Anderson (1947:106) and Miller and Kellogg (1955:182)). Other localities are: Black Bay and L'Anse au Loup (Bangs, 1899:13, and 1912:460); Aillik (A. H. Howell, 1915: 30, fig. 1); near Harrington Harbour (Weaver, 1940:421); Point Amour (Hall and Kelson, 1959, 1:322, map 211).

Lacs Aulneau, Cramolet, and Effiat lie within the zone of permafrost, as delimited by Jenness (1949:map 1) and by Thomas (1953: chart 8–1). Throughout the range of *Marmota monax* east of the Rockies, there appears to be only one previous record within that zone—from York Factory, Manitoba (Preble, 1902:48).

Tamias striatus quebecensis Cameron
Quebec Chipmunk; Suisse rayé de Québec (Fr.). (Map 11.)

The records of this Chipmunk in the Ungava Peninsula—and on its immediate borders—extend from Mattagami and Waswanipi lakes eastward to Lakes Mistassini and Albanel, the Lake St. John area, Godbout, lower Ste. Marguerite River, Moisie Bay, and Matamek River (A. H. Howell, 1929:20, fig. 2; Anderson, 1947:113; Cameron and Orkin, 1950:102; Cameron, 1950:347; Cameron and Morris, 1951: 126; Hall and Kelson, 1959, 1:295, map 196).

Tamiasciurus hudsonicus laurentianus Anderson
Laurentian Red Squirrel; Écureuil roux (Fr.); Nikotshash or Annikotsash (M.). (Map 12.)

The present subspecies of the Red Squirrel ranges from the Strait of Belle Isle westward along the North Shore of the Gulf to Lake St. John and the St. Maurice River (Anderson, 1947:118). Its type locality is Lac Marchant (?"Lac Mechant" of the Clarke City-Mingan map in the National Topographic Series), near Moisie Bay. I found it moderately common in the vicinity of Seven Islands, and particularly in spruce woods, May 23 to 31. One was feeding on fresh twig tips or cones in a white spruce. I also noticed several well-marked trails (presumably made by this species rather than by Snowshoe Rabbits) that extended through beds of *Cladonia alpestris* from one clump of spruce to another; they were three to four inches wide. At one place in the woods there was a mound formed by fragments of black spruce cones, with several entrances to subterranean tunnels of this species. At a dump near the airport a squirrel crossed some open ground into a thicket where I was, began squeaking at me, and descended a balsam overhead to within two feet of my face. In some spruce woods along the Gulf shore, one pranced or pattered with its hind feet as it squeaked at me and gave its rolling chatter. The squeaks had an impudent questioning tone: *tseek?*, *tseek?* One or two other squirrels were noted at the airport dump on October 11. Several were kept in a cage at the Indian reserve near Seven Islands.

Red Squirrels reported at Lac de Morhiban by Philip Loth, and at

Gad Lake (as abundant) by A. E. Boerner, are presumably of the same subspecies.

The following records from the literature may be attributed to *laurentianus*: Matamek area (Eidmann, 1935:48, fig. 9); Moisie River to Pigou Harbour (C. F. Jackson, 1938:432); Cross River and Kecarpoui (Weaver, 1940:418,419); and Lake St. John area (Cameron and Orkin, 1950:102). See also Hall and Kelson (1959, 1:401, map 257).

Tamiasciurus hudsonicus ungavensis Anderson
Ungava Red Squirrel; Écureuil roux d'Ungava (Fr.). (Map 12.)

The type locality of this subspecies is Lake Waswanipi (Anderson, 1942*b*:33), which is outside the limits of the Ungava Peninsula as defined by Bell (1895:335) and by Low (1896:19), and almost outside the southwestern boundary at the Nottaway and Saguenay rivers, as defined in the present paper (p. 26, *antea*). Thus there may be some question as to the appropriateness of the subspecific name. There may have been some typographical errors in the original description, for the foot measurement (38–42 mm.) seems much too small, and the total length (up to 407 mm.) a great deal too large. Neither Anderson (1947:118,121) nor Miller and Kellogg (1955:264) account for *any* representative of the species in the wooded areas of the northeastern part of the peninsula (east of Fort Chimo and north of Hamilton Inlet). Palmer (1954:193) maps this part of the range with reasonable accuracy. The name *ungavensis* is only provisionally applied to my records and specimens from the interior of the peninsula. Since the type localities of both *laurentianus* and *ungavensis* are in the Canadian Life-zone, it is just possible that the population of the Hudsonian Life-zone is subspecifically distinct from either.

In the vicinity of Knob Lake (and elsewhere) Red Squirrels were the mammalian autocrats of the garbage dumps—except at such times as a Black Bear might choose to make a visit. Here they made merry over the perennial feast spread before them, although it was doubtless far less wholesome than the natural foods available to them in the adjacent green timber. I noticed one with a domineering or dog-in-the-manger attitude; it resented the close approach of one or two of his kind, chasing them away and scolding at them. They would delve into the piles of garbage, bringing out small morsels or even good-sized bones. They not only freely allowed me to film them at half a rod's distance; one even came and gnawed at a knapsack resting at my feet. Their confiding nature in this region is in noteworthy contrast to the excessive shyness of their relatives in far-away Keewatin.

On one of my visits (on June 6) a Red Squirrel approached and kept scolding me; I could see its lower jaw drop with each note—something like *tsick, tsŏok*, or *kŏok*—delivered at a rate up to two per second. Presently a second squirrel appeared on a stump and added its voice, with saucy flirts of its tail, while the first one stamped with its hind feet. One of them continued to scold with a prune pit in its mouth. A ragged stage of molt was evident, the old fur remaining especially on the hind quarters. (Molt continued in evidence up to June 10.) On the same day, far up on the slopes of Ruth Lake Ridge, a squirrel came up behind me, squeaking within a yard, while another appeared on a black spruce, nibbling at the tips of the twigs. On June 9, near Camp Pond, another one scolded at me from a vantage point some 9 feet overhead in a burned black spruce, flirting its tail and stamping its feet at me. It had a cone in its mouth, and presently proceeded to gnaw it contentedly. Later it made a flying leap of about 6 feet to another burnt tree.

At Attikamagen Lake single Red Squirrels were noted on a number of occasions, July 3 to 20. Here, as at Knob Lake, their narrow trails extended through the woods. One of them passed beneath a fallen limb in a space too small for a Snowshoe Rabbit. Many of the spruces are too far apart to permit leaping from one to another; hence, probably, the ground trails. One of the squirrels was noticed with a white spruce cone in its mouth. Some of the big trees had piles of cone fragments about their bases. On July 13 I met with another squirrel on the summit of a ridge north of the Iron Arm. At first it retreated into some alders, where it uttered some *kŏok* or *klŏok* notes, punctuating them with flicks of its tail in alternate directions—upward with one note and downward with the next. Presently it perched on the limb of a small white spruce, where I filmed it at decreasing distances, until the camera was only two feet from it. Perhaps the animal had never before had an experience with a human being and was thus unaware of the latter's dangerous potentialities.

Before I arrived at Lac Aulneau on July 22, an Indian boy was said to have killed about a dozen Red Squirrels with a slingshot in the camp area. Yet the species still appeared as abundant there as in any other locality I visited in that season. They were attracted particularly to the ample supply of food in the garbage pit. One was seen frequently in pursuit of another—perhaps not altogether in mere playfulness, but in some sort of rivalry for food. There was some evidence of feeling of the latter sort between the squirrels and their fellow-scavengers, the Labrador Jays. For example, when one of the squirrels was feasting on a discarded loaf of bread, a jay appeared to be more or less competing for it. It was amusing to notice their air of unconcern in close proximity to several predatory Northern Shrikes. On one occasion a couple of them were frisking about a brush pile, from the top of which two of the shrikes were interestedly observing the squirrels. They also bounced about in apparently complete indifference to the rain. In late July they appeared to be in full summer pelage, with a black lateral stripe. As I was walking along a path in the camp area, a squirrel ran across it ahead of me and came to a pause beneath a spruce about 6 feet away. There it seized upon a cluster of black spruce cones, picked one off, and sat up on its haunches to gnaw at a great rate, deftly turning the cone with its hands as the chips fell to the ground. Presently a second cone was handled in like maner. On another day an individual was seen holding a fresh twig of black spruce and gnawing on one of the cones attached to it. Finally one was collected with a cone of this spruce in its mouth. On August 1 one gnawed a little on a loose bird wing, but soon ran over to a tree, and stamped at me with all four feet, meanwhile uttering its rubber-doll squeaks. One was still active in the early dusk at 8:38 p. m. On a gravelly knoll near the camp there was a well-marked squirrel trail (pl. 2, fig. 2) extending across a mat of *Cladonia alpestris* between two clumps of black spruce about 15 feet apart. Robert Slipp reported having seen a squirrel feeding upon this "caribou moss" (*Cladonia*). Sebastien McKenzie said that Red Squirrels do not build tree nests here, but live in holes in the ground. (Tree nests might not be very habitable in the low winter temperatures.) He indicated that the squirrel numbers remain about the same from year to year.

In August, September, and October one of the animals was frequenting the rather bare camp area at Knob Lake, where it may have made its home in one of the buildings or in the ground. At Slimy Lake, on August 8, one came running along a log to within a yard of me. Here, among some unusually large white spruces, remains of the squirrels' repasts on the cones were in evidence on all sides. Peter Norman, at the commissary in Burnt Creek, told of a squirrel that would come to the window and take food from his hand, and even enter the building to filch chocolate bars and the like.

At Mollie T. Lake I recorded no squirrels, and at Leroy Lake only two. One of these was familiar enough to let one of my Montagnais friends knock it over with a paddle. In the latter area (and elsewhere) the animals had left spruce cone fragments in piles, but never in such enormous heaps as have been seen in the Athabaska region. In the vicinity of Mile 224 Airstrip, in late August and September, there were a considerable number of Red Squirrels, seen for the most part at a big garbage dump, but also to some extent in the balsam and spruce woods. One vociferated at me to the accompaniment of jerks of its body, giving 10 *tsŏŏk* calls in 10 seconds. At Carol Lake, in September, there was an apparent dearth of squirrels, but at the neighboring Stevens Lake a very small one was seen leaping from spruce to spruce.

Three specimens were collected: adult male, Lac Aulneau, August 1; adult male, Leroy Lake, August 21; and adult female, Knob Lake, September 30. All were taken in woods composed at least in part of spruce. Since about 35 mm. of the tail of the first specimen was missing, the measurements for length as well as tail in that specimen are omitted from the following data: length, —, 308, 305; tail, —, 128, 125; foot, 51, 50.5, 48; ear, 23, 21, 21; weight, 201.4, 195.5, 161 g. The testes of the males measured 9×5 and 8×4; the uterus of the female was small. The hide of the first was almost prime; that of the second, slightly unprime on nose and throat; that of the female, unprime on dorsum from crown to rump. These specimens are well matched in size and color by two from Davis Inlet in the United States National Museum. Fleas (*Orchopeas caedens durus* (Jordan)) were collected from all three: one female from the first, two females from the second, and three males and one female from the third. The third also yielded two lice (*Hoplopleura sciuricola*).

In 1949 Dr. F. D. Foster found Red Squirrels at Wishart, Menihek, Astray, Evening, Molson, Whiteman, and Ashuanipi lakes. The species was reported in the Fort McKenzie area in 1952 by Arthur C. Newton. At Trough Lake, according to Remi Kelly, the animals were numerous and troublesome in 1953, invading the mess-tent to eat cakes; one even jumped on a member of the party and, when shaken off, landed on still another person! They were of general occurrence at various small lakes west and southwest of Wabush Lake (Garth D. Jackson). Two individuals were noted on February 11, 1955, on the headwaters of the Nemiscau River (J. L. Véronneau, *in litt.*, June 26, 1955).

The following records from the literature pertain to the territory from Lakes Waswanipi and Mistassini northward in the western part of the peninsula, and from the Canadian Life-zone boundary northward in the eastern part (these presumably representing the subspecies *ungavensis*): east coast, north at least to Fraser River (Bangs, 1898b:497; Prichard, 1911:43; Strong, 1930:8; Hall and Kelson, 1959, 1:403, map 257); in the central north as far as Fort Chimo (Bangs, 1898b:497), False River (Gabrielson and Wright, 1951:128), and Finger Lake south of Leaf Bay (Bateman, 1953:7); and west coast at Great Whale River (Anderson, 1942b:33). Interior records include the following: East Main River, Sandgirt Lake, Atikonak River, but not Ashuanipi River (Low, 1896:320); The Forks (Bangs, 1898b:497); Lower Susan River (Wallace, 1906:63); middle and upper Fraser River (Prichard, 1911:43,44,54); Eskimo (=St. Paul's) River (Cabot, 1920: 331); Flour Lake (Merrick, 1933:106); Lake Waswanipi and Mistassini district (Anderson, 1942b:33; Hall and Kelson, 1959, 1:403, map 257); Lower Seal Lake (Doutt, 1942:65); Mushalagan, Sawbill, and Panchia lakes (Manning, 1947:83); headwaters of Manicouagan River (Pomerleau, 1950:14); Lakes Mistassini and Albanel (Cameron and Morris, 1951:126); Clearwater Lake (Doutt, 1954:242).

"Squirrel" skins to the number of 92,519 were taken in Quebec in 1950–51 (Cowan, 1955:169). For 1954–55, 37,755 skins were reported (Canada Year Book 1956:606). In all likelihood the vast majority of these were Red Squirrels.

"Specimens referred to *ungavensis* have not been examined, but to judge from Anderson's description of the subspecies, the specimens from Knob Lake, Leroy Lake, and Lac Aulneau may be tentatively referred to it, although they are apparently grayer and duller colored, particularly on the head. Proportions of the rostrum, used as diagnostic characters by Anderson, are extremely variable in northeastern populations." (C. O. H., Jr.)

Glaucomys sabrinus sabrinus (Shaw)
Hudson Bay Flying Squirrel; Écureuil volant du Nord (Fr.);
Oponikotsash (M.). (Map 13.)

Several individuals, probably of the present subspecies, were trapped and released in the summer of 1953 at Gad Lake, where they came into a mess-tent at night (A. E. Boerner). On February 19, 1955, J. L. Véronneau (*in litt.*, June 26, 1955) observed two individuals pursuing each other at the headwaters of the Nemiscau River. They flew from the top of a tamarack to a distance of 50 to 60 feet from its base.

This Flying Squirrel ranges through the southern portion of the peninsula from Lakes Mistassini, Kallio, and St. John, Tadousac, and

Godbout eastward at least as far as Matamek River (A. H. Howell, 1918:31, fig. 3; Eidmann, 1935:49; Cameron and Orkin, 1950:103; Cameron and Morris, 1951:127; Hall and Kelson, 1959, 1:411, map 260); perhaps also north in the James Bay drainage to the vicinity of Fort George (Doutt, 1954:242).

Glaucomys sabrinus makkovikensis (Sornborger)
Labrador Flying Squirrel; Écureuil volant du Labrador (Fr.).
(Map 13.)

Flying Squirrels seem to be rather sparingly distributed in the interior. They may, however, be somewhat commoner than the few records indicate, for their nocturnal habits shield them from ordinary observation.

In the early part of the summer four of the animals were taken in a cage trap at a camp area among spruce woods at the north end of Ashuanipi Lake. Two of them presently escaped, but one, through the good offices of Fred Farah, was shipped alive by air express in the latter part of July to the Army Medical Center in Washington, for purposes of serological and parasitological investigation. While I was in that vicinity myself on September 7, a subadult male was captured in the same area by John Macko, who kindly presented it to me. The data for it were: length, 334; tail, 164; tail pencil, 34; foot, 45; ear, 20; greatest length of skull, 41; weight, 127.1 g.; testes, 3.5 × 1 (not descended); dorsum unprime. It yielded 10 males and 6 females of a flea (*Opisodasys pseudarctomys* (Baker)).

Although the specimen is not fully adult, nearly all its measurements equal or exceed the maxima given by A. H. Howell (1918:34-35) for *G. s. makkovikensis* or two adjacent subspecies; it is therefore referred provisionally to *makkovikensis*, the largest of these three subspecies. Since some of its colors differ considerably from those ascribed to adults of that subspecies by Howell, the following notes on it are presented: dorsal coloration near Saccardo's Umber, or much darker than that of an adult from Goose Bay (USNM No. 282890); sides of face Light Neutral Gray; eye-ring blackish; ears short-haired, dusky internally and externally; upper surface of flying membrane (mostly) blackish, lower surface Pale Pinkish Buff; upper surface of feet Fuscous; tail near Mouse Gray above, becoming black toward tip, and with a slightly buffy median anterior area; a broad, indistinct blackish median stripe, beginning toward base and becoming gradually more unmixed blackish to the tip; under side of tail Light Grayish

Olive near base and becoming progressively darker toward tip, with a blackish border at and near tip.

"Although differing in tail length and cranial proportions from *G. s. makkovikensis* (specimens from Cartwright area), this immature specimen agrees most closely with that subspecies and is tentatively referred to it" (C. O. H., Jr.).

At the guest house on the north shore of Knob Lake, located in an extensive growth of black spruce, Mr. and Mrs. Yeo told me on October 6 of a squirrel there that differed from the Red Squirrels. They pointed out two spruces fully 25 feet apart, where it jumped from one to another. That alone settled its identity as *Glaucomys*, at its northernmost known point in the interior. They also showed me its globular nest, located close to the trunk of a 35-foot black spruce, at a height of about 28 feet. (This was the tree to which it was said to leap.) The nest was about 14 inches in diameter and constructed, apparently, of tree lichens and papers. (Red Squirrels are said not to make outside nests in this region.) There appeared to be an entrance-hole at the middle of the side.

A Montagnais of Seven Islands, Georges Michel, spoke of Flying Squirrels getting into his fur traps (probably at a considerable distance to the north, in the interior). Howard Jackson reported the animals coming into a cabin at Sawyer Lake. Leopold Gelinas described a squirrel as "flying" about 20 feet from a dead tree he had struck one morning in July, a mile north of Wabush Lake.

G. s. makkovikensis ranges along the east coast from Makkovik southward a little past the Strait of Belle Isle, with records at Northwest River, Paradise, Cartwright, L'Anse au Loup, Bonne Esperance, Stick Point, and St. Augustin (Cartwright, 1792, 2:179; Stearns, 1883: 115; A. H. Howell, 1918:34, fig. 3; Hall and Kelson, 1959, 1:410, map 260). The area of intergradation with *G. s. sabrinus* in the interior of the peninsula has not been ascertained but may conform in part (from Lake Mistassini eastward) to the boundary between the Canadian and the Hudsonian life-zones. Makkovik and Knob Lake evidently represent the northernmost points of known occurrence in the peninsula (*cf.* map 13).

Castor canadensis labradorensis Bailey and Doutt
Labrador Beaver; Castor du Labrador (Fr.); Amisk (M.). (Map 14.)

In the central interior Beavers seem to be rather scarce. I myself found no trace of them. Sebastien McKenzie seemed to attribute the local scarcity to a dearth of mud for building lodges. Ben McKenzie said there were not many Beavers in the Menihek-Bringadin-Wakuach lakes area, but in 1945 there were more in the middle or upper Hamilton River basin, where there might be as many as 10 lodges on a creek. Dr. F. D. Foster noted a dam and fresh cuttings at Evening Lake in 1949. Allen Thompson reported lodges, fresh cuttings, and the splash of a tail in the summer of 1951 in the Michikamau Lake area. In the same season James Murdoch noted a considerable number of old dams on little rivers running into the upper Hamilton. Remi Kelly saw a Beaver on Donald Lake in 1951. Gilbert Simard mentioned beaver cuttings on alders and willows in 1953 between Mollie T. and Greenbush lakes. In this season Kom Pinette secured a Beaver near Ashuanipi Lake. According to some of the Montagnais whom I met at Knob Lake and whose trapping grounds were in that general area, a family in the old days might capture 70 Beavers in a season.

From J. L. Véronneau I learned that in the early fall of 1953 a lodge was found on an expansion of Swampy Bay River south of Lac Le Fer (about lat. 55°15′ N.); this is one of the more northerly locality records in the central interior. A quantity of alders had been freshly cut and stored near it. The animals would come out to feed about 6:15 p. m. From this family (reported to number five) some Montagnais secured an adult female and a young one. The former was estimated to weigh 70 lb.; the length of its flat skin (without tail) was 1065 mm.

The foregoing records presumably pertain to *C. c. labradorensis*, which may belong mainly to the fauna of the eastern part of the Hudsonian Life-zone in the peninsula.

The wild fur production in Quebec, for the season of 1950–51, included 25,143 beaver skins (Cowan, 1955:169). For 1954–55, 32,901 skins were reported (Canada Year Book 1956:606). These statistics cover both *labradorensis* and *acadicus*.

Previous records attributable to *labradorensis* are: common along east coast south of Hamilton Inlet, including Charles and Alexis rivers, 1770–1783 (Cartwright, 1792: *passim*); extremely rare in the north—no sign about Fort Chimo or thence to George River (McLean, 1932 (1849):202,209,251); becoming extinct on [east] coast (Packard, 1891:442); Hamilton River up to Sandgirt Lake, very rare toward Michikamau Lake (Low, 1896:70,86,100,318,320); tributary of Susan River (Wallace, 1906:79); near Namaycush Lake (Wallace, 1907:79); lower Naskaupi River (Mrs. Hubbard, 1908:31); lower Eagle River (Durgin, 1908:83); interior streams west of Hopedale, but not farther north (Strong, 1930:7); Kenamu River (Leslie, 1931:210); Flour Lake to Ossokmanuan Lake (Merrick, 1933:98,146,183); 1,000 skins per year formerly traded at Northwest River, but Indians at Davis Inlet never have skins to sell (Tanner, 1947, 2:622); fur statistics (Elton, 1942:254); 5 miles above Grand Falls (type locality of *labradorensis*), Gull Lake, Northwest River, 25 miles above Winokapau Lake, and Paradise River (Bailey and Doutt, 1942:86); George River (Rousseau, 1949: 102).

Castor canadensis acadicus Bailey and Doutt
New Brunswick Beaver; Castor du Nouveau-Brunswick (Fr.).
(Map 14.)

The northern and eastern limits of this subspecies on the north side of the St. Lawrence are not definitely known. I am only provisionally attributing to it, within the peninsula, all records from the Canadian Life-zone and all those from the drainage system of Hudson and James bays in the Hudsonian Life-zone.

Sebastien McKenzie said that in his 20 years (1916–36) at Fort McKenzie he had traded only three skins; and these came from Great Whale River. Willé Pinette reported taking 18 Beavers at Eric Lake in the winter of 1952–53. J. L. Véronneau (*in litt.*, April 5, 1954) reported seeing old beaver dams in the winter of 1953–54 on every small lake in the vicinity of Lake Paterson, where Indians from Pointe Bleue, near Roberval, had hunted in previous years. In mild weather on February 3, 1954, he saw a Beaver come out of a hole on Paterson Creek, walk 15 feet in the snow, and return to the hole. From January to March, 1955, Mr. Véronneau (*in litt.*, June 26, 1955) found many beaver lodges and dams on lakes about the head of Nemiscau River. By mid-February several Indian families thereabouts had taken 75 skins—apparently less than a normal catch. They were eating the meat.

Published records of Beavers from the provisionally stated range of *acadicus* include the following: a tributary of Mistassini River in 1792 (Michaux, 1889:79); inland ponds along the south coast (Stearns, 1883:115); Lake Nichicun, East Main River, and Richmond Gulf (Low, 1896:86,100,320); lower Peribonca River and vicinity of Nekebau Lakes (Chambers, 1896:189); 40 a good season's catch for two trappers in the 1860's in the Trinity Bay–Godbout area (Comeau, 1923:75); Matamek River and Trout Lake (Eidmann, 1935:50); Lake St. John, Godbout, and Ste. Marguerite River (Bailey and Doutt,

1942:87); extinct near Lake St. John (Cameron and Orkin, 1950: 104); near Otish Mountains (Pomerleau, 1950:14); Mistassini River (Cameron and Morris, 1951:127); Clearwater Lake (Doutt, 1954: 243).

In the Lake Mistassini area "skulls are always scraped clean [by the Indians], and set up on poles facing the sun" (Low, 1890:25).

An immensely inspiring story of beaver conservation has come from the Rupert House area on James Bay. Forty years ago the Beaver population had dwindled to the point where only four skins were traded by the Indians in a whole season. Since the Caribou had largely disappeared, the Beavers had become one of the most essential sources of food for the natives, and many of them starved for lack of this food. At this juncture J. S. C. Watt, manager of the Hudson's Bay Company's post at Rupert House, with the help of Mrs. Watt, persuaded the Indians to spare the remaining Beavers for a period of years. By degrees they secured the co-operation of the Department of Indian Affairs at Ottawa and the provincial Department of Fish and Game. Mrs. Watt was made "sole proprietor of 7,200 square miles of beaver territory" surrounding Rupert House. In 1933 an official count revealed 162 Beavers; in 1938, 3,300; in 1939, more than 4,000. The following year, when trapping was resumed, each Indian trapper was licensed and allowed an exact quota based upon the number of beaver lodges in his territory. "Today the family cash incomes of the Indian hunters average between $1000 and $1500 from the catch of beavers alone.... By any standards the Indians are now prosperous." (W. A. Anderson, 1959.)

Peromyscus maniculatus maniculatus (Wagner)
Labrador White-footed Mouse; Souris à pattes blanches du Labrador (Fr.). (Map 15.)

This subspecies is reported from parts of three life-zones in the Ungava Peninsula. Its occurrence on both east and west coasts (north to Port Burwell and Great Whale River) is remarkable in constituting almost the only known cases where *Peromyscus* ranges into the Arctic Life-zone (*cf.* Osgood, 1909:pl. 1; Hall and Kelson, 1959, 2:614,615, maps 355,356). The apparent absence of the White-footed Mouse throughout the central and northern parts of the interior (in the Hudsonian Life-zone, where it might logically be expected on the basis of its occurrence in this zone in western Canada) is likewise an anomaly. I can scarcely escape the conclusion that it reached the coastal settlements in the Arctic Life-zone through transportation on ships. According to Bangs (1912:461), "it seems to be much more abundant in [buildings and huts] than in the woods and among rocks." Very few of the records to date are at any considerable distance from settlements.

The mean January daily temperature in the heart of the Ungava Peninsula (approximately –10°) is actually higher than that in the Hudsonian Life-zone of western Canada (approximately –20°). The mean annual snowfall, on the other hand, is more than twice as great in the former region—approximately 120 inches compared with 50 inches (Thomas, 1953: charts 1–1 and 4–3). Since *Peromyscus* seems inclined to run over the top of the snow rather than in runways beneath it on the surface of the ground (*cf.* Soper, 1944:346), this situation might be an important factor in its apparent failure hitherto to penetrate the far interior of the peninsula under its own locomotive power and to become established there.

Previous records of *P. m. maniculatus* include: eastern part of North Shore of the Gulf (Stearns, 1883:115), west to Natashquan (Weaver, 1940:419); Northwest River (Low, 1896:321); Hopedale, Makkovik, Nain, Rama, Windsor Harbour, and Great Whale River (Osgood, 1909:40); Gready, Indian Harbour, Nachvak, and Nain Bay (Austin, 1932:63,69,177); Port Burwell (Hantzsch, 1932:8; Anderson, 1934:99); east James Bay coast (Anderson, 1947:135; Manning and Macpherson, 1952:14); Lakes Mistassini and Albanel (Cameron and Morris, 1951:127). Maps indicating continuous distribution across the central part of the base of the peninsula, as far north as latitudes 52° or 53° (Osgood, 1909:pl. 1; Eidmann, 1935:51, fig. 4; Palmer, 1954:227) or even Fort Chimo (Hall and Kelson, 1959, 2:615, map 356), are obviously based upon supposition rather than actual records. The population of this subspecies on the east coast would appear to be separated by a gap of hundreds of miles from that on the west coast.

Peromyscus maniculatus plumbeus C. F. Jackson
North Shore White-footed Mouse; Souris à pattes blanches de la côte nord (Fr.); Mistapokosho (M.). (Map 15.)

So far, this subspecies is known only from the middle part of the North Shore. It may, however, even prior to the present era of industrialization in the interior, have found a livable habitat for some distance to the northward and eastward.

Sebastien McKenzie, while familiar with *plumbeus* about Seven

Islands, indicated that no representative of the species occurred at Menihek Lake or at Fort McKenzie. A. E. Boerner reported two *Peromyscus* (with white feet and long tail) drowned in a pail of water at Gad Lake in 1953.

I venture to predict that this mouse will presently penetrate the central interior (if it has not already done so) by means of the railway that began operating in 1954 between Seven Islands and Knob Lake. The various settlements that have become established along the railway should offer *Peromyscus* a good chance of winter survival.

The possibility of transportation by other means than ship or rail came to light in the latter part of the 1953 season, when two prospectors in a seaplane, coming from the south, landed at Ashuanipi Lake and reported having a mouse "stowaway" aboard. At a previous landing-place they had seen it traveling down one of the supports of the fuselage to go ashore, but apparaently it had returned to its unusual abode. With the permission of the prospectors, Fred Farah and I searched through the baggage on board without discovering the mouse. Its agility in negotiating the smooth metal supports of the plane suggested *Peromyscus* rather than some microtine species.

C. F. Jackson (1938:432) found this White-footed Mouse abundant in 1935 and 1937 at all his collecting stations along the North Shore, from Seven Islands to Pigou River. Subsequently (1939:101) he described it as a new subspecies. As he suggests, there may be periodic fluctuations in its numbers. I secured none in several nights of trapping in May and June near Seven Islands, and Weaver (1940: 418,419) had a similar experience in 1939 along this part of the North Shore. Eidmann (1935:50) recorded one specimen from Matamek River.

Peromyscus maniculatus gracilis (Le Conte)
Le Conte's White-footed Mouse; Souris à pattes blanches
de Le Conte (Fr.). (Map 15.)

This subspecies has been recorded from Godbout (Osgood, 1909: 42) and from Lake St. John, where its "rarity . . . was most remarkable" (Cameron and Orkin, 1950:104). These localities represent the northeasternmost limits of its known range (*cf.* Hall and Kelson, 1959, 2:615, map 356).

Dicrostonyx hudsonius (Pallas)
Labrador Varying Lemming; Lemming varié du Labrador (Fr.).
(Map 16.)

In the Knob Lake – Burnt Creek area I heard accounts of the "millions" of Lemmings that had overrun the land there in 1949—a year of peak abundance. They were said to have even gnawed the straps of packsacks, perhaps in broad daylight. This mass occurrence had been so quickly and so thoroughly wiped out (by unknown agencies) that apparently not a single one had turned up during a couple of succeeding years. In 1953 they had just begun to reappear, but in such small numbers that I secured just two specimens from Sunny and Geren's mountains in August.

In 1949 the great numbers had appeared at Burnt Creek rather than at Knob Lake. The former is 250 feet higher than Knob Lake and is more closely invested with treeless or semi-barren country. The Lemmings appear to be restricted to Barrens or to a terrain closely simulating such a habitat through destruction of its forest cover by fire.

On August 12 I picked up a weather-cleaned skull in the "alpine garden" at the foot of the perpetual snowbank (alt. *circa* 2,000 feet) above timber-line on Sunny Mountain. I noticed also a grass nest and a good many scats, probably of this species, on the rocky borders of the snowbank. On the following day I secured a Lemming as the sole catch of 20 traps placed thereabouts. It was beneath a shelving rock near the top of a rock slide on the border of the snowbank. Plants in the immediate vicinity included low willow, crowberry, mountain cranberry, blueberry, dandelion, *Oxyria digyna, Dryas, Carex, Cladonia,* and *Parmelia centrifuga.* On bringing the specimen back to camp, I was astonished to find that several of my Montagnais friends were totally unfamiliar with such an animal! (Apparently the Lemming ranges only slightly into present Montagnais territory, and perhaps scarcely at all into their formerly more restricted territory.) On the next day, however, two of my friends—Georges Michel and Ben McKenzie—brought back a live individual from a point about a mile west of the summit of Geren's Mountain, at an altitude of perhaps 2,500 feet. This one had made the mistake of seeking refuge in a shallow hole, while three or four others had been sighted but had made their escape.

"These specimens agree in pelage and cranial characters with Payne Lake and Fort Chimo material. On the basis of cranial characters the former is a juvenile, the latter a subadult. The one is molting from the first or juvenal pelage to the second or subadult pelage; the other, from the subadult to the third or adult pelage" (C. O. H., Jr.).

Two pelages are represented in different parts of each specimen, according to Handley. The sides and belly are subadult in the first specimen, adult in the second. The chest, anal area, and dorsum are immature in the first, subadult in the second. The first specimen was unprime on the dorsum from crown to upper rump, also on chest and in inguinal area; the second was unprime on dorsum and chest.

Both are males, with the following measurements: length, 116, 122; tail, 12, 15; foot, 17.5, 19; ear, —, 7; testes, 3×2, 2.5×1.5 (not descended); weight, 31.1 (rather fat), 36.4 g.

About 15 mites (*Hirstionyssus isabellinus, Laelaps alaskensis,* and *L. kochi*) were preserved from the first individual.

The second individual (pl. 3, fig. 2) was kept in a wire cage until it succumbed on August 21. Here its associates were a Spruce Mouse and several immature Redbacks. When one of the Redbacks would meet the Lemming in these confined quarters, the latter would rather viciously repel the other's advances, to the accompaniment of husky squeaks. These apparently emanated from the Lemming, although the squeaks of the Redbacks resemble those of the Lemmings.

On August 21 John Stubbins showed me the decomposed remains of one of two individuals that had been found about 10 days previously in a powder house at Burnt Creek. A cased skin of an adult, without skull or legs, was presented by Jérôme St. Onge, whom I understood to say that he had secured the animal about August 20 somewhere southwest of Leaf Lake. "This skin is rich brown dorsally, much like Fort Churchill examples of *D. groenlandicus richardsoni,* and quite unlike other Ungava specimens examined. Perhaps it did not actually come from Leaf Lake" (C. O. H., Jr.). However, after this note was written, T. H. Manning showed me, at the National Museum of Canada, some specimens of *Dicrostonyx* from Ungava that evidently represent two color phases. One of these phases, resembling the cased skin from Leaf Lake and other specimens from Keewatin, does not seem to have been recorded in the literature on *D. hudsonius.* This circumstance would seem to substantiate the provenance of the cased skin from Leaf Lake.

In the two complete skins (juvenal and subadult) the dorsum is near Deep Olive-Gray, having a narrow blackish vertebral stripe from nose to upper rump (not reaching tail); tail blackish above, overlaid with longer, pale buffy hairs; upper side of feet Dark Grayish Olive; underparts Deep Olive-Buff, Dark Olive-Gray on chest; more or less Cinnamon-Buff on sides, and a little deeper-colored at arm insertion, sides of throat, and aural region.

On October 5 microtine tracks, with alternate steps (*cf.* Murie, 1954:226, fig. 115a–c), seemed to constitute about four-fifths of the mouse tracks on the snowy upper slopes of Ruth Lake Ridge. I took their makers to be *Dicrostonyx* rather than *Microtus, Clethrionomys,* or *Phenacomys.*

Previous records, mostly coastal, are detailed by G. M. Allen (1919: 514), Hinton (1926:157,420), Anderson and Rand (1945:302), and Hall and Kelson (1959, 2:767, map 427). On the east coast the range is from Port Burwell to Hamilton Inlet (Bangs, 1898*b*:493). No actual specimen seems to have turned up to substantiate G. M. Allen's remark (1919:517), "probably . . . to the Straits of Belle Isle." His record from Great Caribou Island (*cf.* maps in Hall and Cockrum, 1953:482, fig. 129, and in Hall and Kelson, 1959, 2:766, map 427), near Battle Harbour, is evidently based merely upon "the rather characteristic deposits of dung made during winter in certain parts of their tunnels in the snow." I have found quite similar piles of scats in *Microtus* runways near Carol Lake, where *Dicrostonyx* does not occur. Hamilton remarks (1940:426) concerning *Microtus* runways in general: "At regular intervals occur midden heaps composed of the little green dung pellets."

North coast points include False River (Gabrielson and Wright, 1951:132); Fort Chimo, Cape Hope's Advance, Stupart Bay, Cape Wales, and Sugluk (Anonymous, 1948:35); George River post (Hildebrand, 1949:310); and Irony Lake south of Leaf Bay (Bateman, 1953:4). West coast records extend from Digges Islands south to Belcher Islands and Great Whale River, and even to Kakachischuan Point (about lat. 54°06′ N., not "50° N.") (Anderson and Rand, 1945:302; Doutt, 1954:244). Interior records include: Michikamau Lake (Low, 1896:321); George River (Mrs. Hubbard, 1906:537); 25 miles north of Port Harrison, and Minto and Scoter lakes (Manning, 1947:83); Indian House Lake (Clement, 1949:372); and Chubb Crater area (Martin, 1955:491). Eklund and Cool (1949:21) refer to a "high cycle" in 1949 in northwestern Ungava, without mention of precise localities; these, however, are eventually provided by Eklund (1957:74): Aigneau, Payne, Ptarmigan, Maryland, and Gregory lakes and Povungnituk and Leaf rivers. Practically all records are from the Arctic Life-zone proper or from isolated patches of tundra within the Hudsonian Life-zone. Thus the range is far from being continuous north of a line extending from Great Whale River to the Strait of Belle Isle, as one might surmise from the maps of Hall and Cockrum (1953:482, fig. 129), Palmer (1954:242), and Hall and Kelson (1959, 2:map 427). The southernmost points that are on record from the interior seem to be Michikamau Lake and Burnt Creek.

At Stupart Bay the animals were said to be heard at night burrowing through the snow, and were thus captured by foxes (Payne, 1887:73).

Synaptomys cooperi cooperi Baird
Cooper's Lemming Mouse; Campagnol lemming de Cooper (Fr.).
(Map 17.)

Cooper's Lemming Mouse has been obtained at the following localities in the Quebec portion of the peninsula, which constitutes the northeasternmost area occupied by the species: Lake Mistassini, Godbout, Ste. Marguerite River, and Mingan (Hinton, 1926:169,420; A. B. Howell, 1927:14; Anderson, 1947:144; Cameron and Morris, 1951:127; Wetzel, 1955:8; Hall and Kelson, 1959, 2:762, map 435). These localities are in the Canadian Life-zone.

Synaptomys borealis innuitus (True)
Ungava Lemming Mouse; Campagnol lemming d'Ungava (Fr.).
(Map 18.)

This subspecies has been recorded from Payne Bay, Payne Lake, Lower Seal Lake, Irony Lake south of Leaf Bay, Fort Chimo, Swampy Bay River, Ste. Marguerite River, and Godbout (True, 1894: 243; A. B. Howell, 1927:28, fig. 11; Cross, 1938:378; Anderson and Rand, 1943b:102; Bateman, 1953:4; Doutt, 1954:243; Eklund, 1957: 74; Hall and Kelson, 1959, 2:764, map 426). Thus it occurs in three different life-zones of the peninsula. The presence of the species in any part of the Arctic Life-zone is noteworthy.

Synaptomys borealis medioximus Bangs
Labrador Lemming Mouse; Campagnol lemming du Labrador (Fr.). (Map 18.)

Determination of *Synaptomys* material from the Ungava Peninsula is rendered difficult by the small number of previously recorded specimens of S. b. *innuitus* (True) and S. b. *medioximus* Bangs (about 13 of the former and 6 of the latter), and further by the fact that the type specimen of the former is an alcoholic, while that of the latter is subadult.

On June 13, in woods of large white spruce near Little Slimy Lake (⅝ mile west of Knob Lake, Quebec), I induced a Labrador Jay to drop a mouse held in its bill. This proved to be an adult male *Synaptomys*. Its scapular region was eaten out, but a few eggs of blowflies on the body and the apparent absence of ectoparasites suggested that the animal had succumbed sometime previously to some enemy other than the Jay. On June 16 an adult female (fig. 2) was trapped on a mossy log in a swamp along Camp Brook, among tall and low willows, dwarf birch, *Carex*?, sphagnum, and liverwort. On July 17 an adult male was taken on a rock in a little side channel of a brook flowing through mossy woods and entering the Northwest Bay of Attikamagen Lake; the surrounding vegetation included white spruce, tamarack, alder, willow (tall and low), Labrador tea, *Viburnum edule, Cornus canadensis, Rubus, Coptis groenlandica, Viola, Trientalis borealis, Usnea,* and *Sphagnum*. In the animal's mouth were several bits of a moss (*Hylocomium pyrenaicum*)—a species that I did not collect otherwise during the season. The nature of the last two collecting areas suggested a semi-aquatic habit of the species. Fairly close associates here were *Microtus, Clethrionomys,* and *Phenacomys.*

The measurements and weights of the two males (June 13 and July 17) and the female (June 16) were: length, 130 (approx.), 139, 150; tail, 25, 22, 23; foot, 20, 19, 21; ear from crown, 14, 15, 15; weight, —, 40.6, 57.5 g. (all specimens somewhat fat). Skull: condylobasal length, —, 25.7, 26.8; rostral length, 7.1, 6.6, 7.0; rostral breadth, 5.1, 4.9, 5.1; interorbital breadth, 3.2, 3.5, 3.1; zygomatic breadth, —, 15.9, 18.0; lambdoidal width, —, 12.5, 13.5; incisive foramina, —, 5.6, 5.6; height, —, 9.1, 10.3. These measurements indicate larger animals, in general, than the specimens from the Ungava Peninsula that have hitherto been recorded (A. B. Howell, 1927:29; Cross, 1938:378; Anderson and Rand, 1943*b*:103).

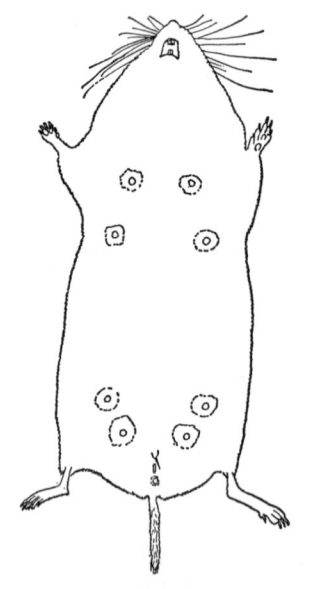

Fig. 2.—*Synaptomys borealis medioximus,* mastology (×½). Adult female, No. 1280. Knob Lake, Quebec. June 16, 1953.

In the first male the testes measured 7.5×6; the dorsum was largely unprime except on the rump; lateral glands greatly developed, 15×7; ears black internally. In the second male the testes measured 8×5; the hide was generally prime; lateral glands greatly developed, 14×8, and 2 mm. in thickness; an apparently similar but less developed glandular area between each ear and foreleg; forelimbs having enormous muscular development and strong bones, suggesting fossorial prowess. The female of June 16 had seven 13-mm. embryos; vagina perforated; mammary glands greatly enlarged; mammae eight (fig. 2); lateral glands slightly developed, 10×4.5.

Upper parts in all three specimens near Saccardo's Umber, lined with blackish hairs; a little less bright on sides, and a little brighter in aural region and on sides of snout; a small patch of grayish white hairs over lateral glands in each specimen; underparts Smoke Gray, with faint buffy tinge on chest in one or two specimens; upper side of feet Deep Mouse Gray; tail Dark Mouse Gray above, Mouse Gray below (not sharply bicolor).

The female of June 16 yielded mites (*Haemogamasus alaskensis*, *Laelaps alaskensis*, and *Haemolaelaps glasgowi*). The male of July 17 yielded mites (*Laelaps alaskensis* and *Haemolaelaps glasgowi*) and a female flea (*Megabothris asio asio*).

Mammalogists have not been in complete agreement on the number of mammae in the two subgenera of *Synaptomys*. A. B. Howell remarks (1927:7): "There are said to be eight mammae in Mictomys [*S. borealis*] and only six in true Synaptomys [*S. cooperi*], but the full number are not always functional in young mothers with small litters." On subsequent pages (9, 11, 19, 21) he indicates that six "seems to be the maximum" in the subgenus *Synaptomys*, and eight in *Mictomys*, but he still holds that "young females may develop a fewer number."

In specimens of *S. cooperi* from Indiana, Quick and Butler (1885: 114) found only four mammae; two were pectoral and two inguinal. In specimens (*S. c. gossii*) from Kansas, Linsdale (1927:54) noted four pectoral and two inguinal mammae. Burt states (1946:211): "There are eight mammae, two pairs inguinal and two pectoral," in *S. c. cooperi*. Hall and Cockrum (1953:474,476) attribute six mammae to the subgenus *Synaptomys*, and eight to the subgenus *Mictomys*. Hall and Kelson (1959, 2:761,763) do likewise. Mastological sketches of *S. c. cooperi* made by myself in Michigan in 1924 (MS) and in New York in 1925 (1929:100, fig. 22) show six mammae, while the sketch of *S. borealis medioximus* made in Quebec in 1953 (fig. 2 of the present report) shows eight. Howell's statement (1927), quoted above, evidently remains valid as to the maximum number of mammae in the two subgenera.

S. b. medioximus has been found along the east coast: Nain, Rigolet, Red Bay, and L'Anse au Loup (A. B. Howell, 1927:29, fig. 11; Anderson and Rand, 1943b:103; Doutt, 1954:243; Hall and Kelson, 1959, 2:764, map 426).

"The specimens from Little Slimy, Knob, and Attikamagen lakes differ from referred specimens of *innuitus* (Payne Lake) in having much darker, brighter coloration of upper parts, and differ from the type of *innuitus* and from Payne Lake specimens in having the incisors less decurved, the pterygoid fossae longer, and the braincase not so [nearly] flat dorsally. They agree fairly well with descriptions of *medioximus* and are tentatively referred to that subspecies" (C. O. H., Jr.).

Clethrionomys gapperi gapperi (Vigors)
Ontario Red-backed Mouse; Campagnol à dos roux de Gapper (Fr.); Kaoappikoshishapokoshish (M.). (Map 19.)

Three specimens, taken a mile north of Seven Islands on May 24 and 25, differ from all those collected in the interior, and are referred to *C. g. gapperi*. The mossy woods of their environment included black spruce, jack pine, balsam, Labrador tea, willow, sheep laurel, alder, blueberry, common bearberry, mountain cranberry, bunchberry, creeping snowberry, sphagnum?, *Hypnum crista-castrensis*, *Usnea*, and *Cladonia alpestris*. Data for an adult male and two adult females are: length, 145, 145, 136; tail, 41, 43, 39; foot, 20, 20, 18; ear, 14, 14, 12.5; weight, 27.6, 26.3, 19.3 g. (not fat to slightly fat); hide prime in all three; lateral glands evident in the male, 12×5, but only in the smaller female, 15×10. The testes of the male were 12.5×8 (descended). The larger female (May 25) contained six 6-mm. embryos; vagina perforate. The smaller female (May 25) contained no embryos; vagina perforate and uterus swollen. The male (May 24) yielded 18 lice (*Hoplopleura acanthopus*) and 2 female fleas (*Megabothris quirini*); one female, five of the same lice and four of the same fleas; and the other female, two of the same lice.

The measurements and weights of these specimens correspond closely to those of *C. g. gapperi* from the Adirondacks (*cf.* Harper, 1929:103); on the other hand, they average smaller than those of *C. g. proteus* from the interior. In comparison with the latter, these specimens have tails averaging darker above, with an apparently blacker tip; the dorsum seems to have less admixture of lighter-colored hairs. Their underparts average less buffy, but can be matched in a Carol Lake specimen of *proteus* (No. 1342). The upper side of the feet is not so light-colored as in *some* specimens from the interior. Their faces seem to average slightly less gray, more buffy.

In extensive collecting of *gapperi* in New England, New York, and Pennsylvania, I have never collected any color phase but the red-backed. The three specimens from Seven Islands are likewise redbacked. However, in the National Museum of Canada one of three specimens from Moisie Bay (just east of Seven Islands) is a representative of a gray phase. It is perhaps significant that out of more than 40 specimens reported by C. F. Jackson (1938:433) from the North Shore, between Seven Islands and Pigou River, only two were melanistic. The proportion of such specimens among populations of *proteus* is evidently much higher.

Several authors (Eidmann, 1935:54; C. F. Jackson, 1938:433; Anderson, 1947:153; Hall and Kelson, 1959, 2:716, map 401) have recorded the population of Seven Islands and vicinity as *proteus*. On the other hand, Weaver (1940:420) remarks that "two males ... from Seven Islands and Mingan ... were allocated to this subspecies [*C. g. gapperi*] by Dr. [Glover M.] Allen." Dr. Allen had at his disposal in the Museum of Comparative Zoölogy ample material of *proteus* for comparison, and I am following his judgment.

The only other record of the subspecies *gapperi* in the Ungava Peninsula seems to be from Godbout (Bailey, 1897:122). Hall and Cockrum (1953:386, fig. 8) and Hall and Kelson (1959, 2:713, map 401) extend its range eastward along the North Shore only to that point.

A. E. Boerner reported many mice as seen runnig about in daytime at Gad Lake in the summer of 1953. Probably these consisted largely of Redbacks. The local population more likely represents *gapperi* than *proteus*.

"Intergradation between *C. g. gapperi* and *C. g. proteus* seems to occur on the North Shore in the region of Seven Islands and Mingan. The Seven Islands specimens, though not typical, are more like *C. g. gapperi* in all characters and should be allocated to that race. *C. g. hudsonius* may enter the picture here, but material of that form available for comparison is too inadequate to be commented upon" (C. O. H., Jr.).

Clethrionomys gapperi proteus (Bangs)
Labrador Red-backed Mouse; Campagnol à dos roux du Labrador (Fr.). (Map 19.)

The type locality of *proteus*, originally indicated by Bangs (in Bailey, 1897:137) as "Hamilton Inlet," was later stated more specifically by him (1898b:495) to be "Rigoulette, Hamilton Inlet." This restriction of the type locality has been subsequently overlooked by compilers of check-lists.

This subspecies appears to be the one that is distributed through the central interior. I preserved 30 specimens from the following localities: Ashuanipi Lake (3); Carol Lake (8); Knob Lake (2); Attikamagen Lake (10); Mollie T. Lake (3); and Leroy Lake (4). Many others were secured but discarded owing to lack of time for preparing them.

"Specimens from interior localities other than Lac Aulneau closely resemble examples of *C. g. proteus* (Lake Melville) in coloration, although they approach *C. g. ungava* in size" (C. O. H., Jr.).

Ecology.—The habitats of this subspecies included mossy upland woods of black and white spruce, tamarack, and balsam (*cf.* pl. 2, fig. 1); muskegs with spruces and tamaracks; garbage heaps; thickets of willow and alder near streams and lakes; tents and bare camp areas. Plants recorded at least five times as occurring within a few yards of the places of capture of 30 specimens were the following (listed in approximate order of frequency): *Ledum groenlandicum, Betula glandulosa, Cornus canadensis, Vaccinium uliginosum, Sphagnum* spp., *Equisetum sylvaticum, Pleurozium schreberi, Cladonia alpestris, Cladonia rangiferina, Picea mariana, Picea glauca, Salix planifolia* (and other tall willows), *Larix laricina, Salix vestita, Petasites palmatus, Epilobium angustifolium, Rubus chamaemorus, Empetrum nigrum, Sanguisorba canadensis, Calamagrostis canadensis,* and *Viburnum edule.* In Ungava, as elsewhere in the range of *Clethrionomys,* mosses seem to form a more or less essential element in the environment. In spruce woods at Leroy Lake, where this was the predominant mouse, I noticed trails (presumably of its making) extending here and there on top of the moss; they were little more than one inch wide. At Carol Lake I saw a Redback moving along a more or less covered runway through a growth of hair-cap moss (*Polytrichum*) beneath dwarf birches.

Trapping returns as well as visual observations indicated that this was the most numerous of all the mammals of the region during 1953 —a year of extraordinary abundance; *Microtus pennsylvanicus* was the only other species that could begin to compare with it. It was commonly seen running about in broad daylight in practically all localities in the interior. Some of the muskegs were fairly honeycombed with holes and runways and littered with scats. Sebastien McKenzie informed me that, in all his 68 years, he could recall only one other season when mice occurred in such amazing abundance; that was in the Opiscoteo Lake area, about 50 years previously—quite possibly 1905, when Cabot (1912a:288 ff.) found a peak population of mice in the Assiwaban River area. Despite the superabundance of

Clethrionomys and *Microtus* in 1953, there was no visible concentration of predators to reduce their numbers—such as hawks, owls, foxes, or weasels.

On June 29 I glimpsed a mouse-sized animal running down the vertical trunk of a dead spruce beside Camp Brook. My suspicion that it was a Redback has been confirmed by reading in Bangs (1897: 239): "Several times while walking through the forest [at Hamilton Inlet] Mr. Goldthwaite discovered one sitting upon a spruce branch 'like a squirrel.' I have never known of this arboreal habit being noticed in other species [of *Clethrionomys*]." (See also Palmer, 1954: 247.) On July 13, near the Iron Arm of Attikamagen Lake, I had a brief view of a reddish mouse (presumably *Clethrionomys*) running actively about among the shrubbery (alder or dwarf birch); part of the time it appeared to be on the stems above the ground. In the mess-tent at Mollie T. Lake the cook found a small quantity of rice grains in folds of a cloth hung over a frame of poles about 5 feet off the ground; they must have been stored there by a mouse, and no other local species is known to have scansorial ability equal to a Redback's. Near the Ashuanipi River one of these mice entered a trap placed on a leaning log 4½ feet above the ground.

Food.—On June 25, near Knob Lake, I noticed mouse gnawings on the bark of *Ledum groenlandicum*, that had been made probably beneath the snows of winter, and *Clethrionomys* was the mouse most likely to have been operating there, in the midst of spruce woods. On July 9, at the Iron Arm of Attikamagen Lake, I released a female on the shore where it had been taken in a live-trap. It walked off a few feet to a little spring and spent a minute or two there eagerly lapping up the water. Then it ran along and disappeared into a hole in the bank. This was the only mouse in the wild that I had ever seen in the act of drinking. In a drizzling rain on the morning of July 19, at the Northwest Bay of this lake, a Redback came scurrying along a path toward me. When a couple of yards away, it left the path and paused beside a couple of twigs. These were thickly covered with a dark green lichen (*Alectoria implexa*) spreading in every direction like the fur on an animal's tail. There were also a few bits of a gray foliose lichen that seems to be common on dead spruce twigs. The mouse began immediately to nibble on the lichens—apparently the *Alectoria*, but perhaps the other. After a few moments it returned to the path, crossed it, and paused 2 feet from me to nibble on some spilled food (perhaps flour). Its unmindfulness of my presence indicated how readily it might fall victim to some predaceous foe. Near Camp

Brook at Knob Lake, on August 9, an individual in the gray phase came scurrying along the base of a small cliff. Presently it poked its nose out of a hole and chewed on some green leaves growing there (possibly *Coptis groenlandica*). A little farther along it paused beneath a small fallen log and proceeded to devour a sizable leaf (perhaps *Solidago*).

Behavior.—When two Redbacks would chase each other about in a shipping cage, or merely encounter each other without coming to blows or bites, they would utter their characteristic husky squeaks: ööch, ööch (the vowels as in German pronunciation). Probably the same vocal sounds take place when two individuals, moving in opposite directions, meet in the narrow subterranean passages. A slaty-black individual at Leroy Lake, while posing for motion pictures in an empty aquarium jar, gave an exhibition of "washing its face."

Enemy.—A new enemy of the species, in the form of the Domestic Cat, had arrived in the Knob Lake area. Here, at the seaplane base on September 27, a Redback was rescued from a cat that was playing with it, and it was dedicated to scientific purposes.

Molt.—Evidence of molt, in the shape of dark, unprime areas on the inside of the skin, was obtained as follows:

June 20, adult: a few dark spots on rump.
July 4, adult: patches on head, shoulders, and venter.
July 9, adult: crown, nape, and rump.
July 14, adult: middle of back and right axilla.
July 18, adult: crown and nape.
August 17, juvenile: dorsum generally.
August 17, juvenile: occiput and nape.
August 19, subadult: a few streaks on rump.
August 19, juvenile: sides of head and dorsum from crown to rump.
August 20, subadult: on nape and about ears.
August 26, subadult: middle of throat.
August 26, adult: posterior dorsum.
September 9, adult: mostly unprime except on snout and nape.
September 10, juvenile: unprime except on snout, throat, and limbs.
September 13, juvenile: crown and nape.
September 17, adult: streaks on dorsum, occiput to rump.
September 17, subadult: nape, scapular region, posterior rump, and posterior venter.
September 17, juvenile: generally unprime.
September 27, subadult: dorsum from interscapular region to rump.

It thus appears that molt was in progress in at least two-thirds of the specimens from June 20 to September 27.

Lateral glands.—These glands were evident in most adult males from June 20 to September 17, varying from 15×9 (July 4) to 26×11 (July 9) and 16×7.5 mm. (September 17). They were not noticed in most of the adult females, but were evident (14×6 mm.) in one large subadult and pregnant female (August 19). Their presence is probably indicative of sexual maturity. In at least two adult males the position of the glands was marked externally by patches of grayish hairs.

Ectoparasites.—Approximately 29 of the specimens yielded about 11 species of mites, 2 species of lice, and 2 species of fleas. Acarina: *Haemogamasus alaskensis*—Attikamagen Lake, July 4; Mollie T. Lake, August 17; Leroy Lake, August 19; Carol Lake, September 10; *Haemogamasus ambulans*—Attikamagen Lake, July 14; Mollie T. Lake, August 17; *Hirstionyssus isabellinus*—Mollie T. Lake, August 17; Phytoseiidae (non-parasitic)—Attikamagen Lake, July 3; Knob Lake, September 27; *Laelaps alaskensis*—Attikamagen Lake, July 21; Carol Lake, September 14; *Laelaps kochi*—Attikamagen Lake, July 21; Carol Lake, September 9 and 17; *Laelaps* sp.—Attikamagen Lake, July 21; *Haemolaelaps glasgowi*—Attikamagen Lake, July 14; Mollie T. Lake, August 17; Ashuanipi River, August 25; Carol Lake, September 14 and 17; *Dermacarus* sp. (non-parasitic)—Leroy Lake, August 19 and 20; Ashuanipi River, August 25 and 26; Carol Lake, September 9 and 17; Analgesoidea—Knob Lake, September 27; *Nothrus* sp. (non-parasitic)—Carol Lake, September 13. Anoplura: *Hoplopleura acanthopus*: Knob Lake—3, June 20; 2, September 27; Attikamagen Lake—1, July 3; 3 and 3, July 4; 24, July 14; 5, July 17; 9 and 2, July 21; Mollie T. Lake—1 and 7, August 17; Leroy Lake—19, 1, and 22, August 19; 2, August 20; Carol Lake—2 and 8, September 13; 2, September 17; *Polyplax borealis*: Attikamagen Lake—1, July 3; 1 and 2, July 4; 1, July 17; 4, July 18. Siphonaptera: *Malaraeus penicilliger athabascae*: Knob Lake—1 female, June 20; Mollie T. Lake—2 females, August 17; *Megabothris quirini*: Attikamagen Lake—2 males and 1 female, July 9; 1 male, July 14.

Reproduction.—From June 20 to July 21 the testes of adult males varied from 12×7 to 14×8 mm.; late in the season, from 4×2 (August 26) to 2.5×1.5 (September 17). From August 19 to September 27 the testes of juvenal or subadult males varied but little, from 2.5×1.5 to 3.5×2. Data on females were: adults, mammary glands developed, July 3 and 4; adult, uterus swollen, July 14; subadult, four 4-mm. embryos, August 19. It would appear from these records that mating may have ceased by mid-August. It seems rather strange that so few data on reproduction turned up in a year of peak abundance. Every specimen was examined for such evidence.

Growth.—At Lac La Cosa, about July 4, Gilbert Simard found three very young, practically hairless mice (apparently *Clethrionomys*) in a rotten stump close to the ground; and he kindly preserved two of them for presentation to me. The eyes and ears are closed. The vibrissae are about 3 mm. long; there are a few shorter hairs on chin and crown. The umbilicus is not entirely healed. One of the specimens is about 45 mm. in length; tail, 7; foot, 7.

Two small individuals, probably no more than a few weeks old, were secured in live-traps at Attikamagen Lake, July 20 and 21; one of them had a length of 120 mm. and a weight of 13.25 g. From August 17 to September 27 young of the year were collected much more frequently than adults; 16 of them were preserved in that period, compared with only three adults. Perhaps the adults that had attained such an unusual peak of abundance earlier in the year were already dying off, leaving a population composed predominantly of individuals born that season. As far as may be judged by the records of 13 juvenal or subadult individuals, there was little or no general increase in length or weight as the season advanced from mid-August to late September: three, August 17, 130–136 mm., 18–20.8 g.; three, August 20–26, 135–139 mm., 19.2–20 g.; four, September 10–14, 119–135 mm., 14.3–20.25 g.; three, September 17–27, 127–132 mm., 19.3–22.7 g. This situation might almost suggest that the successive litters were dying off as they reached this approximate size, at an age of only two months or so. However, Hamilton's studies (1937:503) on marked young individuals of *Microtus pennsylvanicus* indicate a "rapid growth until the twelfth week, when the steady increase is retarded." In this connection it may be useful to consult Scheffer's interesting study (1955) of "body size with relation to population density in mammals."

Color phases.—Several color phases are represented among 29 specimens from the interior.

RED-BACKED: Five adults (including one not quite fully grown) and six subadults (Attikamagen, Mollie T., Leroy, and Carol Lakes and Ashuanipi River), more or less normally "red-backed" (that is to say between Chestnut and Auburn); ears much like dorsum; face and sides between Deep Olive-Buff and Buffy Citrine (face intermixed with blackish hairs); tail varying from near Tawny-Olive to near Citrine-Drab above, Deep Olive-Buff below; upper sides of hands and feet Olive-Buff to Deep Grayish Olive; underparts Olive-Buff to Deep Olive-Buff. Subadults have darker backs, grayer sides, brighter-colored ears (Tawny), and generally darker upper surfaces of hands, feet, and tail.

RUFESCENT: An especially bright-colored subadult from Knob Lake (No. 1354, September 27) differs from first group in having dorsum and ears between Tawny and Russet; face and sides between Cinnamon-Buff and Tawny-Olive; tail near Hazel above, near Deep Olive-Buff below; upper sides of hands and feet Pale Brownish Drab; underparts Olive-Buff. Area about eyes and on each side of nostrils more buffy than in any of the six subadults of first group. Measurements of this specimen are: length, 132; tail, 35; foot, 19; ear, 14; testes, 3.5×2; weight, 22.7 g.

No. 1354 bears considerable resemblance to two rufescent subadults of *C. g. athabascae* from Nueltin Lake, Keewatin (No. 1087, September 2, and No. 1146, October 26) (*cf.* Harper, 1956:33). Individuals of similar size and appearance were taken also at Mollie T. and Leroy lakes. I have not met with equally bright specimens of adults among either subspecies. It may thus be suspected that this bright subadult phase of pelage is succeeded by some duller adult pelage.

BUFFY: Six adults (Knob, Attikamagen, and Carol lakes) represent the lightest color phase; dorsum (including ears) between Cinnamon-Brown and Dresden Brown; face and sides near Ecru-Olive (the face intermixed with blackish hairs); tail Dark Olive-Buff above, Deep Olive-Buff below; upper sides of hands and feet Light Drab to Hair Brown; underparts near Olive-Buff.

BROWN: Two adults and two subadults (Attikamagen and Carol lakes and Ashuanipi River) resemble last-mentioned group, but are distinctly darker; dorsum of adults between Cinnamon-Brown and Mummy Brown; face and sides Buffy Olive (face has some blackish hairs); upper sides of hands, feet, and tail Dark Grayish Olive; underparts near Deep Olive-Buff; subadults somewhat darker, both above and below.

SLATY: In four subadults (Mollie T., Leroy, and Carol lakes) dorsum between Chaetura Drab and Chaetura Black; face and sides Light Grayish Olive; ears and upper sides of hands, feet, and tail Chaetura Drab; underparts Olive-Buff.

BLACKISH: Three subadults (Attikamagen, Leroy, and Carol lakes) represent darkest phase of all; extreme specimen (No. 1327, Leroy Lake; pl. 4, fig. 1) almost entirely Sooty Black or Slate-Black above, and a trifle less intensely colored below; two others intermediate between No. 1327 and slaty group; dorsum nearly Chaetura Black; pelage elsewhere on body a mixture of lighter and darker hairs, with a general tone near Dark Olive.

The slaty and blackish phases were especially in evidence at Leroy

TABLE 2.—AVERAGE MEASUREMENTS AND WEIGHTS OF ADULTS OF *C. G. PROTEUS*

Locality	No. of specimens	Length	Tail	Foot	Ear from crown	Weight (grams)
Knob and Attikamagen lakes	6 ♂	150.3	41.6	19.4	14.0	31.7
Ashuanipi and Carol lakes	2 ♂	154.0	44.3	19.5	14.5	27.4
Attikamagen Lake	3 ♀	156.6	43.7	19.5	15.5	31.0
Carol Lake	1 ♀	163.0	50.0	19.0	15.0	32.3

Lake. In these the dorsal pelage is distinctly more glossy than in any of the other groups.

Measurements and weights.—In view of the small number of specimens involved, the local variations in size of adults (table 2) need not be considered as of any special significance. It may be noted, however, that these specimens of *proteus* average larger than those of *gapperi* from Seven Islands.

Distribution.—Previous records of this subspecies are mainly from the east coast, north to Assiwaban River and Nain (Bangs, in Bailey, 1897:137; Bangs, 1912:462; G. M. Allen, 1927:248; Anderson, 1934:35, 1939:82, 1940:76, and 1947:153; Hall and Kelson, 1959, 2:716, map 401). There are also a few along the North Shore of the Gulf, west at least to Washicoutai (Weaver, 1940:418,420). Published records from the interior seem to have been wanting.

Clethrionomys gapperi ungava (Bailey)
Ungava Red-backed Mouse; Campagnol à dos roux d'Ungava (Fr.).
(Map 19.)

Taxonomy.—Perhaps the most trenchant character attributed to *ungava* in Bailey's original description (1897:130) was a dental one: "Molars as in *gapperi*, except the first upper, in which the edges of the first and second inner salient loops meet and coalesce, inclosing a dental core." This, however, is nearly matched in an adult specimen of *proteus* from Attikamagen Lake (USNM No. 298648); furthermore, it is *not* matched in two subadult topotypes from Fort Chimo (USNM), collected by David H. Johnson, and consequently it may be regarded as a mere individual variation. In the alcoholic type specimen such characters as "tail and feet slender" and "ears very small" are more or less meaningless, and the colors are quite unreliable.

On the other hand, "Lac Aulneau specimens differ from *C. g. proteus* in larger size, indistinct dorsal band, and much more buffy or yellowish coloration. In these respects they agree with referred specimens of *C. g. ungava* (Lac Aigneau and Payne Lake) and should be allocated to that subspecies" (C. O. H., Jr.).

Ecology.—At Lac Aulneau seven specimens were preserved, July 22 to 31, and about 21 others were secured but not preserved. Their habitats included buildings, tents, muskegs, an alder thicket on the wooded lake shore, and Barrens above timber-line (this last habitat being at an elevation 450–500 feet above the others). Plants recorded at least three times as occurring within a few yards of the places of capture of these individuals were the following (listed in approximate order of frequency): *Picea mariana, Ledum groenlandicum, Salix vestita, Empetrum nigrum, Cladonia alpestris, Larix laricina, Sphagnum* sp., *Alnus* sp., *Rubus chamaemorus, Myrica gale,* and a tall willow (*Salix* sp.).

Here the Redback was certainly the principal, if not the sole, mouse that was given to entering the buildings and tents. It was an unwelcome visitor in the kitchen, where its was known to nibble bread and perhaps other food. There was also complaint of damage to clothing. In my tent, where I trapped several specimens, it was evidently an individual of this species that attacked two freshly stuffed mice (a *Clethrionomys* and a *Phenacomys*), pulling the head off one and chewing at the face of the other.

Behavior.—At dusk on July 23 a Redback came into an open area of *Cladonia alpestris* in front of my tent and began nibbling on something. After an alarm, it soon returned and resumed its feeding on what I found to be the flattened remains of a young *Clethrionomys.*

When a new individual was introduced to one or more others being kept for a few days in the confined quarters of a shipping cage before starting on their air journey to Washington, considerable squeaking, chasing, and sparring were apt to result. There was no evident damage, however, even when two or three together might engage in a rough-and-tumble fight. A common attitude of contestants was sitting up on haunches and sparring with forefeet. In wire cages the Redbacks would crawl not only up the sides but also along the ceiling.

Molt.—Dark areas on the inside of the skin, indicative of the molting process, were noted as follows: July 22, juvenile, everywhere except on crown and throat; July 27, two subadults, dorsum from crown to rump; July 27, subadult, nearly entire head, except throat; July 28, adult, spots between shoulders and on lower back.

Lateral glands.—These glands were evident in two adult males (July 24, 20×9, and July 31, 18×12 mm.) and in one adult female (July 28, 15×9 mm.).

Ectoparasites.—At Lac Aulneau seven specimens yielded seven species of mites, two species of lice, and two species of fleas. Acarina: *Haemogamasus alaskensis*—July 27 and 28; *Haemogamasus ambulans*—July 24; *Hirstionyssus isabellinus*—July 22, 24, 27, and 28; Phytoseiidae (non-parasitic)—July 27; *Laelaps alaskensis*—July 27; *Haemolaelaps glasgowi*—July 22 and 24; *Dermacarus* sp. (non-parasitic)—July 27 and 31. Anoplura: *Hoplopleura acanthopus*—1, July 22; 4, July 24; 9, 4, and 24, July 27; 2, July 28; 34, July 31; *Polyplax borealis*—9, July 27. Siphonaptera: *Malaraeus penicilliger athabascae*—1 female, July 27; 1 female, July 28; *Megabothris quirini*—1 female, July 24.

Reproduction.—Testes of adult males remained large through July: 12.5×7 on July 24, and 13×8 on July 31. Those of three juveniles, July 22 and 27, were 4×2.5, 2.5×1.5, and 3×1.75. An adult female, July 28, contained five 12-mm. embryos.

Coloration. (No color description of *ungava*, based upon non-alcoholic specimens, seems to have been hitherto available.)—In three adults: dorsal area between Chestnut and Auburn; rim of ears (internal) near Verona Brown; face Olive-Buff, intermixed with blackish hairs; small Cinnamon-Buff area on each side of nostrils; sides near Deep Olive-Buff (one male with a light grayish area over lateral glands); tail Citrine Drab above, intermixed with blackish hairs, and near Deep Olive-Buff below; upper side of hands and feet varying from Light Drab to Grayish Olive; underparts Light Buff to Light Ochraceous-Buff.

One subadult and two juveniles are somewhat darker on back and sides, and have brighter-colored ears (near Tawny). Another juvenile (No. 1313) represents a distinct color phase; it is practically as dark as a *Microtus pensylvanicus*, the dorsum having a tinge near Saccardo's Umber, intermixed with blackish hairs. The coloration of this last specimen is closely matched in some specimens (brown phase) of *proteus.*

Measurements.—Two adult males, July 24 and 31: length, 146, 150; tail, 36, 39; foot, 19, 19.5; ear, 15, 15; weight, 28.2, 35.9 g. An adult, pregnant female, July 28: 159–43–20–15; 42.7 g. Two juvenal males and one subadult female, July 27, varied from 126 to 131 mm. in length, and from 15.8 to 21.9 g. in weight. A still smaller juvenal male, July 22: 96–23–16.5–8; 8.6 g.

Distribution.—Previous records in the literature are from Fort Chimo (Bailey, 1897:130; Bangs, 1912:462; Anderson, 1934:100, and 1939:83), Irony Lake south of Leaf Bay (Bateman, 1953:4), Payne

Lake and Lac Aigneau (Eklund, 1957:74), and Lower Seal Lake (Anderson, 1940:76; Hall and Cockrum, 1953:391, fig. 8; Hall and Kelson, 1959, 2:716, map 401). Specimens from Lower Seal Lake are recorded by Doutt (1954:244) under the name of *C. g. hudsonius* Anderson.

Clethrionomys gapperi hudsonius Anderson
Hudsonian Red-backed Mouse; Campagnol à dos roux d'Hudson (Fr.). (Map 19.)

Records of *C. g. hudsonius* from the Ungava Peninsula include the following: east coast of Hudson and James bays at Richmond Gulf, Great Whale River, Fort George, Sheppard Island, Eastmain, and Rupert House (Anderson, 1940:73); Lake St. John area (Cameron and Orkin, 1950:104); and Lakes Mistassini and Albanel (Cameron and Morris, 1951:127).

Phenacomys ungava ungava Merriam
Ungava Spruce Mouse; Phenacomys d'Ungava (Fr.). (Map 20.)

During a season when traps were apt to be filled up with the superabundant *Clethrionomys* and *Microtus*, I felt fortunate to have secured two specimens of this attractive mouse at Lac Aulneau. Most of the previous records of *ungava*, as well as of *P. u. crassus*, have been from coastal areas. Perhaps the former is more characteristic of the Barren Grounds or their borders, and the latter, of the boreal forests.

"Although resembling *crassus* in size, specimens from Lac Aulneau agree with *ungava* (specimens from Fort Chimo) in other characters, *i.e.*, narrower, more fragile rostrum, smaller auditory bullae, and paler, duller coloration. They may be referred to the latter form." (C. O. H., Jr.)

An adult female and a subadult female were trapped on July 24 among rocks on the Barrens (altitude about 950 feet) above timberline on the west side of Lac Aulneau. The surrounding vegetation included small tamaracks, *Salix*, *Betula glandulosa*, *Ledum groenlandicum*, *L. decumbens*, *Vaccinium uliginosum*, *V. vitis- idaea* var. *minus*, *Empetrum nigrum*, *Carex*, *Cladonia alpestris*, *Alectoria ochroleuca*, and *Parmelia centrifuga*. In the adult the hide was prime except on the mid-venter; in the subadult it was unprime on rump, sides, chest, and posterior venter. The former contained five 7-mm. embryos. There were eight mammae: four pectoral, two postabdominal, two inguinal. Other data for the two specimens were: length, 158, 138; tail, 35, 26; foot, 18, 18; ear, 14, 14; weight, 45.6, 25.8 g. (each with little fat). The body measurements of the adult indicate that this is a larger animal than suggested by previous measurements of alcoholics (cf. A. B. Howell, 1926:26). *Phenacomys* is also a larger and heavier animal than the local *Clethrionomys*.

In adult female, dorsum, including ears, and sides are near Buffy Olive (mixed with blackish hairs), becoming Buffy Brown on rump; snout near Buckthorn Brown or Tawny-Olive, not sharply defined; tail Dark Mouse Gray above (but browner basally), Mouse Gray below; upper sides of hands and feet Light Drab; underparts Pale Olive-Gray. Subadult similar, but rump not appreciably brighter than back.

Three species of Acarina (*Hirstionyssus isabellinus, Laelaps alaskensis*, and *Haemolaelaps glasgowi*) were collected from the two specimens.

This subspecies has been reported previously from comparatively few localities in the peninsula: Fort Chimo, Irony Lake south of Leaf Bay, Harrington Harbour, Seal River, St. Charles Point, Godbout, Seal and Clearwater lakes (Merriam, 1889:33,34,35; Miller, 1897a:83, 84; Bangs, 1912:461; A. B. Howell, 1926:25, fig. 6; Anderson, 1934: 100, 1939:81, and 1942a:57,60; C. F. Jackson, 1938:433; Weaver, 1940:418,419; Hall and Cockrum, 1953:395, fig. 20; Bateman, 1953:4; Doutt, 1954:244; Hall and Kelson, 1959, 2:718, map 403—under the name of *P. intermedius celatus*). While it was found in an Arctic-Alpine area at Lac Aulneau, it does not seem to push out for an appreciable distance, if at all, into the main Barren Grounds in the north of the peninsula.

I have pointed out (1956:40) what would appear to be reasonable objections to the recently proposed common name of "Heather Vole" for *Phenacomys*. Yet it still persists. A further objection to "vole" is the difficulty of inducing the lay public to accept such a bookish name. There is too much likelihood of confusion with "mole."

Phenacomys ungava crassus Bangs
Labrador Spruce Mouse; Phenacomys du Labrador (Fr.). (Map 20.)

Of three individuals taken in the interior, two (Attikamagen and Ashuanipi lakes) were made up as specimens, and another (Leroy Lake) was shipped alive to Washington.

"Available specimens of this genus are too few for satisfactory judgments. However, on the basis of large size, broad, heavy rostrum, large auditory bullae, and dark, bright coloration, specimens from Attikamagen and Ashuanipi lakes agree fairly well with a topotype

and near-topotypes of *crassus* from Rigolet and 'Grosswater Bay.'"
(C. O. H., Jr.)

The first specimen was taken on July 18 at the Northwest Bay of Attikamagen Lake. The place was the mossy bank of a brook in thick woods of white spruce, with a lower growth of willows, *Viburnum edule, Ledum groenlandicum, Rubus, Cornus canadensis, Streptopus, Viola, Coptis groenlandica, Mitella nuda,* and *Sphagnum*. The animal was an adult male: length, 150; tail, 27.5; foot, 17.5; ear, 14.5; testes, 8×5.5; lateral glands, 28×10; weight, 40.4 g. (somewhat fat). There was a small unprime area along one shoulder, and small dark streaks elsewhere. There were three fragments of some green leaf in its mouth.

On the subject of lateral or hip glands, A. B. Howell remarks (1926: 7): "No observations in this regard seem to have been made in the field upon fresh material."

In the burnt tract at Knob Lake, on August 7, I noticed evidence of activity by some mouse (perhaps *Phenacomys*) in the shape of some dwarf birch twigs that had been dragged into the entrance of a hole beside a rock. Foster remarks (1956:21) that "Phenacomys, more than any other Churchill small mammal, has the habit of pulling freshly cut shoots of plants to its burrow." He reports this habit in Quebec as well as in Manitoba.

While we were setting up camp in an area of lichen woodland at Leroy Lake on August 18, one of these mice apparently came out of a hole by a stump, whereupon it was run down and captured within a few rods by the agile Georges Michel. The vegetation here included black and white spruce, tamarack, *Betula glandulosa, Ledum groenlandicum, Vaccinium uliginosum, V. angustifolium, Empetrum nigrum, Cornus canadensis, Cladonia alpestris, C. rangiferina, C. gracilis, Pleurozium schreberi,* and *Stereocaulon fastigiatum.* The mouse was kept in a cage for several days before being shipped by air to Washington, meanwhile providing rare opportunities for observing its attributes and securing photographs of it. When it was first put in the cage, there was a little bickering between it and a Lemming (*Dicrostonyx*), but not much more than squeaks resulted. The *Phenacomys* was of such mild demeanor that on the next day it let a young Redback of half its size spar at it vigorously; meanwhile it made practically no defense, except to sit back on its haunches and face the aggressor. It even submitted without protest when one of the young Redbacks perched on top of it. It gave the impression of having a longer neck than other local mice, as it habitually thrust its head forward and held it at a lower level than its back (pl. 4, fig. 2). The short tail was generally tucked out of sight beneath the body. The ears were fairly prominent. This animal had a distinctly more convex profile than *Clethrionomys* (*cf.* pl. 4, figs. 1 and 2; also Harper, 1956: 37, fig. 6a). This is the outward manifestation of a "markedly depressed" rostrum (A. B. Howell, 1926:25, pl. 2, fig. 7)—a character which should help to keep the *ungava* group separate from the *intermedius* group of *Phenacomys*.

The final specimen (subadult male) was trapped on September 6 on the boggy border of a small pond (pl. 1, fig. 2) on the southeast side of Mile 224 Airstrip. Plants of this environment included black spruce, *Ledum groenlandicum, Myrica gale, Chamaedaphne, Rubus chamaemorus, Empetrum nigrum, Smilacina trifolia, Equisetum sylvaticum, Sphagnum,* and *Pleurozium schreberi.* The length was 126; tail, 31; foot, 18.5; ear, 14; testes, 2.5×1.5; weight, 20.8 g. (with little fat); dorsum unprime from crown to rump.

Three species of Acarina (*Haemogamasus ambulans, Hirstionyssus isabellinus,* and *Laelaps alaskensis*) were collected from the specimen at Attikamagen Lake.

The adult male closely resembles the adult female of *P. u. ungava* from Lac Aulneau, but is a little darker above (near Buffy Brown, approaching Brussels Brown or Cinnamon-Brown on the rump). The snout is Tawny-Olive, the tail Saccardo's Umber above and Light Buff below, the upper sides of the hands and feet Light Buff, and the underparts light Olive-Gray. In the fresh specimen the skin of the ears is notably whitish, in contrast to the black of *Synaptomys*. The subadult male is similar, but its rump is not appreciably brighter than the back, and the tail is Dark Mouse Gray above and Mouse Gray below.

The present subspecies has been known hitherto from the east coast—Rigolet and L'Anse au Loup (Bangs, 1900:39; A. B. Howell, 1926:27, fig. 6; Hall and Cockrum, 1953:396, fig. 20; Hall and Kelson, 1959, 2:719, map 403). Various records from Hamilton Inlet and "Grosswater Bay" (Lake Melville) may pertain chiefly or even wholly to Rigolet, which is on a channel between these two bodies of water.

Microtus pennsylvanicus pennsylvanicus (Ord)
Pennsylvania Meadow Mouse; Campagnol des champs (Fr.); Assioapokoshish (M.). (Map 21.)

Several days of trapping in May and June in the vicinity of Seven Islands yielded no *Microtus*, though I noted runways and scats at the airport and near the marshy outlet of a brook on the shore of the Gulf. A nest, probably of this species, was found in a meadow bordering the bay. Apparently the species was not so abundant here as in the interior to the northward.

Previous records from the North Shore and adjacent areas have been generally attributed to *M. p. fontigenus* Bangs (type locality, Lake Edward, Quebec), which appears, at best, only weakly differentiated from *M. p. pennsylvanicus*. Some of the localities are: Godbout (Bailey, 1900:21); Matamek River (Eidmann, 1935:54); Seven Islands to Pigou River and Cape Whittle (C. F. Jackson, 1938:433); from Natashquan westward (Rand, 1944a:119; Hall and Kelson, 1959, 2:726, map 406); the Lake St. John area (Cameron and Orkin, 1950:105); and the Ste. Marguerite and Kegashka rivers (Snyder, 1954:227). Weaver (1940:418,420), with the concurrence of Glover M. Allen, considered *fontigenus* invalid and recorded as *pennsylvanicus* a series of specimens from the North Shore (Johan Beetz Bay to Mutton Bay).

Microtus pennsylvanicus enixus Bangs
Hamilton Inlet Meadow Mouse; Campagnol des champs du Labrador (Fr.). (Map 21.)

It is perhaps symptomatic of the long-standing confusion as to the real taxonomic status of the various forms of *Microtus pennsylvanicus* so far described from the Ungava Peninsula that *enixus* has gone by the name of Labrador Meadow Mouse, and *labradorius* by the name of Ungava Meadow Mouse! The material secured in the interior in 1953 is here referred tentatively to *enixus*. This is regarded as a large form by Bangs (1896b), Bailey (1900), Anderson (1940:78), and Rand (1944a), but as a small form by Davis (1936). Measurements of a series of topotypes by Bailey and by Rand on the one hand, and by Davis on the other hand, are widely at variance. (I have collected an adult female of *M. p. pennsylvanicus* in New Hampshire whose measurements (210–65–23) are almost exactly those of the huge female type of *enixus*.) Apparently little dependence can be placed upon mere size in the discrimination of the subspecies (*cf.* Snyder, 1954).

"Non-geographic variation is exceedingly great in Ungava series. *M. p. labradorius* is not certainly distinguishable from *M. p. enixus*. Pending a thorough review, interior specimens are referred tentatively to the older name, *enixus*" (C. O. H., Jr.).

In the original description of *Microtus enixus*, Bangs (1896b) designated the type locality merely as "Hamilton Inlet." Later (1898b:

494) one of the few localities he listed for *enixus* was "Rigoulette." Finally (1912:462) he definitely indicated that "Rigolet" was the type locality. This restriction seems to have been overlooked by subsequent authors.

After *Clethrionomys*, this was obviously the most abundant mammal of the interior in 1953. My 16 specimens were secured at or near Ashuanipi, Carol, Knob, Attikamagen, and Aulneau lakes. Many others that came to hand were not preserved. In this species, as in *Clethrionomys*, the proportion of adults in the population seemed to become very small toward the end of the summer.

Four years later there was evidently another peak of abundance. In July, 1957, David B. Harper sent me from Lac Montagni the flat skin of a female, "which had a nest in the cook tent." He reported: "Dozens of these things have little trails in the swamp next to camp and on the hillsides. The other day I saw eight or ten at one time, running around within ten feet square."

Habitats.—The habitats where these mice were found included muskegs of black spruce and tamarack; drier coniferous woods, generally near the banks of streams and lakes; moss-sedge bogs; burnt tracts; willow thickets; fairly open, dry areas of shrubs, grasses, mosses, and lichens; garbage dumps; camp clearings (some rather bare of vegetation); and buildings. On two occasions, when alarmed and beating a hasty retreat, these mice did not hesitate to take to shallow water in a muskeg and a swamp. (See also, under *Enemies*, accounts of their being fed upon by Lake Trout.) I found this species to be the most abundant mammalian inhabitant of the terrestrial strips in a "string bog" near Carol Lake; I also found numerous runways and scats in a similar bog near Mile 224 Airstrip. Though I took no specimens above timber-line, I noticed runways, evidently made by this species, in a moss-sedge bog on the higher slopes of Lorraine Mountain, at an altitude of about 2,575 feet.

Plants recorded at least four times in the immediate vicinity of the places of capture or observation of some 77 individuals were the following (listed in approximate order of frequency): *Sphagnum* spp., *Carex* spp., *Salix vestita*, *S. planifolia*, *Ledum groenlandicum*, *Larix laricina*, *Betula glandulosa*, *Picea glauca*, various grasses, *Picea mariana*, *Viburnum edule*, *Myrica gale*, *Equisetum* spp., *Cornus canadensis*, *Rubus ?pubescens*, *R. chamaemorus*, *Linnaea borealis* var. *americana*, *Empetrum nigrum*, *Potentilla fruticosa*, *Smilacina trifolia*, *Menyanthes trifoliata*, *Pleurozium schreberi*, *Viola* spp., and *Mitella nuda*.

Diurnal habits.—Like the Redbacks, these mice were distinctly diurnal, and frequently appeared running about at various hours of the day, especially at such well-favored spots as the garbage heaps. Occasionally one would dart along at very considerable speed.

Nests.—In the burnt tracts about Knob Lake I noticed numerous old, flattened nests exposed on the surface of the ground, obviously remaining from the previous winter when they were safely concealed beneath the snow. They were composed largely or perhaps wholly of common hairgrass (*Deschampsia flexuosa*). Their makers were probably *Microtus*. *Clethrionomys* would presumably prefer the green timber to these burnt tracts, where the lichens had scarcely begun to become regenerated since the fire seven years previously, though some mosses (such as *Polytrichum*) had reappeared.

Food.—On June 9 I observed a mouse, apparently a *Microtus*, on the border of a streamlet in a muskeg adjacent to Camp Pond. A movement in a little hollow at the waterside resolved itself into this mouse, hunched up, perhaps alarmed at my approach but not to such an extent as to retreat out of sight. For several minutes it remained there, making a few nervous movements, while partly concealed by some willow stems. Presently it moved a few inches in my direction, seized a grass or sedge stem, and returned to its original stand to gnaw on the rhizome. Then it repeated the performance. Watching through binoculars at 25 feet, I could make out its beady little untamed eyes. While chewing the stem, it held it up with both hands, knuckle sides uppermost. Presently it scurried along a log with very nimble movements and disappeared. A few minutes later, however, the same or a similar individual was watching me from just outside a stump near the same spot.

On June 18 a friend brought me a *Microtus* that had entered a livetrap at Burnt Creek and had probably been overlooked for a day or so. It was obviously very weak when released at the border of a muskeg area. After an hour or two it was still there, gradually gathering strength from the food it was securing. When I presented the rhizome ends of a couple of grass stems to the mouse, it nibbled on them while I held the other ends. In feeding, it sat up and grasped the stem with both hands, in the same way as described in the preceding paragraph.

At Attikamagen and Aulneau lakes I found leaves of *Salix vestita* and *Polygonum ?viviparum* in runways of *Microtus*, apparently as remnants of its repasts. At the damp border of Goldeneye Pond, and likewise at a small pond near Mollie T. Lake, there were chewings on buckbean (*Menyanthes trifoliata*)—probably the work of *Microtus*. At Knob Lake there were similar chewings on fireweed (*Epilobium angustifolium*).

In a muskeg at Lac Aulneau three mice, apparently of this species, scuttled away along runways and tunnels from a trap in which I found the fairly skeletonized remains of a *Microtus*—evidently a case of cannibalism. On the next day, in the same muskeg, a small *Microtus* ran away from a spot where there was a chewed Redback in a trap.

Enemies.—On July 25 members of a geological party secured a Lake Trout (*Cristivomer namaycush*) in a river at the north end of Lake Wapanikskan. It was about 23 inches in length and was estimated to weigh 4 lb. In its stomach were about six partly digested mice, whose tails were of about the right length for *Microtus* (too long for *Synaptomys* or *Phenacomys*) and whose incisors were not grooved. Since *Microtus* is much more aquatic than *Clethrionomys*, I concluded that these belonged to the former genus. It was still a mystery how so many of them, at one time and place, could have entered the watery habitat of the Lake Trout. Further evidence was obtained in September at Carol Lake, where Wilfrid Emond caught at 6.5-lb. Lake Trout whose stomach contained a mouse similar to those mentioned above. In the course of several days four or five dead Meadow Mice were found floating in this lake. This circumstance suggests that the individuals both at Lake Wapanikskan and at Carol Lake had succumbed in the water before being swallowed by the Lake Trout. But what had induced them to enter such wide bodies of water—perhaps with a view to crossing them—that they had perished in the attempt? Was it possibly population pressure in a year of peak abundance that brought on an explosive exodus that did not turn aside for such obstacles as lakes and rivers? Or could it have been some internal disease whose aggravations drove them to seek relief in the water? (For further accounts of mice found in the stomachs of Lake Trout and Brook Trout in the Ungava Peninsula, see Cabot (1912*a*:288–289) and Dunbar and Hildebrand (1952:95).) Voluntarily swimming individuals of *M. p. pennsylvanicus* have been observed in Michigan (Blair, 1939) and in Ontario (Peterson, 1947).

On July 27, at Lac Aulneau, I induced a Northern Shrike (*Lanius excubitor borealis*) to drop a furry object, which proved to be the fresh hind quarters of an immature *Microtus*.

The largest adult male specimen of the season was salvaged from the clutches of a Domestic Cat on September 28 at Knob Lake.

Ectoparasites.—From 15 specimens I collected 9 species of mites, 1 species of louse, and 1 species of flea. Acarina: *Haemogamasus alaskensis*—Attikamagen Lake, July 16 and 18; *Haemogamasus ambulans* —Carol Lake, September 13; *Hirstionyssus isabellinus*—Attikamagen Lake, July 4; *Laelaps alaskensis*—Knob Lake, June 15 and 19; Attikamagen Lake, July 4, 16, and 18; Lac Aulneau, July 27; Ashuanipi Lake, August 23; Carol Lake, September 10; *Laelaps kochi*—Knob Lake, June 14, 19, and 27; Attikamagen Lake, July 4, 16, and 18; Lac Aulneau, July 27; Ashuanipi Lake, August 23; Carol Lake, September 10; *Haemolaelaps glasgowi*—Knob Lake, June 15; Attikamagen Lake, July 16 and 18; *Dermacarus* sp. (non-parasitic)—Lac Aulneau, July 28; Carol Lake, September 13; *Camisia* sp. (non-parasitic)—Knob Lake, June 27; *Heminothrus* sp. (non-parasitic)—Lac Aulneau, July 27. Anoplura: *Hoplopleura acanthopus*: Knob Lake—5, June 14; ±60, June 15; 7 and 3, June 19; 5, June 27; Attikamagen Lake—28, July 4; 13, July 16; ±100, July 18; Carol Lake—1, September 13. Siphonaptera: *Megabothris asio asio*: Carol Lake—1 male, September 10.

Reproduction.—The testes of adult males, from June 14 to July 18, varied from 17×10 to 16×10 mm.; those of another, on September 28, were 7×5. In subadult males (July 27 to September 13) the variation was from 3.5×2 to 4×2.5. Data from adult females were: June 19, six 11-mm. embryos; June 27, seven 15-mm. embryos; July 16, mammary glands much developed; July 28, no embryos; from juvenal females: June 19, vagina perforate; July 16, vagina imperforate.

Growth.—Lengths and weights of juvenal or subadult specimens were: June 19, 113 mm., 14.2 g.; July 16, 135 mm., 21 g.; July 27, 147 mm., 30.4 g.; August 23, 146 mm., 29.1 g.; September 10, 139 mm., 29 g.; September 13, 144 mm., 27.7 g. Much as in the case of *Clethrionomys*, these samples showed no increase in size of members of the subadult population as the season advanced from July 27 to September 13. The similarity of conditions in both species may be significant of a high mortality rate among the young of the year at this season, when food should be ample. Since no considerable numbers of predators were evident, the decline may be due to disease rather than to predation. (See discussion of *Clethrionomys*, p. 66.)

Molt.—Change of pelage was indicated by dark areas on the inside of the skin as follows: June 14, adult, most of dorsum and part of venter; June 15, adult, sides of neck and lower back and rump; June 25, adult, crown and dorsum; July 16, juvenile, entire hide; July 27, subadult, a few dark streaks on dorsum; August 23, subadult, dorsum from crown to rump; September 10, subadult, dorsum from snout to rump.

Coloration.—The present series of specimens is darker, less brown or buffy, than specimens of *pennsylvanicus* from Maine and Massachusetts; dorsum a mixture of blackish and light buffy hairs, producing a general effect near Saccardo's Umber; sides slightly paler and buffier; facial area similar to dorsum; tail Fuscous or Fuscous-Black above, Grayish Olive below; underparts Pale Smoke Gray to Pale Olive-Buff; upper side of feet Hair Brown. A series of *enixus* from Goose Bay (USNM), collected by David H. Johnson, is appreciably browner; the measurements are approximately similar. A subadult male and an adult female from Lac Aulneau are a sort of buffy brown—thus lighter-colored than the specimens from more southerly localities in the interior. They match fairly well three specimens collected at Fort Chimo by Johnson, and are probably referable to *M. p. labradorius*, provided that is a good subspecies.

Measurements and weights.—The averages and extremes of five adult males from Knob, Abel, and Attikamagen lakes are: length, 169.8 (156–183); tail, 43.8 (36–50); foot, 20 (19–21); ear, 12.8 (12.5–13); weight, 51.1 (42.5–56.6) g. (somewhat fat to rather fat). Three adult females from Knob and Attikamagen lakes: length, 184 (167–200); tail, 49.8 (44–56.5); foot, 20.5 (20–21); ear, 13.5 (12.5–14); weight, 61.2 (47–70.4) g. (two pregnant, the other with mammary glands much developed). The adult female from Lac Aulneau shows almost no difference in size from the others: length, 179; tail, 47.5; foot, 20.5; ear, 12.5; weight, 54.8 g. (somewhat fat, and fur a little damp).

Distribution.—Previous records of *enixus* are mainly from the Hudsonian Life-zone: near Petitsikapau Lake (Low, 1896:321); Rigolet, 50 miles north of Fort George, and Black Bay (Bangs, 1898*b*:494, and 1899:12); Gready (Austin, 1932:63); Hamilton River, Windsor, Nain, Davis Inlet, Hebron, Charlton Island, Cape Hope Islands, Fort George, and near Cape Jones (Rand, 1944*a*:117); Panchia Lake (Manning, 1947:83); Red Bay and Battle Harbour (Snyder, 1954:227). See also Hall and Kelson (1959, 2:726, map 406). From zonal considerations, Austin's record (1932;69) of *enixus* from Nachvak would seem more likely to be attributable to *labradorius*.

Cabot's classic account (1912*a*:171,233,287–292) of "mice" overrunning the Assiwaban River area in 1905, a year of peak abundance, is apparently regarded by Anderson (1939:84) as pertaining to *M. p.*

enixus. This identification is, in all likelihood, correct—at least as to the species.

Microtus pennsylvanicus labradorius Bailey
Ungava Meadow Mouse; Campagnol des champs d'Ungava (Fr.).
(Map 21.)

The records of *labradorius* are mainly from the Arctic Life-zone and the outer edge of the Hudsonian: Fort Chimo (Bailey, 1900:22); Port Burwell, George River, Port Harrison, Richmond Gulf, Second River, and Great Whale River (Rand, 1944a:118); Povungnituk and Mistake Bay (Manning, 1947:83); Koksoak and Nastapoka rivers (Snyder, 1954:227); south of Leaf Bay (Bateman, 1953:4,7). See also Hall and Kelson (1959, 2:726, map 406).

Microtus chrotorrhinus chrotorrhinus (Miller)
New England Rock Vole; Campagnol des roches (Fr.). (Map 22.)

Records for Quebec localities within (or nearly within) the peninsula are: lower Moisie and Seal rivers (C. F. Jackson, 1938:433); Val Jalbert (Cameron and Orkin, 1950:105); Lake Mistassini (Cameron and Morris, 1951:128); Seven Islands and Fort McKenzie (Schad, 1954:217—without subspecific determination). See also Hall and Kelson (1959, 2:741, map 413).

Microtus chrotorrhinus ravus Bangs
Labrador Rock Vole; Campagnol gris des roches (Fr.). (Map 22.)

There seems to be only one authentic locality record in the literature on this subspecies: Black Bay (Bangs, 1898c:188, and 1912:463). It has also been reported by Anderson (1939:85) from Port Manvers and Curlew Harbour. However, the Port Manvers specimen was misidentified (Charles O. Handley, Jr., *in litt.*, February 3, 1956), and the other, a mutilated skin without skull, is of uncertain identity (Karl F. Koopman, *in litt.*, February 12 and 23, 1960).

Ondatra zibethicus zibethicus (Linné)
Eastern Muskrat; Rat musqué (Fr.); Otshisk (M.). (Map 23.)

This subspecies is not definitely known to range northeastward beyond the area of Lakes Mistassini and St. John in the Canadian Life-zone of Quebec, whence the following records come: south of Lake Mistassini in 1792 (Michaux, 1889:82); headwaters of Peribonca River (Low, 1890:17); Lake St. John (Hollister, 1911:16, pl. 1; Cameron and Orkin, 1950:106); Lake Mistassini (Neilson, 1948:154); Mistassibi River (Cameron and Morris, 1951:128). The following records from farther eastward in the same life-zone may, however, pertain to the same subspecies: lower Natashquan River (Townsend, 1913:176); Trout Lake (Eidmann, 1935:54, fig. 7); Mingan (Weaver, 1940:421).

Gilbert Simard spoke of some Montagnais, in a previous year, setting snares in muskrat houses on the Romaine River 75 miles above its mouth, and thus securing four or five of the animals but losing them to a Lynx that came along and ate them up. There are many Muskrats at Lac de Morhiban (Philip Loth). A. E. Boerner saw one at Gad Lake in the summer of 1953.

Ondatra zibethicus aquilonius (Bangs)
Labrador Muskrat; Rat musqué du Labrador (Fr.). (Map 23.)

In the central interior of the Ungava Peninsula the severity of the winters and the dearth of suitable marshy areas may deter the Muskrats from building many "houses" of the type that is so familiar in more southerly regions. At any rate, I observed none, and I have found only one published reference to their presence in the peninsula; Wallace (1907:131) reported them as numerous at the head of George River. I also had reports of houses on the Romaine River (75 miles above its mouth) and perhaps in the Menihek Lake area. In the absence of houses, the presence of Muskrats may be determined chiefly from their droppings on rocks along the shores. They excavate burrows in the banks in lieu of houses.

In June I saw several Muskrats that had been captured by a workman at Knob Lake, either in traps or by being struck with a stick.

The only live animal that came under my observation was a hundred yards offshore in a cove of Northwest Bay, Attikamagen Lake, on the morning of July 17. As it swam along, head, body, and tail appeared slightly and perhaps separately above the surface. After a number of dives, it made toward the mouth of an inlet brook, where there were droppings on rocks.

Two of my Montagnais friends, Joseph Georges St. Onge and Georges Michel, presented me with a Muskrat that they secured on the evening of August 20 along the outlet of Leroy Lake. It was an adult female (but probably in early maturity, since the cranial sutures are distinct); length, 536; tail, 230; foot, 77; ear, 22; weight, approximately 2 lb. (not very fat). Skull measurements are: basal length, 60.4; zygomatic breadth, 37.3; length of nasals, 20.9; breadth of nasals, 8.6; alveolar length of upper molars, 15.4. Nearly all of the measurements are smaller than the average of four specimens from Hamilton Inlet and L'Anse au Loup (*cf.* Hollister, 1911:20). The animal contained no embryos, but its mammary glands were developed. The hide was unprime on crown and nape. It was swarming with thousands of mites (*Laelaps kochi, L. multispinosus,* and *Dermacarus* sp.—the last non-parasitic).

Jérôme St. Onge presented a cased skin that he obtained on September 25 on Swampy Bay River about 8 miles south of Lac Le Fer. Both skins are quite comparable in color with several specimens (USNM) collected by Turner at The Forks and Fort Chimo.

"The specimens resemble one in similar pelage taken in Lake Melville, not far from the type locality of *aquilonius,* and are darker than specimens from Maine and Massachusetts. The skull of the Ungava specimen, although not fully mature, is considerably smaller than those of similar age from the northeastern United States. However, the hind foot measurement is larger than is usual for *aquilonius,* and it may indicate an approach toward *zibethicus*" (C. O. H., Jr.).

In the early fall Kom Pinette secured one at or near Ashuanipi Lake. Three "baby Muskrats" (possibly grown *Microtus?*) were reported in a Lake Trout's stomach at Shabogamo Lake. Members of a geological party saw a Muskrat in Carol Lake, September 9. Cyrille Dufresne reported the species in Gilling River and in Comeback Lake; James Murdoch reported it in Ossokmanuan Lake, mostly in little coves where the "grass" was thick. Robert Slipp saw two in Lac Aulneau in 1953. J. L. Véronneau saw one and plentiful evidence of others at a small lake near Leroy Lake. In 1949 Dr. F. D. Foster noted small numbers at Evening, Astray, and Knob lakes.

In one year at Fort McKenzie (between 1916 and 1936), Sebastien McKenzie traded 1,100 muskrat skins, but in other years the animals would disappear almost completely—perhaps killed off in severe winters. He knew of "push-ups" on the ice, such as are reported in northern Mackenzie (Porsild, 1945:17), southwestern Keewatin (Harper, 1956:44), and other northern localities. Fuller (1951:14–15), writing of the Athabaska-Peace Delta in Alberta, provides the most complete account of "push-ups" that has come to my notice.

Ben McKenzie spoke of the occurrence of the species in the Menihek-Bringadin-Wakuach lakes area. At Oskoas Lake (perhaps in this same area) he and two companions secured 300 Muskrats in approximately 15 October days, about 1943. They operated by night, from a canoe; while one paddled from the stern, another in the bow struck the animals with a paddle, and the man in the middle finished them with a stick. They took still others by placing a bag over the under-water entrance to a burrow, and then striking on the ground above to drive them into the bag.

Thoreau (1877:211-212) tells how his Indian guide, Joe Polis, endeavored to call a Muskrat on a stream near Chesuncook Lake, Maine, by making "a curious squeaking, wiry sound with his lips . . . . An acquaintance of mine who was hunting moose in those woods a month after this, tells me that his Indian in this way repeatedly called the musquash within reach of his paddle in the moonlight, and struck at them." Is it perhaps by this same means that the Montagnais get within range of their Muskrats on the nocturnal waters of Ungava?

According to Porsild (1945:17), the identical technique is employed by the natives (Eskimos or Indians) on the far-away Mackenzie Delta: "Experienced hunters can 'call' the rats, often from a considerable distance, by a high-pitched squeaky note made with the lips."

The wild fur production in Quebec, for the season of 1950-51, included 180,648 muskrat skins (Cowan, 1955:169); this was by far the largest catch of any fur-bearing animal. For 1954-55, 122,709 skins were reported (Canada Year Book 1956:606).

Previous records from the peninsula that may be referred to *O. z. aquilonius* are: south coast—Kecarpoui (Weaver, 1940:421); east coast—from Strait of Belle Isle north to Nain (Cartwright, 1792, 3:14, 32,228; Bell, 1884:49; Bangs, 1899:11; Hollister, 1911:19, pl. 1; Cabot, 1912*a*:45; Hall and Cockrum, 1953:465, fig. 117; Hall and Kelson, 1959, 2:755, map 423); north coast—Fort Chimo (Hollister, 1911:19; Bangs, 1912:463; Anderson, 1934:102); Killinek area (Hantzsch, 1932:9); south of Leaf Bay (Bateman, 1953:7); west coast—Cape Jones (Bell, 1884:49); Great Whale River to Kikkerteluk River (Doutt, 1954:244). Interior localities are: Nichicun Lake and upper Hamilton River (Low, 1896:100,321); lower Naskaupi River and Seal Lake (Mrs. Hubbard, 1906:536, and 1908:31); Mountaineer Lake (Wallace, 1906:88); Crooked River and head of George River (Wallace, 1907:53,131); The Forks (Hollister, 1911:19); west of Davis Inlet (Strong, 1930:7); Kenamu River (Leslie, 1931:210); Flour Lake (Merrick, 1933:70,75,77,86,118); George and Payne rivers (Rousseau, 1949:102,126); Clearwater and Seal lakes (Doutt, 1954:244). The records from the Killinek area and Kikkerteluk and Payne rivers are perhaps the only ones in the peninsula from the main Arctic Life-zone.

Rattus norvegicus (Berkenhout)
Norway Rat; Brown Rat; Rat (Fr.).

Roger Ferguson reported this pest as present at Seven Islands since about 1943. In one case, it carried off a lot of onions from a cellar and stored them elsewhere. It presumably reached this locality by ship.

Roland C. Clement reports (*in litt.*, August 8, 1957): "Norway Rats were abundant in the filthy lumber camps along the Moisie River at Mile 30 on May 23, 1957."

I have come across published records from just two definite localities in the peninsula—at Black Bay (Bangs, 1912:461), and about Lake St. John (Cameron and Orkin, 1950:106). Hantzsch remarks (1932:8) that "rats" are "said to reach the coast [localities not specified] occasionally on ships, but apparently they soon perish."

Mus musculus domesticus Rutty
House Mouse; Souris commune (Fr.).

This species has probably been overlooked in many places where it must occur, especially along the coast. There is a single definite record for the peninsula—at Havre St. Pierre (Weaver, 1940:418, 421); and one just over the border at Val Jalbert on Lake St. John (Cameron and Orkin, 1950:106).

Zapus hudsonius ladas Bangs
Labrador Meadow Jumping Mouse; Souris sauteuse du Labrador (Fr.). (Map 24.)

A male was obtained on May 29 in a thicket of sweet gale and alder in a wet meadow bordering Seven Islands Bay. In this locality, where the average daily minimum temperature for April is 23°, and for May 34°, it had probably just recently emerged from hibernation. Its length was 212; tail, 130; foot, 30.5; ear, 13; testes, 7×3.5 (not descended); weight, 13.7 g. (somewhat fat). The hide was prime, and the cheek-pouches were empty. The specimen yielded several mites (*Haemolaelaps glasgowi*). No further trace of Jumping Mice was found in the interior.

"On the basis of excellent Labrador material, but extremely inadequate Quebec material, it seems probable that the Seven Islands specimen is intermediate between *ladas* and *canadensis*, but nearer the former, which it most resembles in coloration" (C. O. H., Jr.).

The range of *ladas* extends across the more southerly portions of the peninsula westward to approximately longitude 70° (*cf.* Krutzsch, 1954:420, fig. 47). South coast records include: Godbout (Anderson,

1934:103); Moisie Bay (Eidmann, 1935:56); between Seven Islands and Pigou River (C. F. Jackson, 1938:433); Belles Amours, Kecarpoui, Mutton Bay, and Johan Beetz Bay (Weaver, 1940:418,421). Along the east coast *Zapus* has been found from Black Bay north to Makkovik (Bangs, 1897:237; Krutzsch, 1954:449, fig. 47; Hall and Kelson, 1959, 2:773, map 428). Interior localities include: 3 miles above mouth of Naskaupi River, Northwest River, Flour Lake, and "northwest Ungava" (Krutzsch, 1954:449).

Certain early records from the peninsula, published under the name of *Zapus hudsonius* (by Stearns, 1883:115; Packard, 1891:442; Bryant, 1894:55; and Low, 1896:321) may have pertained to either *Zapus* or *Napaeozapus*. *Napaeozapus* was not distinguished from *Zapus* until 1899 (Preble, 1899:33), and then only as a subgenus. No form of the single species *insignis* (described in 1891) from the Ungava Peninsula had been recognized as such and recorded in print at the time when Stearns, Packard, Bryant, and Low were publishing. At least one of the specimens referred to by Low was evidently *Napaeozapus*. For Bangs writes (1912:463): "I have seen but one Labrador specimen of this species [*N. i. 'abietorum*,' since *saguenayensis* was not described till 1942], a mounted specimen from the Geological Survey of Canada collection, taken by Low at Hamilton River."

Krutzsch (1954:420, fig. 47) uses the specimen vaguely recorded as from "northwest Ungava" to place a mark on his distributional map at approximately 56°40' N., 69° W. This record, if correctly placed, would be the only published one in the peninsula from within the zone of permafrost (*cf.* Thomas, 1953:chart 8–1). Yet Richard S. Peterson (*in litt.*, March 18, 1961) informs me of having recently secured several specimens in the Kaniapiskau Basin. Krutzsch also indicates the range of *Z. h. hudsonius* as including York Factory, southwestern Keewatin, the entire surroundings of Great Slave Lake, and nearly the whole Mackenzie River valley, and thus as invading the zone of permafrost to a very considerable extent. However, there is no actual record for Keewatin, and apparently none in the Mackenzie district north of Fort Rae and Fort Simpson.

Zapus hudsonius canadensis (Davies)
Quebec Meadow Jumping Mouse; Souris sauteuse du Québec (Fr.).
(Map 24.)

Z. h. canadensis ranges eastward to the Lake St. John area (Cameron and Orkin, 1950:107) and to Lakes Mistassini and Albanel

(Cameron and Morris, 1951:128; Hall and Kelson, 1959, 2:773, map 428).

Napeozapus insignis saguenayensis Anderson
Saguenay Woodland Jumping Mouse; Souris sauteuse
des bois du Saguenay (Fr.). (Map 25.)

As remarked in the account of *Zapus hudsonius ladas*, some of the records of *"Zapus hudsonius"* from the Ungava Peninsula, published between 1883 and 1896, may have actually pertained to *Napaeozapus*. Among the subsequent records, attributed to *N. i. abietorum* before the publication of *saguenayensis* in 1942, the following may now be assigned to the latter subspecies: Godbout (Preble, 1899:36); Hamilton River (Bangs, 1912:463); Moisie Bay (Eidmann, 1935:56); Moisie River (C. F. Jackson, 1938:434); Black Bay (Anderson, 1939:88). See also Hall and Kelson (1959, 2:779, map 431).

Napeozapus insignis algonquinensis Prince
Algonquin Woodland Jumping Mouse. (Map 25.)

This subspecies ranges eastward at least as far as Lake Edward (about 50 miles south of Lake St. John, in Quebec County) (Bangs, 1896a:50; Hall and Kelson, 1959, 2:778, map 431); and apparently to the very margin of Lake St. John and the Ashuapmuchuan River (Cameron and Orkin, 1950:107) which form part of the southwestern boundary of the Ungava Peninsula, as defined on page 26 (*antea*).

Napeozapus insignis abietorum (Preble)
Northern Woodland Jumping Mouse; Souris sauteuse
des bois du Nord (Fr.). (Map 25.)

As far as available records go, this Jumping Mouse reaches its eastern limit at Lakes Mistassini and Albanel (Cameron and Morris, 1951:129; Hall and Kelson, 1959, 2:778, map 431).

Erethizon dorsatum dorsatum (Linnaeus)
Eastern Canada Porcupine; Porc-épic du Canada (Fr.);
Kak (M.). (Map 26.)

On June 25 a Porcupine was reported dead on a road near John Lake, 2 miles northeast of Knob Lake, and I secured it for a specimen. It had perhaps been struck by a motor vehicle, for there was a gash in its back and its skull was broken. It was an adult male: length, 810; tail, 180; foot, 100; ear, 25; testes, 55 × 20; weight, 17 lb. (a little fat). The hide was prime. Four rudimentary pectoral mammae were evident (fig. 3). The general color of the upper parts is Fuscous-Black; there are comparatively few guard hairs with lighter (pale brownish) tips; these arise chiefly from the occiput and the middle of the back, and are not at all conspicuous. The quills on rump and tail are predominantly Olive-Brown; comparatively few of them are Pale Olive-Buff to white. The underparts are uniformly Chaetura Black. The incisors are dull yellow. In these characters the specimen answers to the description of *E. d. picinum* Bangs.

Porcupine gnawings in the forests about Attikamagen Lake impressed me as the most extensive I had ever seen. Some groups of trees had been stripped so thoroughly that the bare, light-colored trunks were noticeable from a distance of a mile across the lake. On July 11 I came upon two feeding areas in the coniferous forest near the northwest end of the Iron Arm. Each, with a radius of 15–20 feet, involved from about 15 to 30 trees. On some of the trees (about 35 feet in height) scarcely any bark remained between the base and a point, say, 6 feet from the top. In one of these areas most of the trees seemed to be balsams, with a maximum diameter of about 6 inches. Some of the stripped trees were obviously dying; but in that vast green wilderness the economic effects were quite negligible. The ground about the trees was strewn with chips of the outer bark, discarded in favor of the inner layers. On the next day a similar group of a dozen or more trees (at least some of them balsams) was noticed. In the same vicinity, in dense woods, I found a den beneath an old stump, whose top was decorated with a bed of the attractive moss, *Hypnum crista-castrensis*. The threshold was carpeted with a clubmoss, *Lycopodium annotinum*, and was thickly strewn with half a bushel of clean-looking scats. Elsewhere about the Iron Arm I noticed gnawings on medium-sized spruces (4 to 6 inches in diameter) rather than on the larger trees. The tooth marks were evident on the wood beneath the bark. Here the white spruce seemed to be selected a little

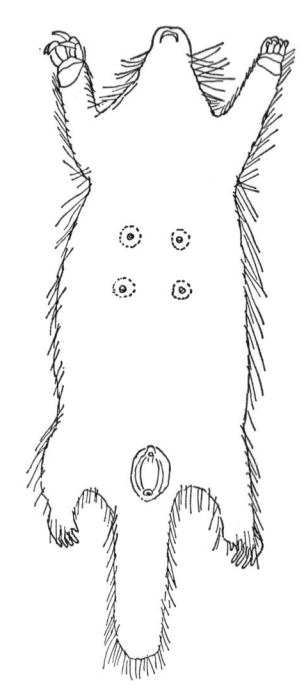

Fig. 3.—*Erethizon dorsatum dorsatum*, mastology ($\times \frac{1}{10}$). Adult male, No. 1285. John Lake, Quebec. June 25, 1953.

more frequently than the black spruce, although Hustich remarks (1951*b*:178) concerning the Knob Lake area: "When the four coniferous species occur together, porcupines prefer balsam fir, black spruce, tamarack, and white spruce, in the order mentioned."

About 6:30 a. m. on August 11 a Porcupine came waddling along near the shore of Mollie T. Lake. I induced it to climb a tree, but it did not remain long. It seemed distinctly less black—more brownish —than the John Lake specimen. On the next day I noticed some scats in a sort of ice cave at the head of the perpetual snowbank on Sunny Mountain, at an altitude of about 2,050 feet, well above timber-line. This case of a normally arboreal species occurring in an Arctic-Alpine area, while interesting, is not unique. Rousseau (1949:102), in discussing the mammals of the George River area, remarks that the Porcupine takes refuge in summer beneath rocks in elevated, treeless parts.

An adult male was obtained by James A. Dewey in spruce woods at the north end of Ashuanipi Lake on September 4, and presented by him. Its length was 709; tail (after skinning), 201; foot, 100; ear, 20; testes, 35×16 (only right one descended); weight, 17 lb. (not especially fat). This specimen shows less tooth wear than the other (from John Lake), and is presumably not so old; the molariform teeth are larger, and the tooth-row is longer (23.5 vs. 21.5); the width of the rostrum is less (21.5 vs. 22); the length of the nasals is greater (31.7 vs. 30.7); the incisors are dull orange. The general color of the upper parts is between Mummy Brown and Blackish Brown—more blackish on snout, rump, and tail; lighter (pale buffy) guard hairs arising from occiput and quite conspicuous; others, less conspicuous, arising from middle of back and sides; pale buffy to white quills on rump and tail much more numerous and conspicuous than in the other specimen; other quills Olive-Brown; underparts of body quite uniformly Fuscous, but underside of tail blackish, having brownish median area. Most of the diagnostic characters of *dorsatum*, as pointed out by Anderson and Rand (1943*a*:300), seem applicable to this specimen. The hide was prime. Numerous small nematodes *(Wellcomia evoluta)* and a cestode *(Monoecocestus variabilis)*, found in the abdominal cavity, were probably derived from the ruptured intestines.

On the basis of current literature, the differences noted between the two specimens would seem to fit them neatly into two distinct subspecies, *picinum* and *dorsatum*. However, Handley comments as follows:

"Individual variation is great in porcupines of eastern Canada and adjacent portions of the United States. *E. d. picinum* of the eastern and northern sectors of Ungava appears to be unrecognizable as a distinct race. The characters ascribed to it, far from being unique, apparently will not even distinguish it as average differences."

In 1949 Dr. F. D. Foster noted evidence of Porcupines in the vicinity of Menihek Lake and at Howell's River, and Allen Thompson found the species fairly common about Mackenzie and Kasheshibaw lakes, on the east side of Michikamau Lake. In 1951, about the middle of July, James Murdoch found an approximately half-grown individual in a tree on the upper Hamilton River. In 1952 Sebastien McKenzie secured and ate a Porcupine at Lac Aulneau, and Arthur C. Newton reported the animals in the Fort McKenzie area. The next year Robert Slipp saw one of the animals, a den among rocks, and many gnawed trees about Lac Aulneau. In June, 1953, Ron Barrett saw one near Sucker Creek. Gilbert Simard reported several in the Greenbush Lake area—one rather brownish, the others black. H. E. Neal and Glenn Hogg found droppings at Al's Lake, and William C. Hood, Jr., noticed evidence at Lac Hayot. At Trough Lake one of the animals was killed by Remi Kelly. At various field camps a Porcupine would be destroyed after damage to stored goods, or occasionally in anticipation of such damage.

The field party of Peter Almond reported single Porcupines seen in the summer at Shabogamo, Wabush, and Carol lakes. At the first-mentioned locality one of them ate a rubber pipe, according to Leopold Gelinas (*cf.* Seton, 1929, 4:627). I saw porcupine work on two or three balsams at Carol Lake. Garth D. Jackson saw one of the animals and many gnawed trees just east of Huguette Lake. A. E. Boerner reported many at Gad Lake. On the other hand, according to Willé Pinette, the Porcupine has disappeared from the vicinity of Eric Lake—and likewise its predator, the Fisher.

Dr. Bertram H. Harper writes (*in litt.*, September 28, 1955) of what might appear to be a diminutive local population on the east side of Hudson Bay:

"I saw several porcupines killed by the Indians in and around Richmond Gulf and, on remarking that they must be small young ones, was advised by the trader there that any he had seen in that area were only half the size of those found farther south."

The following method of extracting porcupine quills (from the flesh of man or other animals), advocated by a machinist at Mile 224 Airstrip, is offered for what it may be worth: "Cut the quills off rather short and immerse them in coal oil, which will penetrate the hollow center and so soften the barbs that the quills may be pulled out." Otherwise (as I can testify from personal experience), a quill has to be fairly dissected out.

The strong, stout, stiff, muscular tail, when applied to a tree, evidently serves the Porcupine much as a feathered tail does a woodpecker—for support (*cf.* Murie, 1926:112; Seton, 1929, 4:621). The fur on the underside of the tail in the present specimens seems much worn from such usage.

I have never succeeded in finding any ectoparasites on a Porcupine. Perhaps its fur is not dense and warm enough to harbor many of them in the cold regions it inhabits. The animal must depend largely upon its winter fat for protection from low temperatures.

The range attributed to the hitherto recognized subspecies *picinum* extends along the east coast, to the Ungava Bay region at Fort Chimo, and as far northwestward as Lower Seal Lake and Richmond Gulf (Anderson and Rand, 1943*a*:298; Doutt, 1954:245; Hall and Kelson, 1959, 2:783, map 432). The subspecies *dorsatum* has been assumed to be limited to the rest of the peninsula, west and south of the above-mentioned areas. The following distributional summary covers the peninsula as a whole, with *dorsatum* as the sole recognized subspecies in eastern Canada: south coast—very common generally (Stearns, 1883:115); Matamek (Eidmann, 1935:56); Kecarpoui (Weaver, 1940:421); east coast, from Strait of Belle Isle north to Nain (Cartwright, 1792:*passim*; Bell, 1884:491; Bangs, 1900:37; Strong, 1930:8; Anderson and Rand, 1943*a*:298,300, fig. 1); in the north, only at Fort Chimo (Low, 1896:321; Bangs, 1898*b*:492; Anderson and Rand, 1943*a*:298,300); in the west, at Great Whale River (Low, 1896:321) and Richmond Gulf (Doutt, 1954:245). Interior localities include: Hamilton River and above Cambrian Lake (Low, 1896:321); Susan River (Wallace, 1906:75,271,272,296); lower Naskaupi River and George River below Indian House Lake (Mrs. Hubbard, 1906:536; 1908:29,192); Grand Lake and Crooked River (Wallace, 1907:21,22, 60); Natashquan River above fifth falls (Townsend, 1913:176); Big Romaine River (Comeau, 1923:83); Voisey's Bay to Hopedale in interior valleys (Strong, 1930:8); Tikkoatokak Bay (Wheeler, 1930: 456); Traverspine River, Hamilton River above Minipi Rapids, and Flour Lake (Merrick, 1933:20,41,106); Little Mecatina River (Stainer, 1938:157); Lake St. John area (Cameron and Orkin, 1950:107); Lakes Albanel and Mistassini (Cameron and Morris, 1951:129); and Lower Seal Lake (Doutt, 1954:245).

Nearly a hundred years ago there were great numbers of Porcupines in the territory extending eastward from the Manicouagan River to the headwaters of the Ste. Marguerite. About 1880 there was a large migration of Fishers into this area, and in two years the Porcupines were "completely destroyed." After another year the Fishers, too, disappeared (Comeau, 1923:82).

Delphinapterus leucas (Pallas)
White Whale; Beluga; Marsouin blanc (Fr.); Mistimek (M.).
(Map 27.)

On May 21 a White Whale, dirty grayish white in color, breached a number of times in succession in the harbor at Rimouski. In its leisurely gliding to the surface—quite different from the active rolling of a *Tursiops*—it would expose perhaps 6 feet of its back at a time and remain in view for several seconds.

Flying Officer W. A. McKenzie, RCAF, spoke of sighting from the air about a dozen of these animals in the St. Lawrence on October 5, 1952; some of them were as far up as Quebec City, and all of them within 15–20 miles of that point. He referred to these animals, and to the Blackfish (*Globicephala scammonii*) of the Pacific Coast, as a distinct menace to Canso aircraft in landing on or taking off from the water. If one were struck, it would demolish the Canso. The pilots need to watch carefully to avoid such a mishap.

The species has been recorded from three coasts of the peninsula: south coast (Stearns, 1883:114; Low, 1896:317; Grenfell, 1922:356; Anderson, 1934:73; Eidmann, 1935:46; A. B. Howell, 1935); north coast (Bell, 1884:52; Payne, 1887:75; Turner, 1888b:83; Low, 1896: 122; Wallace, 1907:236; Binney, 1929:19; Hantzsch, 1932:8; Anderson, 1934:73, and 1940:101; Gabrielson and Wright, 1951:128; Dunbar, 1952:7); and west coast, including the Belcher Islands (Bell, 1879:29, 1884:52, and 1886:12,14; Spencer, 1889:79; Turner, 1894: 174; Low, 1896:122; Flaherty and Flaherty, 1924:53; Anderson, 1934: 73; Manning, 1947:84; Doan and Douglas, 1953:1,20). In an extensive account of the pursuit, the biology, and the economic utilization of the White Whale in the St. Lawrence, Vladykov (1944:46,59,61, figs. 48–49) points out that it occurs throughout the year from Ile aux Coudres to Pointe des Monts, and in the lower Saguenay; in summer only, along the North Shore from Trinity Bay to Seven Islands, Mingan Islands, and Natashquan; and in autumn, up the St. Lawrence past Quebec City. The same author (1946) presents detailed food studies of the species at Manicouagan and Les Escoumains.

Bangs' statement (1898b:492; 1912:459) that it is "common everywhere along the Labrador coasts" would seem to apply to the east coast of the peninsula as well as to the others. However, Vladykov (1944:51) "could find no precise records of white whales from the Labrador coasts, and we have none" (Sergeant and Fisher, 1957:92).

Canis lupus labradorius Goldman
Labrador Wolf; Loup du Labrador (Fr.). (Map 28.)

The existing uncertainty in regard to the exact ranges of *C. l. labradorius* and *C. l. lycaon* in the Ungava Peninsula is not likely to be resolved in the near future. Goldman (1944) was handicapped by dearth of material in determining their respective ranges or the area of intergradation between them. Of the former he says (p. 434) that it "appears to be an inhabitant of the barren grounds"; yet his map (p. 414, fig. 14) indicates that it ranges not only over the Arctic Life-zone of the peninsula, but throughout the Hudsonian and even into part of the Canadian. It would seem more logical to consider it an inhabitant of the same territory as the Labrador Barren Ground Caribou (*Rangifer caboti*), and to assign to *lycaon* a northward range coextensive with that of the Eastern Woodland Caribou (*R. caribou caribou*). The original range of the latter Caribou presumably extended north at least to the East Main River, Nichicun, Wakuach, and Michikamau lakes, and the Naskaupi River. Both species of Caribou probably occupy some territory jointly in the northern part of the Hudsonian Life-zone (*cf.* maps 44 and 45); and in the winter there may be some overlapping in the ranges of the two subspecies of Wolves, in the general area of the 55th parallel of latitude.

The following records may be assumed to apply, at least in large part, to *labradorius*.

More than a century ago Schubert (1844:col. 419) reported— apparently for the northern part of the east coast—that Wolves were rarer than Black Bears, and that few were killed. Low (1897:31) had never seen or heard a Wolf in the interior; the animal was rarely met with anywhere, even where there were great herds of Barren Ground Caribou. Records from definite localities in the western half of the peninsula are exceedingly few (*cf.* map 28).

"The old [Eskimo] natives say that wolves were formerly quite numerous in the Labrador interior. They followed the great bands of migratory reindeer [Caribou], on which they fed. In the winter they approached the coast and rifled traps and tore down meat caches, and even attacked the dogs in the villages." They were baited and killed by means of a sharp strip of whale bone tied up in folds inside a chunk of blubber. (Hawkes, 1916:85.)

Further records are: Stupart Bay (Payne, 1887:71); Ungava district (Turner, 1888b:83); Michikamau Lake and Hudson Bay coast (Low, 1896:315); middle George River, Indian House Lake, and mouth of Whale River (Wallace, 1907:153,155,197,198); Michikamats Lake and lower George River (Mrs. Hubbard, 1908:119,191); east of Indian House Lake (Prichard, 1911:90,94); Assiwaban River, Nain, near Davis Inlet, and Mistinipi Lake (Cabot, 1912a:165,193, 217,233,266,269); Adlavik, Hopedale, Kaipokok, and Fort Chimo (Goldman, 1944:434); Lower Seal Lake area (Doutt, 1954:239). See also Hall and Kelson (1959, 2:850, map 444).

"It is now abundantly clear that the wolf is the master herder, culling the herd of unfit individuals, and therefore should be rigidly protected" (William O. Pruitt, Jr., in review of Lois Crisler's *Arctic Wild* (1958), in *The Beaver*, outfit 290:55, 1959).

Canis lupus lycaon Schreber
Eastern Timber Wolf; Loup des bois de l'Est (Fr.);
Meiken (M.). (Map 28.)

The New York Times for April 14, 1953, carried the following dispatch from Shelter Bay:

Wolves became so hungry in this remote northeastern Quebec district that a pack invaded this village and tried to mingle with the local dogs.

Thirty of the pack were killed by Game Warden Alphonse Bourgeois and residents who joined in the hunt.

Anything that resembled a wolf or a shepherd dog was shot on sight by the villagers, as the wolves were so thin they easily passed for ordinary hounds. Some of them weighed less than half their normal weight—125 pounds to 140 pounds.

In order to obtain more details regarding this remarkable incident, I called upon M. Bourgeois in Seven Islands on the day of my arrival there (May 22). That afternoon he kindly took me on a 45-mile drive to Shelter Bay, for a first-hand investigation. There, with the guidance of two of his friends, we located two maggot-ridden bodies that had been thrown out in the woods, and the head of a third in the back yard of Antonio Carby. The hunters had not bothered to skin the animals, but had apparently clipped the ears of each for a $15 bounty. M. Carby said he had taken four of the animals in traps—all or nearly all in the preceding January. The published account appeared to be largely correct except as to the numbers of Wolves killed. (Communication with my Shelter Bay acquaintances was hampered somewhat by language difficulties.) An informant later in the season gave the total number in the pack as ten.

At least one of the Wolves was so emaciated that it was said to have weighed only 45 lb. When two of the men held it up by the hind legs to be photographed (pl. 5, fig. 1), its toes were on a level with the tops of their heads, while its nose grazed the ground. Its length was probably a little more than 5 feet (say 1,600 mm.). The color was light grayish. It was presumably a local dearth of Caribou or other food animals that had driven the Wolves to the outskirts of the village, where apparently the inhabitants had become concerned for the safety of their children.

The Shelter Bay episode is not quite unparalleled in the annals of the North Shore; for J. J. Audubon (in M. R. Audubon, 1897:407) remarked on Wolves killing dogs at the very doors of a cabin at Baie de Portage, 75 miles west of Bradore. This had happened sometime prior to his visit in 1833.

In the St. Lawrence drainage on the north side of the Gulf, where Woodland Caribou have survived locally in moderate numbers, the Wolves may not have diminished to the same extent as in the more northerly interior. In the vicinity of Harrington Harbour they are said to be very scarce (Wallace Mansbridge). Some droppings were noted in 1953 about 40 miles east of Gad Lake (A. E. Boerner). During the winter of 1951–52, on the headwaters of the Rivière aux Rats (about 80 miles north of Lake St. John), J. L. Véronneau heard Wolves howling and reported one caught in a trap. One day a lake was full of tracks. According to an old man of that area, no Wolves had appeared there previously for years. Lloyd Hogan saw a Wolf on the ice of Wacouno Lake; soon thereafter (in April, 1951) it went into a surveying camp, among the dogs, and was shot.

There are a few Wolves about Ashuanipi Lake (Willé Pinette). Mathieu André secured five during the winter of 1952–53 in the area east of Menihek and Ashuanipi lakes (Sebastien Mackenzie). Francis McKenzie reported "plenty" of them about "Kapikitiapiskao" Mountain, about 40 miles east of Knob Lake, where Barren Ground Caribou also are found. On the other hand, after considerable experience in trapping in the Menihek and Knob lakes area, Ben McKenzie had never seen a Wolf. The general opinion is that none is left about Knob Lake. The Wolves do not seem to maintain their stand where the Caribou have largely disappeared.

Wallace (1906:308) reports a Wolf attacking a man on Lake Melville, near Kenamish River. "However, Wolves . . . have never been known to kill a man in Labrador" (Grenfell, 1930:289).

Young reports (1944:243, *fide* Clarence Birdseye) on three Wolves attacking a large male [Woodland?] Caribou in the fall of 1912 at Ticoralak, on the north shore of Hamilton Inlet.

It seems worth while to present the following notes on a blackish female Wolf, although it was taken a little south of the Ungava Peninsula, in Charlevoix County, Quebec. The details were kindly supplied by Dr. D. A. Déry (*in litt.*, October 22, 1956). At 8 a. m., March 24, 1956, it was pursued by J. B. Desgagné in a truck along the national highway between Bagotville and St. Urbain, at a speed of 50 miles per hour. The Wolf could not gain the forest, owing to the high banks of snow. When it made an attempt to surmount them, it fell back and was killed by the truck. The animal was nonpregnant, and was reported to weigh 100 pounds. The skin and skull were obtained by Captain Alphonse Déry. The total length of the skin (probably stretched somewhat in the skinning and tanning processes) was about 1,780 mm.; of the tail, 483 mm. (both measurements including the hairs at the tip of the tail). A photograph of the skin corresponds closely to the color pattern of a specimen from 50 miles north of Quebec, as described by Goldman (1944:438). An X-ray of the skull and mandible is reproduced here (pl. 5, fig. 2) by the kind permission of Dr. Viger Plamondon, who made it. He reported (*in litt.*, January 25, 1957) that the teeth showed no decay, abnormality, pathology, or tartar.

Certain cranial measurements of this specimen (taken from the X-ray), compared with the averages of three females of *lycaon* from Gatineau and Pontiac Counties, Quebec (Anderson, 1943:391), show a close correspondence: greatest length, 236, 231.7; condylobasal length, 214, 218.0; zygomatic breadth, 130, 123.6; length of mandible, 166, 170.8; lower carnassial, crown length, 26, 26.4. The X-ray also appears to bear out Goldman's comment (1944:437) on the "remarkably slender rostrum" of *lycaon*.

The wild fur production in Quebec, 1950–51, included only 44 wolf skins (Cowan, 1955:169). For 1954–55, a "few" were reported (Canada Year Book 1956:606). A different sort of picture is presented by Bourque (1958) in describing the destruction of Wolves by means of poisoned meat dropped from planes. In this way 500–600 Wolves, besides 1,000 Foxes, are killed annually in the Montreal district alone. These statistics probably apply mainly to the subspecies *lycaon*.

The following records may be assumed to pertain wholly to *C. l. lycaon*: Charles River and Sandwich Bay areas (Cartwright, 1792: *passim*); Sheldrake River (Couper, 1877:300); "seldom met with in the southern regions since the extermination of the caribou there," but one "was seen at the post at Northwest River" (Low, 1896:315); Godbout (Comeau, 1923:317); Trout Lake (Eidmann, 1935:46); Porcupine (Goldman, 1944:434); Lake Mistassini area (Neilson, 1948:154); Lake St. John area (Cameron and Orkin, 1950:100). See also Hall and Kelson (1959, 2:850, map 444).

Canis tundrarum ungavanensis N. M. Comeau (1940), with type locality 35 miles north of Godbout, is regarded by Goldman (1944: 440) as "undoubtedly synonymous" with *lycaon*.

"Examples are cited to show that wolves tend to take sick and injured game animals, that wolves do not exterminate game herds, that the real limiting factors for caribou and other game animals are space and food supplies, that these factors may completely extirpate a game population where there are no significant predators, and that wolves have interest and value in themselves" (from abstract of Murie (1957) in *Wildlife Review* 90:44, 1957).

Alopex lagopus ungava (Merriam)
Ungava Arctic Fox; Renard arctique (Fr.);
Oapi tseshish (M.). (Map 29.)

According to Sebastien McKenzie, an occasional White Fox would come to the Fort McKenzie area in the period from 1916 to 1936. The wild fur production in Quebec, 1950–51, included 181 skins of the Blue Fox (a color phase) and 12,241 of the White Fox (Cowan, 1955:169). For 1954–55, 19,201 White Fox skins and 264 Blue Fox skins were reported (Canada Year Book 1956:606).

This species normally inhabits the northern Barren Grounds, but it is inclined, at least sporadically and probably more often in winter than at other seasons, to move southward along both coasts, as far as the head of James Bay in the west and to the Strait of Belle Isle in the east (Cartwright, 1792, 1:89,94,133; 2:50,63,67,139; McLean, 1932 (1849):222,251; Payne, 1887:72; Spencer, 1889:76; Low, 1896:53,122, 314, and 1898:22; Wallace, 1907:181,193,197,236; Bangs, 1912:465; Hantzsch, 1932:9; Anderson, 1934:95; Hall and Kelson, 1959, 2:854, map 446). In 1922 there was a notable invasion along the North Shore of the Gulf; the animals appeared in April and May and remained through the summer, causing havoc among nesting ducks on the islands from Piashte Bay eastward (Lewis, 1923:136). Fetherston

(1947) presents a record of the numbers of this species traded over a period of years at the following posts: George River, Fort Chimo, Payne Bay, Sugluk, Wolstenholme, Cape Smith, Povungnituk, and Port Harrison.

About 1917 forty skins were traded in the Lake St. John area, and one in 1944–45; these animals were presumed to have reached that area from the North Shore (Cameron and Orkin, 1950:99), although it is perhaps equally likely that they came south through the interior. Other interior localities are: Nichicun and Michikamau lakes (Low, 1896:314); east of Indian House Lake (Prichard, 1911:119); east of Mistinipi Lake (Cabot, 1912a:172); George River (Rousseau, 1949: 101); Mistassini River (Cameron and Morris, 1951:124); (Lower) Seal Lake (Doutt, 1954:239); and Chubb Crater area (Martin, 1955: 490).

Although Cartwright found and trapped numbers of Arctic Foxes between Sandwich Bay and the Strait of Belle Isle, he does not seem to have recorded any of them during his various summer seasons later than June 16—at St. Lewis Bay, in 1771 (1792, 1:133). Perhaps the majority moved farther north at that season.

Vulpes fulva bangsi Merriam
Labrador Red Fox; Renard roux du Labrador (Fr.); Oishao tsesho (M.). (Map 30.)

Scats came to my notice near Abel Lake on June 5 and 8; one of them was in a tractor trail. After snow came in the fall, in late September and early October, tracks appeared rather commonly in the Knob Lake area (Goldeneye Pond, Camp Pond, Dolly Ridge, and Ruth Lake Ridge). A track in a burnt tract followed a wood road for a considerable distance. One of the prints on Ruth Lake Ridge was about 2½ inches long and 2 inches wide.

The remaining observations were by friends and acquaintances. Warden Alphonse Bourgeois spoke of Red Foxes (in three different color phases) as rather common about Seven Islands. On August 3 Richard Powell reported a den on Dolly Ridge, where one of the animals allowed him to approach fairly close. On September 24 James Stewart saw a Red Fox cross the Right of Way 10 miles south of Knob Lake. At about the same time a Black Fox was seen 3 miles north of Burnt Creek by Howard Jackson, who spoke of that color phase as fairly common locally. Robert Slipp found a track on a treeless ridge west of Lac Aulneau. In late June or early July Gilbert Simard saw a Fox, and heard it yap, in Barrens 10 miles southwest of

Wakuach Lake. J. L. Véronneau reported a young Fox, with yellow fur, killed in the Barrens at or near Scott Lake on September 6 by a Montagnais in his party; he also saw a Silver Fox at the south end of Harris Lake on September 15. In early August Arthur C. Newton (*in litt.*, August 5, 1953) observed a group of 10 about 30 miles north of the junction of the Larch and the Kaniapiskau rivers.

In the area about Mile 224 Airstrip, near the north end of Ashuanipi Lake, Red Foxes were reported by several observers (R. Gordon Racey, William Schrøpfer, and J. Malkin) as seen fairly frequently in 1953. In the Grand Falls area many scats were noted in 1951 (James Murdoch). Eight individuals were taken about Eric Lake during the winter of 1952–53 (Willé Pinette). J. L. Véronneau (*in litt.*, June 26, 1955) reported a good number of Red Foxes in January, 1955, about the headwaters of the Nemiscau River.

The wild fur production in Quebec, 1950–51, included 10,252 skins of Red Fox, 496 of Cross Fox, and 106 of Silver Fox (Cowan, 1955: 169). For 1955–56, 4,958 Red Fox skins and 537 Cross Fox skins were reported (Canada Year Book 1956:606).

This Red Fox apparently occurs more or less throughout the peninsula, in the Arctic, Hudsonian, and Canadian life-zones: south coast (Stearns, 1883:112; Merriam, 1900:667; Comeau, 1923:91–92; Eidmann, 1935:45; C. F. Jackson, 1938:432); east coast (Cartwright, 1792:*passim*; Bangs, 1898*b*:505; Cabot, 1912*a*:214; Strong, 1930:7; Elton, 1942:265–272, 278–297; Frazer, 1950:126); north coast (McLean, 1932 (1849):251; Bell, 1884:49; Low, 1896:53,122,314; Hantzsch, 1932:11; Bateman, 1953:7; Hall and Kelson, 1959, 2:856, map 447); and west coast (Doutt, 1954:239). Interior localities include: between Lake St. John and Lake Mistassini in 1792 (Michaux, 1889:83); Lake Mistassini (Low, 1896:70; Cameron and Morris, 1951:124); Crooked River and middle George River (Wallace, 1907: 46,153); south of Flour Lake (Merrick, 1933:206); Lower Seal Lake (Doutt, 1942:65); Indian House Lake (Clement, 1949:372); and Lake St. John area (Cameron and Orkin, 1950:99). The subspecific allocation of the population in the southwestern part of the peninsula (as at Lakes St. John and Mistassini) remains uncertain. The range of *V. f. rubricosa* evidently extends close to, if not into, this area (*cf.* Hall and Kelson, 1959, 2:856, map 447).

Euarctos americanus americanus (Pallas)
American Black Bear; Ours noir (Fr.); Mask (M.). (Map 31.)

From a naturalist's viewpoint, Black Bears are gratifyingly numerous in the central interior; to some others, they may become a nuisance or even a serious annoyance. Their fondness for garbage and their frequent visits to the disposal heaps bring them to friendly attention; but when they extend their visits to meat-safes and mess-tents, they may suffer from reprisals. Now and then an unarmed prospecting party has been considerably inconvenienced by a bold Bear.

In 1953 solitary animals were in the habit of coming to garbage heaps at Knob Lake and Burnt Creek. At the latter place one would appear at irregular times, and even before darkness, so that a number of persons attempted to photograph it. Several visits for that purpose on my part never synchronized with the Bear's appearances. A workman at Burnt Creek was said to provide food for the animal and to get fairly close to it. The print of a hind foot in a muddy part of a tractor road near the Knob Lake dump measured about 7 × 5 inches.

At the old airstrip east of Knob Lake a Bear did not content itself with the garbage, but finally made off with about 20 lb. of beef from a meat-safe only 25 feet from one of the dwellings. Such boldness made the people somewhat apprehensive as to the safety of their children. So, after watching for an opportunity for a week or so, Leo Huard shot the animal on the evening of August 2, and it came into my possession on the following day. It was an adult male. Selected data are as follows:

Length, 1,550; tail, 72 before skinning, 90 after skinning; foot, 195; ear, 120; estimated weight, 250 lb.; fat 1¼ inches thick on rump and plentiful elsewhere; no ectoparasites found; hide prime; color uniform glossy black nearly throughout; Buffy Olive triangular area on each side of the snout, extending from an apex in front of eye to a base along upper lip; narrow border of same color along lower lip; top of nose Clove Brown; extremely little underfur, grayish.

Another Bear killed at the same airstrip on the morning of October 8 was reported of about the same size as the first one. Willé Pinette remarked concerning the specimen of August 2 that some Bears become larger, weighing up to about 300 lb. in the fall. On September 30 I had been directed to some fresh tracks in 6-inch snow only a rod from a house at the airstrip. One print was about 7 inches long, and there was an interval of 2 feet or a little less between the tracks.

At the Iron Arm of Attikamagen Lake, in early July, I noticed a rotten log that had been torn up, presumably by a Bear, and scats of large size in three different places. Their main content was evidently berries of *Vaccinium vitis-idaea* var. *minus*.

At Lac Aulneau Sebastien McKenzie reported that Bears were not numerous. In 1953 Robert Slipp had seen there just a single small individual up to July 30. At Nachikapau Lake the leader of a prospecting party reported seeing one of the animals.

The next year Fred Farah transmitted to me what he believed to be authentic accounts of two aggressive Bears in the general area of Otelnuk Lake and Lac Romanet. One of them came into the camp of a prospecting party, composed of Norman Hallendy and Jean Brivoisac; it growled and elevated the hair on its back. The men retreated to their canoe, and the Bear followed them around the shore for half an hour so so. Toward dusk the animal departed, and they returned to their camp. Early the next morning, when Brivoisac went outside their tent, the Bear was right there. He kept the animal off by making a banging noise with a stove lid. Again the men retreated to their canoe, and presently they had a chance to move their camp to the opposite side of a large lake, where they were not bothered again.

In the same general area Rudy Gallant and Jack Dwyer had a three-weeks-long encounter with a Bear that kept coming to camp every evening. On one occasion Gallant threw an axe at it and missed. Again he hurled a big rock and struck it in the head, whereupon the Bear ran off.

At Mollie T. Lake, in mid-afternoon on August 9, some of my companions called out, "Come and see the Bear!" On a rather bare hill on the opposite side of the lake (pl. 1, fig. 1), about ⅝ mile away, Bruin was nosing about as if for berries. It was a somewhat lanky animal, rather than rolypoly, and it appeared of about the same size as the specimen of August 2. It took rather long steps, and now and then it even trotted. Gradually it moved down toward the lake and disappeared in the brush on the lower slopes. It was delightful to obtain this view, in the unspoiled Ungava wilds, of a Bear unconscious of being watched by man.

It was apparently another and larger Bear, of perhaps 300 lb., that made almost nightly visits to our camp on the west side of the lake, August 8 to 18. On at least three consecutive evenings (August 9–11) it came quite regularly, in the dusk, at 8:15 or 8:20 p. m., to feed at the garbage pile about 90 feet from the tents. Half a dozen of us would watch it from that distance. It would occasionally pause in its feeding, pricking up its fairly large ears at us without much concern; but when one of us attempted a nearer view, it decamped in a hurry, apparently uttering several huffing or snorting notes. Once it came in the early afternoon. In general, there was a good-natured tolerance on both sides, but Henry Larouche, the cook, was inclined to object to its undue proximity to the mess-tent. One night he met it face to face just outside this tent, and the next night it pulled a tarpaulin off a pile of provisions, whereupon Henry threw sticks of wood at the animal. The same sort of missiles were likewise used several nights later. In each case the Bear seemed to yield the field readily to Henry.

During this period several scats were noticed on Sunny Mountain at the "alpine garden" near the perennial snowbank (altitude 2,000 feet) and in an alpine meadow at a slightly lower altitude. One of them, about 1½ inches in diameter, was in three pieces, varying from 2½ to 4 inches in length. While out on Mollie T. Lake one evening, two of the Montagnais of the camp found a Bear swimming across; as they paddled up to within 10 feet of the animal, it did nothing menacing, but merely swung its head from side to side.

Earlier in the season Pierre Côté, a member of Mr. Simard's surveying party, secured a photograph of a Bear in an interesting pose near Greenbush Lake, and he has kindly allowed its reproduction here (pl. 6, fig. 1).

A winter den of a Bear was reported at Shabogamo Lake by Leopold Gelinas. A canoe stored at a small lake west of Wabush Lake was said to have been damaged by one of the animals. A 65-lb. individual was trapped by Adrien Côté at Seahorse Lake on June 25, and I saw its hide at Ashuanipi Lake in August. At Gad Lake a male was killed after raiding a mess-tent; it was very fat and was estimated to weigh 300 lb. A young Bear also was seen in that vicinity (A. E. Boerner). The species was reported at Lac de Morhiban (Philip Loth).

During the summer of 1953 Jérôme St. Onge reported seeing some Black Bears in the Leaf Lake area, where they dug both mice and some other small mammal out of the ground. About 1948 a party of Montagnais killed seven Bears that they found hibernating together near Elross Lake (Ben McKenzie). In July, 1949, Dr. F. D. Foster found bear sign at Evening and Menihek lakes. In 1952 a Bear raided a camp at Dyke Lake in daytime, in the absence of the owners (Brian M. Meikle). In July, 1957, an adult and a cub made off with all the meat from the camp of a prospecting party at Lac Montagni (David B. Harper).

In March, 1955, near the headwaters of the Nemiscau River, J. L. Véronneau (*in litt.*, June 26, 1955) noticed two bear skulls hung in a tree. This treatment of the skulls is a wide-spread Indian custom, referred to by Low (1890:25) in the Lake Mistassini area: "Skulls are always scraped clean, and set upon poles facing the sun." There is further discussion of the topic by Chambers (1896:315,316, pl. opp. p. 316), Comeau (1923:85), and Speck (1935:102,107, pl. 7). I have observed the practice at a point as far away as the Peace River in northern Alberta.

The fur catch in Quebec, for the season of 1950–51, included 240 (Black) Bears (Cowan, 1955:169). For 1954–55, 257 "bear" skins (presumably of the present species) were reported (Canada Year Book 1956:606).

Previous records indicate that the Black Bear occurs more or less throughout the forested areas of the peninsula but to only a slight extent in the main Barren Grounds (*cf.* map 31): south coast (Stearns, 1883:113; J. J. Audubon, in M. R. Audubon, 1897:368,375; Comeau, 1923:85,89,90,93,95,97,98; Eidmann, 1935:43; Weaver, 1940: 421); east coast, north to Okak and Ramah (Cartwright, 1792:*passim*; Bell, 1884:51; Bangs, 1898*b*:500; J. A. Allen, 1910:5; Anderson, 1934: 94; Tanner, 1947, 2:502; Hall and Kelson, 1959, 2:867, map 451); north to the Fort Chimo area (Turner, 1888*b*:83; Low, 1896:122) and the mouth of the George River (Kohlmeister and Kmoch, 1814:54); west coast, north to Little Whale River and Richmond Gulf (Bell, 1884:51; J. A. Allen, 1910:5; Doutt, 1954:237). Interior records include: lower Mistassini River in 1772 (Michaux, 1889:84); Lake Mistassini, East Main River, Nichicun Lake, and Hamilton River (Low, 1896:70,86,100,316, and 1897:33); area about Lakes St. John and Mistassini (Chambers, 1896:181,188,198,208,214,293; Cameron and Orkin, 1950:99; Cameron and Morris, 1951:124); lower Naskaupi River (Mrs. Hubbard, 1906:537; Wallace, 1907:25); Fraser River (Prichard, 1911:39–125, *passim*); Assiwaban River and Mistinipi and Mistastin lakes (Cabot, 1912*a*:170,199,200,249,266,281); Natashquan River (Townsend, 1913:179); branch of Manicouagan River (Comeau, 1923:90); inland from Davis Inlet (Strong, 1930:5); Kenamu River (Leslie, 1931:210); Traverspine and Hamilton rivers and Flour Lake (Merrick, 1933:20,40,52,66); Lower Seal Lake (Doutt, 1942:65); near Otish Mountains (Pomerleau, 1950:14); and headwaters of Little Whale River (Doutt, 1954:237).

The *Événement-Journal* of Quebec, in its issue of April 20, 1956, announced the payment of bounties on 4,424 Black Bears and 422 Wolves in 12 counties of southwestern Quebec. The greater part of two of these counties, Chicoutimi and Roberval, is included in the Ungava Peninsula. The period covered by the bounty payments, while not stated, was presumably one year. The bounty on Bears was $10; on Wolves, $20. In addition to the $52,680 thus paid in bounties, prizes amounting to $8,960 were awarded to the hunters who killed the largest numbers of the animals. Thus the total sum spent out of the public treasury was $61,640.

Is it at all possible that these animals would have caused damage to that amount? The fallacy of bounties and the waste of public funds in paying them has been pointed out time and again by biologists who specialize in conservation and wild-life management.

Bears, in particular, when living in wilderness areas, cause comparatively little damage to other wild life or to livestock and other human property. Should we not be willing to concede to them the privilege of doing a slight amount of damage in return for our own pleasure and satisfaction in having such extremely interesting denizens in the forested lands of North America?

Ursus sp.
Ungava Grizzly Bear; Ours gris (Fr.).

Some of the various accounts of this animal grant it little more than a semi-mythical status. If the Ungava Barrens once did harbor a Grizzly Bear, we must admit one important difference in its way of life from that of its relatives west of Hudson Bay: there are no ground squirrels (*Spermophilus*) in Ungava to furnish it with a staple food supply, either directly or indirectly (in the latter case, through its caches of plant roots). And if perchance still extant in some remote corner of the Barrens, the Grizzly must be on the extreme verge of extinction.

There is comparatively little of significance to add to Elton's excellent account (1954). It is well to bear in mind that not a single hide or bone of the animal is known to have ever reached a museum. It would be difficult to imagine a more gratifying zoological prize to be obtained from any part of North America.

Stirling (1884) quotes from the original account by McLean (1849), and then adds further remarks, still in quotation marks, as if derived from McLean. But it would appear that the end quotes are misplaced, and that the following passage, with the exception of about the first eleven words, is actually Stirling's own:

> I have traded and sent to England several of these skins from the region of Ungava and many more from the eastern slope of the Rocky Mountains years before. Some time since I called the attention of the late Mr. Mittleberger, of this city [Cleveland, Ohio] to the fact. He assured me that the grizzly was found

in Northern Labrador. Mr. M. had been for a long term of years a factor in the employ of the Hudson's Bay Fur Company, and during this period had traveled over the largest portion of their possessions, handling every kind of fur animals, and was thoroughly acquainted with the fauna of the country.

Turner (1885:234), writing of the Ungava district, mentions "a species of barren-ground bear which I shall not attempt to designate." Later (1888b:83) he refers to it indirectly in remarking that three species of bears are important in that district.

Turner writes again (1894:275) of the species in the same district:

> These mementos [portions of the skin or other part of the body of a large animal; e. g., under lip of a bear] are procured with great difficulty from the hunter who has risked his life in the struggles attending the capture of the beasts, for the barren-ground bear of that region is not a timid creature like the black bear; and unless the hunter is well prepared for the animal he would do well to let it alone.

Bell, after discussing the species in 1884, returns once more (1895:358) to the subject:

> Beyond the edge of the forest the principal fur-bearing animals are . . . and the grizzly. The last named has also been called the "barren-ground bear" and possesses much interest for the zoologist. . . . Captain Kennedy, who was in charge of the Ungava for many years, informed me that he had collected many skins of this animal in the district.

Several references by Low (1896:122,316; 1897:32) are important. In his remarks on the Black Bear, he includes the following statement:

> At Cambrian Lake, on the Koksoak River, the tracks of a large bear were seen along the shores, but it is not known whether these were those of a black bear or a barren-ground bear.

Low's "Cambrian Lake" is not on the main Koksoak, but on its largest tributary, the Kaniapiskau River; it is situated in the forested Hudsonian Life-zone, approximately between latitudes 56°05' and 56°45' N. The later account (1897:32—apparently not seen by Elton) takes on significance by reason of the testimony of Low's Indian canoemen:

> The barren-ground bear . . . is undoubtedly found in the barrens of Labrador, as skins are brought in at intervals to Fort Chimo when the Indians have a favorable chance of killing it. On other occasions they leave it alone, having a great respect and fear for its ferocity and size. While descending the south branch of the Koksoak River in 1894 we saw tracks along the banks which my Indians said were much larger than those of any black bear they had ever seen; unfortunately we did not get a sight of the animal.

Bangs states (1898b:500) that there is no doubt that a huge bear is found in the Barrens; but later (1912:467), with weakened faith, he merely refers to Low's report (1896:122,316), adding that there is no evidence that such an animal occurs in the Barrens of Labrador.

Formerly the barren-ground bear ranged rather widely in the northern districts. ... Peter McKenzie, who has bought their skins at Chimo, says the hair was very dark, even black. Both Eskimo and Indian regard it as aggressive and dangerous. ... The species is probably extinct now, and while it is not unlikely to have been a grizzly, its identity may never be established. (Cabot, 1912b:213; see also 1912a:193.)

Millais (1915:364) considers *"Ursus horribilis richardsoni"* as "nearly extinct in Labrador."

Ekblaw (1926:108) merely says: "The barren-ground bear . . . is northerly in its range, and is very rare" in Labrador.

Seton writes (1929, 2:86):

An interesting experience is awaiting some enterprising collector who will go to Labrador and bring us a skull and skin of the Labrador Grizzly. Apparently, it has never yet been seen alive by white men. And yet, it is, or was, there, as the following records attest.

He then quotes from Bell, Bangs, and Wallace.

Strong (1930:5-6) had the benefit of considerable experience with the Davis Inlet band of the Naskapi Indians when he wrote:

I could obtain no definite records of the so-called barren ground bear which Turner mentions as fairly common in a restricted part of the northeastern interior. The Indians have a term *méh-ta-shue* for a brown bear, which in one of their legends is classed as fiercer than the black or white bear. When shown pictures of the various bear species they identified *méh-ta-shue* with both the grizzly and the brown or cinnamon phase of the black bear. The older people said that some sixty years ago three of these brown bears attacked some Indian women at Petiskapau [=Petitsikapau?] Lake, but were all killed by a man with a muzzle loader. None of the informants saw the dead animals or their killer, but they had talked with the women. Petiskapau Lake is far south of the reputed range of the barren ground bear, and it seems probable that the animals referred to were representatives of the brown phase of the black bear (*Euarctos americanus*). Common tradition over most of North America has it that the brown or cinnamon phase of the black bear is more pugnacious than his normal kinsman. The verbal testimony acquired by Turner, Low, Wallace and others, provides rather strong grounds for the belief in a "barren ground grizzly" in northeastern Labrador, but nearly all these accounts seem originally to have come from Indian sources. Now the Naskapi are closely related to the Cree in language and culture and have evidently been much influenced by them. The Cree know the true grizzly of the barren grounds and call him *mistaya*. It is possible therefore that the Naskapi have carried over tales of this awe-inspiring animal and applied them to the cinnamon bear in Labrador. None of the living Davis Inlet or Barren Ground people, who range from Ungava to Hamilton Inlet, have ever seen the animal they call *méh-ta-shue* or any sign of him. Considering the vast gap between the known range of the true grizzly in the north central barren grounds and that of the reputed barren ground grizzly in Labrador, it seems logical to identify this barren ground bear of Labrador with a somewhat aberrant brown phase of the black bear (*Euarctos americanus*), at least until more conclusive evidence comes to light.

There have been many stories about some kind of grizzly or barren ground bear living in the interior of Labrador, but as these reports have been largely traditional and the district is so far from the ranges of any of the above species, it seems more probable that the legends may have referred to an odd specimen of the Black Bear in the brown or cinnamon phase (Anderson, 1934:94).

Speck (1935:109) suggests a possible relation between the Barren Ground Bear and the mythical "great bear" of the Montagnais; he also refers to Cartwright's report (1792) of "a kind of bear very ferocious, having a white ring around its neck."

The persistent reports of a grizzly bear existing in the barrens of northern Labrador have from time to time been investigated as far as such tales may, but no real evidence that such an animal is found there has been elicited. Even though the tale were true that a skin of a grizzly had once been brought in, this might have been traded from still farther west. In that way one might account for the origin of the reports. (G. M. Allen, 1942:150.)

The barren-ground bear (*Ursus richardsoni*) is restricted to a narrow area in the north and is not plentiful—if found at all in these days—. At Barren Ground Lake [=Indian House Lake] tradition says that in 1894 an Indian killed the last recorded specimen of the red or barren-ground bear [Prichard, 1911]. Once it was common enough to keep the Indians in wholesome dread of its vicious disposition when roused. This animal is of much zoogeographical interest; it is difficult to explain how it lived in such an isolated place, as it is not found in the intermediate country between this and the plains of the far west (*cf.* [Bell, 1895]). (Tanner, 1947, 1:420.)

Some kind of Grizzly or "Big Brown Bear" is legendary in Northern Quebec or Ungava, but no determinable specimen skin has ever been examined critically, and no skulls have been examined. Bears of a brown colour have undoubtedly been taken, and although the "brown" or "cinnamon" colour phase of the Black Bear is more common in the West, it is occasionally taken in Quebec, and we have one brown cub from about 75 miles northeast of Ottawa. . . . I shall not have much confidence in any Grizzly in Quebec until a skin with skull and feet with claws, has been produced, and the specimen should also have a pedigree or abstract of title, to show where it came from. There is of course a possibility that some kind of large Brown Bear was found in Ungava at one time, and a very remote possibility that a few individuals have survived in some remote district. The country is only partially hunted over, for when there has been a series of poor years some districts are avoided for a long time. Eskimos may visit an area at one season and Indians at another, but there is an enormous territory inhabited by only a limited number of people who do not like to go where a food supply is not reasonably promising.

The question of a Grizzly Bear in that region is naturally of interest to me, but I do not regard it with much optimism. (Anderson, 1948:12.)

According to Rousseau (1949:126), not even a memory of the Ungava Grizzly is left among the Indians; he himself found not the least trace of it along the George River in 1947 or along the Kogaluk and Payne rivers in 1948.

Polunin (1949:114) offers a sight record of "a largish brown Bear followed by two smaller ones," as observed by a plane crew between Fort Chimo and Hudson Bay in 1946. Manning (in Elton, 1954:349) supplies further details of this observation.

In a report on his trip in 1953 to Clearwater and Lower Seal lakes, Doutt (1954:237–238) gives the following account of "*Ursus* sp. Grizzly bear":

> I have nothing but hearsay evidence for listing this species. However, stories about a bear, which is neither a black bear nor a polar bear, are so current in this region that they deserve more than casual attention. The descriptions are accurate enough to suggest a grizzly bear. In one case, my informant had seen the skin of a strange bear, but he had seen it many years ago. This past summer, Oshin Agathon and T. Donald Carter of the American Museum of Natural History, New York, conducted an expedition into this region looking for this bear. Unfortunately, they found nothing either to substantiate or discredit the reports.
>
> It seems unlikely that an isolated form could occur in Ungava. (Banfield, 1960*a*:56–57.)

At Lac Aulneau in 1953 Sebastien McKenzie, a 68-year-old Montagnais, referred to a native folk-tale dealing with a black bear and a brown bear, but he added that the latter existed only in stories. (He had no information on Grizzly Bears in Ungava.) Since Sebastien had had wide experience and acquaintance in the peninsula, from Fort Chimo and Indian House Lake to Seven Islands, including 20 years' service as manager of the Hudson's Bay Company's post at Fort McKenzie, his word should go far toward discounting the occurrence of a brown or cinnamon phase of the Black Bear in that region. Comeau (1923:85–101), in his extensive experience with Black Bears on the North Shore of the Gulf of St. Lawrence, makes no reference to a brown phase. Thus it scarcely appears reasonable to identify the brown Barren Ground Grizzly as a mere phase of the Black Bear. Moreover, if the true Black Bear ventures little beyond the forested areas, why should some other color phase of that animal have been reported time and again from the Barren Grounds?

The most compelling evidence has come from the highly intelligent trader, John McLean, who knew the Grizzly of the Rockies, and who testified that he had sent "several" skins from Ungava to England; from the accomplished naturalist, Lucien M. Turner, who resided several years at Fort Chimo and included a "barren-ground bear" in the local fauna; from the distinguished geologist, Dr. Robert Bell, who reported "many" skins collected in Ungava by Captain William Kennedy (who had been the Hudson's Bay Company's agent at Fort Chimo, George River post, and Fort Nascopie); from the widely experienced explorer, A. P. Low, who gave similar testimony; from Dillon Wallace (1907:236–237), who obtained descriptions of local skins from two Hudson's Bay Company traders in Ungava; and especially from the fur returns of the Moravian Mission posts (Elton, 1954). Such evidence can not be dismissed as myth or unsubstantial rumor.

The possibility of any skins of the Grizzly of the western Barren Grounds having reached Ungava through Eskimo channels (by way of Southampton or Baffin Islands) is too remote for serious consideration. After being scuffed about in filthy Eskimo camps for the number of years that such a transfer by barter would have required, certainly no skin would have been in fit condition for acceptance by the fur trade. Furthermore, any Eskimo passage of Hudson Strait was an extremely rare event (McLean, 1932 (1849):233).

Another point to be considered is that the Naskapi Indians were apparently as definitely linked with the Ungava Grizzly as were the Eskimos (*cf.* Low, 1896; Wallace, 1907; Prichard, 1911; Strong, 1930; Tanner, 1947). The long-standing antipathy between these two races would have militated against any likelihood of the barter of Grizzly Bear skins between them.

The application of the name *Ursus richardsoni* to the Ungava Grizzly Bear (Bangs, 1898*b* and 1912; Strong, 1930; Tanner, 1947; Elton, 1954) is scarcely warranted. The type locality of that species is on the west side of Bathurst Inlet, nearly 1,000 miles from the nearest point of the Ungava Peninsula. Nearly all the other terrestrial mammals of the Ungava Barren Grounds (of the genera *Dicrostonyx, Microtus, Canis, Alopex, Vulpes, Lutra,* and *Rangifer*) are at least subspecifically distinct from their representatives on the western Barren Grounds. It is useless to apply any specific name to the Ungava Grizzly, as long as there is not a single hair or bone available to which such a name could be tied. If the animal exists, or has existed, at all, it is almost certainly distinct from the western Grizzlies.

The most definite reports seem to have come from the area between the George River and the Atlantic Coast. There is also some indication of occurrence in northwestern Ungava (Bell, 1884; Polunin, 1949; Elton, 1954; Doutt, 1954). The chief trading centers where the skins were handled were the Moravian Mission posts along the northern Labrador coast, from Hebron to Hopedale (Elton, 1954); Fort Chimo was probably next in importance. The possibility that the Grizzly may have ranged to some extent into the wooded country is suggested by Low's report (1896:316; 1897:32) of a huge bear track at Cambrian Lake and by Strong's report (1930:6) of three aggressive brown bears at Petitsikapau Lake. If Low had only recorded the size of that huge track, it might have been conclusive evidence as to the existence of the Grizzly and its occurrence at a considerable distance from the main Barren Grounds.

It is difficult to understand Strong's statement (1930:6): "The Cree know the true grizzly of the barren grounds and call him *mistaya.*" In olden time the Crees undoubtedly knew the Grizzlies of the Great Plains in southern Saskatchewan and Alberta; but they are far removed from the Barren Grounds of Keewatin and Mackenzie. In the latter region the Yellowknives, the Dogribs, the Hare Indians, and the Loucheux were the ones to come into contact with the distinctive Grizzlies of the Barren Grounds. Strong and Tanner should have had no more difficulty in conceiving of a Grizzly in Ungava than of a *Rangifer,* a *Dicrostonyx,* and other Barren Ground mammals with western representatives.

Two factors that may have been major causes of the depletion and possible extinction of the Ungava Grizzly come readily to mind: first, the introduction of modern firearms among the natives; second, the catastrophic decline in the herds of Labrador Barren Ground Caribou several decades ago, with corresponding reduction in the number of wolf-killed bodies of these animals in which the Grizzly might have shared.

In conclusion, there seems to be very good evidence of the former existence of a Grizzly Bear in the northern part of the Ungava Peninsula, but comparatively little likelihood of its having survived to the present day.

Thalarctos maritimus (Phipps)
Polar Bear; Ours polaire (Fr.). (Map 32.)

In view of the doubtful validity of several other species and subspecies of *Thalarctos* that have been proposed, chiefly by Knotterus-Meyer (*cf.* Anderson, 1947:47), all records of Polar Bears from the Ungava Peninsula are here attributed to *T. maritimus.*

In November, 1956, Dr. D. A. Déry, of Quebec City, kindly sent me a photograph of a Polar Bear (pl. 6, fig. 2) that had been killed by

Henri Gauthier near Peribonca on the north side of Lake St. John. This is doubtless the same animal that was recorded by H. H. T. Jackson (1939), Lewis and Doutt (1942), and Cameron and Orkin (1950:99) as having been killed in that locality on October 20, 1938. Lewis and Doutt summarize a considerable number of other records of Polar Bears on or near the North Shore of the Gulf of St. Lawrence. The Peribonca specimen evidently furnishes the most westerly and the farthest inland record in the St. Lawrence region to date.

Jérôme St. Onge reported a Polar Bear circling over the land in the vicinity of Leaf Bay during the summer of 1953.

The wild fur production in Quebec, 1950–51, was 20 skins (Cowan, 1955:169). A "few" pelts are reported for Quebec in 1954–55 (Canada Year Book 1956:606).

Some of the principal references are: for the peninsula in general —Bell, 1884:50; Low, 1896:122,316; Bangs, 1898b:500, and 1912:467; Anderson, 1939:62, and 1948:12; Hall and Kelson, 1959, 2:878, map 453; for the east coast—Cartwright, 1792:*passim*; Packard, 1866:270, and 1891:357–366,444; Cabot, 1912a:52,195; Tanner, 1947, 1:421–422; for the north coast—Payne, 1887:71; Turner, 1888b:83; Wallace, 1907:236; for the west coast—Bell, 1886:12; Doutt, 1939:235, and 1954:237. Tanner (1947, 1:422) presents no record for the east coast south of Hamilton Inlet later than 1864.

In the 1770's and 1780's, from Sandwich Bay south to the Strait of Belle Isle, Cartwright encountered the species at practically all seasons of the year. He reports (1792, 2:164) that in late April, 1776, one of his men "saw the tracks of near a hundred white-bears which had lately crossed the [Sandwich] bay." On July 22, 1778, he counted (1792, 2:347) 32 of these Bears at a rapid or cataract a few miles above the mouth of Eagle River, where they had congregated to feast upon the Salmon. He added that "there were certainly many more, as they generally retire into the woods to sleep after making a hearty meal." The occurrence of such numbers in a well-wooded part of the Hudsonian Life-zone, in mid-summer, was rather remarkable for an animal that is more fully at home among the ice floes of the Arctic seas. Their presence was doubtless explainable by reason of the great abundance of Salmon.

As Lewis and Doutt point out (1942:372), there is a general westerly movement of water along the North Shore of the Gulf of St. Lawrence, and Arctic ice sometimes drifts with it as far as Natashquan Point. The fact that nearly all the records of Polar Bears along the

North Shore lie to the eastward of that point (*cf.* map 28) suggests the general dependence of the species on the proximity of ice.

Martes americana americana (Turton)
Eastern American Marten; Martre d'Amérique (Fr.); Oapistan (M.). (Map 33.)

In contrast to the thousands of Martens taken for the fur trade, a pitifully small number ever reach museums. It is this great dearth of museum material that constitutes a serious and long-standing obstacle to the determination of the ranges of the subspecies. In the present report there is a rather arbitrary assignment of *M. a. americana* to the Canadian Life-zone, and of *brumalis* to the Hudsonian. Hagmeier (1958:1) expresses the opinion that "partitioning of the species into subspecies" is "completely arbitrary."

Gilbert Simard spoke of the resourcefulness of his Montagnais friend, Jérôme St. Onge, in the pursuit of Martens. About 1944, when a fur-trader offered a high price for live animals, Jérôme made two or three trips by plane to a lake about 80 miles inland from Shelter Bay, and established camp there. He then proceeded to track down Martens, capturing two by hand in their holes beneath the snow, and others in live-traps, baited with Beaver. In March or early April, 1941, Jérôme was with Mr. Simard's surveying party on a tributary of Romaine River, near Lac Allard, when he discovered a marten track about the middle of an afternoon. He followed this for 3½ miles, treed the animal, and killed it with a thrown stone; he returned to the camp with it about 9 p.m.

Willé Pinette secured 25 skins during the winter of 1952–53 in the vicinity of Eric Lake. J. L. Véronneau reported a few marten tracks in the winter of 1953–54 at Lac Boisvert, in the Mistassibi area.

The wild fur production in Quebec, 1950–51, included only 95 marten skins (Cowan, 1955:169)—an indication that the population of this species had reached a dangerously low point in the province. For 1954–55, 738 skins were reported; and "steps are being taken . . . to assist in the re-establishment of marten, the population of which has been steadily decreasing" (Canada Year Book 1956:606,607).

The following records from the literature may be considered to apply to *M. a. americana*: between Lake St. John and Lake Mistassini in 1792 (Michaux, 1889:83); lower Moisie River (Cayley, 1863:78); headwaters of Peribonca River (Low, 1890:17); Lake Mistassini (Low, 1896:70); lower Natashquan River (Townsend, 1913:176); North Shore of the Gulf (Comeau, 1923:76); Musquaro ("Nasquarro") Lake (Merrick, 1933:39); Matamek River (Eidmann, 1935: 44).

Martes americana brumalis (Bangs)
Labrador Marten; Martre du Labrador (Fr.). (Map 33.)

Sebastien McKenzie informed me that in former years (1916–1936) from 100 to 600 marten skins were traded annually at Fort McKenzie; but that they no longer occurred in that area. Ben McKenzie spoke of Wakuach and Oskoas lakes and Howell's River as good places for Martens. He also described the following means for capturing one of the animals: "When you see a Marten, yell at it, and it will go up a tree, where you can shoot it." On October 1, 1953, a marten track was noted at Harris Lake by Gilbert Simard and two Montagnais with him.

The following records (all from the Hudsonian Life-zone) are provisionally attributed to *brumalis*: Atlantic drainage: Charles River (Cartwright, 1792, 1:*passim*); Hamilton ("Northwest") River (McLean, 1932 (1849):214); Okak and L'Anse au Loup (Bangs, 1912: 466); lower Naskaupi River and near Seal Lake (Mrs. Hubbard, 1906:537, and 1908:65); inland from Davis Inlet (Strong, 1930:7); Flour Lake, and north of Lake Winokapau (Merrick, 1933:118,143, 178,337); Okak and Hebron (Elton, 1942:272–279); 1,500–2,000 skins per year formerly traded at Northwest River, but very rare at Nain (Tanner, 1947, 2:622); Okak and Strait of Belle Isle (Hall and Kelson, 1959, 2:899, map 461); Ungava Bay drainage: Erlandson's Lake and west side of George River (McLean, 1932 (1849):206,209); skins traded at Fort George, Nichicun, Fort Chimo, and Northwest River, darker and more valuable than those from farther south (Low, 1896: 314); Larch River (Elton, 1942:353); Hudson and James bays drainage: Lower and Upper Seal lakes (Doutt, 1942:65, and 1954:238). Some of the above-mentioned reports may pertain to the posts (for example, Fort Chimo and Fort George) where the skins were traded rather than to the localities where they were actually collected.

Martes pennanti pennanti (Erxleben)
Eastern Fisher; Pécan (Fr.). (Map 34.)

Willé Pinette trapped a Fisher at Eric Lake about 1933. Subsequently the principal food animal of this species, the Porcupine, disappeared thereabouts, and with it the Fisher itself. (This is possibly the northeasternmost record of the latter.) Joseph Georges St. Onge said that his father caught some Fishers 35 miles up the

Moisie River about 1947–48. J. L. Véronneau saw a track on the Mistassibi River, 90 miles above Lake St. John, in the winter of 1952–53.

In the Ungava Peninsula this species is evidently restricted to the southwestern part. Bell (1884:50) refers to its occurrence in the country about James Bay. Low's statement (1896:314) that it does not occur east of Mingan or north of Lake Mistassini has been repeated by Bangs (1898*b*;1912) and by Anderson (1934;1940). (See also Hall and Kelson, 1959, 2:903, map 462.) According to Comeau (1923:82), it was rare in the territory between the Manicouagan and the Ste. Marguerite rivers up to 1880, when a large migration occurred; in two years it completely destroyed the Porcupines, and the Fisher itself virtually disappeared after three seasons. Rand states (1944*b*:77) that in Quebec the annual take from 1930 to 1940 varied from 411 to 2,123; in the season of 1950–51 it was 1,413 (Cowan, 1955:169). For 1954–55, 1,219 skins were reported (Canada Year Book 1956:606). In the Lake Mistassini area, where the Fisher was formerly common, there are now few (Neilson, 1948:154). In the Lake St. John area 200 to 300 skins are traded annually (Cameron and Orkin, 1950:100).

There may be some significance in the fact that the Fisher ranges northward in western Canada to points where the mean annual temperature is approximately 24°, whereas in the Ungava Peninsula it scarcely extends beyond the annual isotherm of 29° (*cf.* Thomas, 1953:chart 1–9). This may perhaps be accounted for by the difference in the mean annual snowfall: about 40–60 inches from Lake Winnipeg to the lower Mackenzie Valley, and about 130–200 inches in the central and southeastern parts of the peninsula where the Fisher does not penetrate (*cf.* Thomas, 1953:chart 4–3). In the latter region there is no dearth of Porcupines, which supposedly form its favorite food, but deep snow may impede its pursuit of Snowshoe Rabbits and its search for mice that travel on the surface of the ground under the protection of several feet of snow.

Mustela erminea richardsonii Bonaparte
Richardson's Ermine; Richardson's Short-tailed Weasel; Belette de Richardson (Fr.); Socoshish (M.). (Map 35.)

Despite the superabundance of Red-backed Mice (*Clethrionomys*) and Meadow Mice (*Microtus*) in 1953, I saw not a single Weasel and only one set of tracks—at the outlet of Knob Lake, September 30. Wallace Mansbridge reported many at Harrington Harbour; Sebastien McKenzie, some at Lac Aulneau; and Ben McKenzie, some in the Menihek-Bringadin-Wakuach lakes area. One of the animals was seen in September at Long Lake (Garth D. Jackson). Willé Pinette took 45 at Eric Lake in the winter of 1952–53. At Lac Aulneau, in 1954, Fred Farah saw a fairly small Weasel that had a blackish tip to its tail; the animal was light brown above, white below. In late October, 1954, a trapper caught three in the winter pelage between Bean and Redmond lakes (Fred Farah). In January, 1955, J. L. Véronneau (*in litt.*, June 26, 1955) noted weasel tracks on lakes about the headwaters of the Nemiscau River; and the next winter he reported (*in litt.*, January 26, 1956) the animals as abundant about Lac Ochiltrie.

Wild fur production in Quebec, 1950–51, included 47,673 "ermine" skins (Cowan, 1955:169). This catch was exceeded only by those of "squirrel" (doubtless *Tamiasciurus* for the most part) and of Muskrat. Probably two or three species of weasels are included in the report of 47,973 skins taken in Quebec in 1954–55 (Canada Year Book 1956: 606).

Richardson's Short-tailed Weasel seems to be of general distribution in the Ungava Peninsula. The principal sources of information include: south coast—Stearns, 1883:113; Comeau, 1923:78; Eidmann, 1935:44; C. F. Jackson, 1938:432; Weaver, 1940:421; east coast —Cartwright, 1792, 2:46,67; 3:86,103,139,145; Bangs, 1897:240; 1898*b*:504; 1899:18; and 1912:466; north coast—McLean, 1932 (1849):252; Hantzsch, 1932:34 (Killinek area); Bateman, 1953:4 (south of Leaf Bay); west coast, north to Mistake Bay—Bell, 1884: 50; Manning, 1947:83; interior—Low, 1896:315; Prichard, 1911:44 (upper Fraser River); Bangs, 1912:466 (The Forks); Strong, 1930:7 (inland from Davis Inlet); Merrick, 1933:77,118,164,178 (Flour Lake to Ossokmanuan Lake); Anderson, 1934:95; Doutt, 1942:65 (Lower Seal Lake); Cameron and Morris, 1951:124 (Lakes Mistassini and Albanel); Martin, 1955:491 (Chubb Crater area). Hall (1951*b*:110, fig. 25) summarizes the distribution for the entire peninsula, with northernmost points at Okak, Fort Chimo, Richmond Gulf, and Belcher Islands. Although his map includes the entire Arctic Lifezone of the peninsula in the range, his text (p. 111) indicates only the Hudsonian and Canadian life-zones on the mainland of the peninsula. The Belcher Islands, Mistake Bay, the Chubb Crater area, and Killinek are well within the Arctic Life-zone, and there is good probability of the species ranging more or less throughout this zone.

Mustela rixosa rixosa (Bangs)
Least Weasel; Belette pygmée (Fr.). (Map 36.)

Ben McKenzie reported from the Knob Lake area a weasel whose characters fitted this species. A. E. Boerner spoke of a weasel at Gad Lake whose total length was under 6 inches, and which was thus probably of the present species.

There have been very few published records from the peninsula, and apparently none at any considerable distance from the coasts: Natashquan (Anderson, 1934:96, and 1940:64; Hall and Kelson, 1959, 2:909, map 464); Davis Inlet, Eagle River (30 miles up), St. Michael's Bay, and island south of Comb Hills, James Bay (Hall, 1951b:184, fig. 28); Great Whale River and Kogaluk River (Doutt, 1954:238); and Elsie Island, northwest of Port Harrison (Burt, 1958).

Mustela vison vison Schreber
Northeastern Mink; Vison commun (Fr.); Tchékash (M.).
(Map 37.)

The Mink, like the Marten, has a range covering practically all of the forested parts of the peninsula (Canadian and Hudsonian life-zones). As in the case of the Marten also, the peninsular population has been divided into two subspecies, whose ranges can not be exactly defined in the light of present knowledge. The peninsular range of *M. v. vison* is here restricted provisionally to the Canadian Life-zone from approximately longitude 70° eastward, while *lowii* is attributed to the remainder of the Canadian Life-zone and all of the Hudsonian.

Willé Pinette secured 50 skins in the winter of 1952–53 at Eric Lake. The species is reported at Lac de Morhiban (Philip Loth). Three Mink were seen in 1953 at Gad Lake (A. E. Boerner).

According to Couper (1877:300), the value of a North Shore skin in his day was twice that of a skin from the south shore of the St. Lawrence. The wild fur production in Quebec, 1950–51, included 20,290 mink skins (Cowan, 1955:169); these probably represented more than one subspecies. For 1954–55, 17,470 skins were reported (Canada Year Book 1956:606).

Previous records of Mink in the territory here assigned to *M. v. vison* are: abundant along the (south) coast and about inland ponds (Stearns, 1883:113); lower Natashquan River (Townsend, 1913:176); Matamek River (Eidmann, 1935:44). Hall and Kelson (1959, 2:919, map 467) extend the range of *vison* eastward to the Atlantic

Coast, from the Strait of Belle Isle northward approximately to Davis Inlet.

Mustela vison lowii Anderson
Ungava Mink; Vison d'Ungava (Fr.). (Map 37.)

Sebastien McKenzie reported Mink as plentiful in the Fort McKenzie area, where he had formerly traded as many as 600–700 skins per year. Allen Thompson saw one at Kasheshibaw Lake in the summer of 1949. Two were seen at Scott Lake in 1953 (Gilbert Simard). On September 30 I noted tracks in the snow, evidently of this species, going under a bridge near the old airstrip east of Knob Lake. Mr. and Mrs. Yeo reported a Mink as occasionally appearing about a woodpile at the guest house on Knob Lake. Some have been caught on Slimy Creek (Lance Widnall). In early July A. E. Moss caught a Pike (*Esox lucius*) in Howell's River and left it on the shore. Presently a Mink was feeding on it (still alive) within a few feet of him, and another Mink was not far away. In September, 1951, a Mink was seen at Chaulk Lake, and in 1952 one appeared swimming in either Bosh or Sylvia lakes (James Murdoch).

About July 19, 1953, an adult Mink with about six half-grown young appeared at the camp of a geological party at the north end of Wabush Lake, where a young gull was tethered on the shore. Members of the party began a lengthy pursuit and eventually captured one of the young ones. These did not seem much at home in the water and did not swim far. After the young captive had been put in a canoe, the adult returned and rescued it. In the night the young gull was killed and its head was consumed. (Paul Dorion.)

In early September or thereabouts single Mink were noted on the Ashuanipi River below Ashuanipi Lake (J. Malkin) and near Whiteman Lake (Lance Widnall). A male, taken on September 21 by a Montagnais along the Ashuanipi River below Ashuanipi Lake, provided the following data: length, 581; tail, 190; foot, 62; ear from crown, 17; testes, 11×4; weight, 1½ lb. (not much fat). (The measurements of total length and tail exceed the maxima given by Anderson (1945:58–59) in the original description of *lowii*.) The hide was unprime on the dorsum (nape to rump) and on the sides. It yielded several mites: *Laelaps kochi* and an undetermined species of Analgesoidea. The stomach contained one or possibly two mice. The upper parts (head and body) are between Prout's Brown and Mummy Brown; underparts very slightly paler, except for white chin, three small white patches on throat, and one each on chest and in inguinal region; upper sides of hands and feet very slightly darker than dorsum; tail changing very gradually from body color, above and below, at base to Black at tip.

"This specimen is not fully adult, but apparently agrees with Anderson's description of *lowii*" (C. O. H., Jr.).

From January to March, 1955, J. L. Véronneau (*in litt.*, June 26, 1955) observed mink tracks on various lakes and creeks about the headwaters of Nemiscau River; and he reported (*in litt.*, January 26, 1956) that the species seemed abundant about Lac Ochiltrie.

Previous records in the literature, pertaining either certainly or presumably to the present subspecies, are: St. Lawrence drainage—headwaters of Peribonca River (Low, 1890:17); Lake St. John or vicinity (Hollister, 1913:472,479; Cameron and Orkin, 1950:100); Atlantic drainage—Charles River and Sandwich Bay (Cartwright, 1792, 1:33; 2:83,89,122,179,212); lower Hamilton River and "Hamilton Inlet" (=Lake Melville?) (Low, 1896:315); Black Bay (Bangs, 1899:17, and 1912:466); inland from Davis Inlet (Strong, 1930:7); Flour Lake to Ossokmanuan Lake and north of Winokapau Lake (Merrick, 1933:77,118,141,178,210,337); Davis Inlet and Nain (Tanner, 1947, 2:622); Ungava Bay drainage—traded at Fort Chimo (Low, 1896:122); Chimo (Anderson, 1945:57); Hudson and James bays drainage—Lakes Mistassini and Nichicun and upper East Main River (Low, 1896:70,315); Lakes Mistassini and Waswanipi (Anderson, 1945:57); Lake Albanel (Cameron and Morris, 1951:125).

Gulo luscus luscus (Linnaeus)
Wolverine; Carcajou (Fr.); Kwakwatcheo (M.). (Map 38.)

The Wolverine seems to have very nearly reached the vanishing point in the Ungava Peninsula—at least in the forested parts. Various inquiries elicited extremely little information. The present status is in strong contrast to that of a generation or two ago, when, for example, Low (1896:315) and Bangs (1912:466) could report the species as "abundant throughout, especially in the northern portions." Its disappearance is quite possibly linked with the serious decline in the numbers of the two species of Caribou, through its dependence on utilizing the remains of those animals after they have been killed and partly consumed by Wolves.

I gathered from Jérôme St. Onge that he had found some evidence of the Carcajou in the Leaf Lake area in the summer of 1953. Sebastien McKenzie reported some Wolverines in the Fort McKenzie area up to 20 years previously, but no more at present. Ben McKenzie, with considerable trapping experience in the Menihek Lake area, did not even know of the existence of the Carcajou. Gilbert Simard, after years of surveying along the southern coast and in the interior, had never heard any report of it. According to Willé Pinette, there were no Carcajou about Eric Lake even in former years. The species is very scarce about Harrington Harbour (Wallace Mansbridge); its survival there may be correlated with the larger population of Woodland Caribou in that area than in the more westerly parts of the North Shore.

Only two Wolverine skins were reported in the wild fur production in Quebec, 1950–51 (Cowan, 1955:169); and none for 1954–55 (Canada Year Book 1956:606).

Previous records may be summarized as follows: south coast—Stearns, 1883:113 ("rather common"); Eidmann, 1935:45 (Matamek River); east coast—Cartwright, 1792:*passim* (Charles River, Sandwich and Table bays); Audubon and Bachman, 1846, 1:202,211 (Cartwright); Bangs, 1898*b*:501, and 1912:466 (Okak; L'Anse au Loup); Cabot, 1912*a*:289 (60 skins traded at Davis Inlet in 1906); Tanner, 1947, 1:421 (erroneously—as far as North America is concerned—considered "greatest killer of wild reindeer"); Hall and Kelson, 1959, 2:923, map 470; north coast—McLean, 1932 (1849):251; Bell, 1884:50; Payne, 1887:71 (Stupart Bay, where it was the "Eskimo's greatest enemy"); Turner, 1888*b*:83; Low, 1896:53–122,315 (N. to Hudson Strait); Bangs, 1898*b*:501 (Fort Chimo); Wallace, 1907: 236; Hantzsch, 1932:34 (Killinek area); west coast—Spencer, 1889: 77; interior—Michaux, 1889:84 (between Lake St. John and Lake Mistassini, where it was reported as jumping on Caribou); Wallace, 1907:236 (inland from Ungava Bay); Cabot, 1912*a*:144, pl. (Mistastin River); Strong, 1930:7 (very rare, inland from Davis Inlet); Merrick, 1933:106 (Flour Lake); Neilson, 1948:154 (Lake Mistassini area, where it is conspicuously rare, owing to "the Indian's zeal in tracking and killing any that appear on his hunting ground"). There are only a few records from definite localities in the western half of the peninsula (*cf.* map 38).

Mephitis mephitis mephitis (Schreber)
Northeastern Striped Skunk; Moufette du nord-est (Fr.);
Tséka (M.). (Map 39.)

This species occurs about Seven Islands, but not so far north as Eric Lake (Willé Pinette). In August, 1952, Robert Leslie saw a couple of Skunks about and in his tent at the south end of Manitou

Lake; he used to feed them. According to Jos. Potvin, an engineer on the Q. N. S. and L. Railway, the animals occur up to Mile 13 (northeast of Seven Islands) (Roland C. Clement, *in litt.*, August 8, 1957).

The wild fur production in Quebec, 1950–51, included 1,743 skunk skins (Cowan, 1955:169); for 1954–55, 389 (Canada Year Book 1956: 606).

In the Ungava Peninsula this Skunk is apparently restricted to the Canadian Life-zone, occurring north to Rupert House (Doutt, 1954: 239) and Lake Mistassini (Cameron and Morris, 1951:125; Hall and Kelson, 1959, 2:936, map 473) and east at least to Manitou Lake. It is rare at Matamek River (Eidmann, 1935:45) and fairly common in the Lake St. John area (Cameron and Orkin, 1950:101).

Lutra canadensis canadensis (Schreber)
Eastern Canada Otter; Loutre du Canada (Fr.);
Nkok (M.). (Map 40.)

In the Ungava Peninsula this subspecies seems to be restricted to the extreme southern part, from the Lake St. John area to Godbout. The records from this territory are few: 17–18 leagues (*ca.* 45 miles) southeast of Lake Mistassini (and thus in the Saguenay Basin) in 1792 (Michaux, 1889:82); inland from Trinity Bay (Comeau, 1923: 63); Lake St. John area (Cameron and Orkin, 1950:101); Godbout (Hall and Kelson, 1959, 2:944, map 477).

From outside the peninsula, I venture to present the following pleasant picture of otter habits, furnished me by Robert Slipp at Lac Aulneau. The scene was in his native New Brunswick, probably in the vicinity of Woodstock. He had come upon a party of four Otters on a November day. One of them was "oldish, with grayish whiskers." They kept sliding down a snow-covered bank on their bellies into an open place in a brook, meanwhile yipping or barking like a small dog. They would lose no time in getting out of the water and up the bank to slide again. The slide was 10–12 feet in length and pretty steep, probably at an angle of 60° from the horizontal. After watching for 5 minutes or more, Slipp stepped out of cover and the Otters went down the brook.

Comeau (1923:62–63) writes of an observation in the Toulnoustouc River area in 1860: "While crossing this last lake three otters came into view, and catching sight of us began to stretch their necks and rise out of the water upon their fore paws." I was the delighted witness (1932:24) of a somewhat similar scene in Mackenzie in 1914.

Earl Poole has portrayed this attitude in his drawing for the cover of the present report.

Lutra canadensis chimo Anderson
Ungava Otter; Loutre d'Ungava (Fr.). (Map 40.)

The numerous reports of this extremely interesting animal indicate that it is still comparatively common. The subspecies *chimo* is assumed to occur throughout the peninsula except in the extreme north and the extreme south. The latter territory, extending between longitudes 67° and 74°, is in the geographical range assigned to *L. c. canadensis*.

Otters were among the principal furs traded at Fort McKenzie in Sebastien McKenzie's sojourn there from 1916 to 1936. In early July, 1953, Robert Slipp saw an Otter at the brook at the south end of Lac Aulneau. He also spoke of an otter trail or path on the east side of the lake. Another one, between the neighboring Lepage Lake and a small lake 200–300 feet higher up, traverses a steep slope. He has noted still other paths 40 miles or so southeast of Knob Lake. Such paths may be between lakes where the connecting stream is obstructed or subterranean. They are about 8 inches wide and take a very straight course, barely avoiding bushes. Arthur C. Newton reported an Otter in Lake Wapanikstan in July, 1953. Gilbert Simard noticed an otter path between two lakes at about latitude 54°55′ N., longitude 67°; it was 6–8 inches wide and held to a very straight course through green timber. In August J. L. Véronneau found many trails at a small lake northwest of Leroy Lake. A few days previously I had noticed a fairly level place on the bank of the outlet of Leroy Lake where one or more animals had torn up a good deal of moss. Two of the Montagnais in our party, Ben McKenzie and Georges Michel, suggested (without seeing it) that this might be the work of Otters. Long ago Cartwright (1792, 1:xiv), in a Labrador glossary, defined a "rubbingplace" as "a place by the water-side, which otters have frequently made use of to rub themselves on after fishing." Such places seem to be known generally as "rubs"; doubtless they are identical in function with the "wallowing places" in the Adirondacks, which Merriam (1882:89) describes with tantalizing brevity as "either level beds, or slight depressions, in which they play and roll." Wallace (1907:131) remarks on otter rubs near the source of George River. Grinnell, Dixon, and Linsdale (1937, 1:280) throw light on the function of the "rolling" places—to dry the Otter when "it crawls out of the water dripping wet." Robert Slipp was evidently referring to such places when he said that Otters play and dig a good deal in moss about trout pools in streams.

Seton (1929, 2:704–707), in discussing Otter slides, seems to overlook the "rubs" entirely. He even cites Cartwright as if on the subject of slides, whereas the latter mentions "rubbing places" time and again and supplies a definition thereof.

A rare eye-witness account of an Otter indulging in this habit in the Yellowstone Park, Wyoming, is provided by Wright (in Wright and Thompson, 1935:34–35), although he apparently did not realize the particular significance of what he saw. This Otter was using an occupied Trumpeter Swan's nest for a rubbing place! "It reached out toward the center and pushed aside the material covering the eggs. Then the commotion started." It "rooted around in the dry nest material, heaving up here and digging in there, until it was more haystack than nest. Then the otter started to roll, around and around, over and over. This went on for a number of minutes." The parent birds, at distances of about 240 and 600 feet from the nest, "gave no evidence of concern," as if they realized the lack of harmful design on the Otter's part. All five eggs remained intact.

In Wye Lake, about the end of July, William C. Hood, Jr., saw two Otters playing and diving. He reported many otter "rubs" in the "bush" about Lac Hayot, where the moss was torn up; also a very straight trail, 6–9 inches wide, extending from one rub to another. I found an otter skeleton at a trapper's camp on the Iron Arm of Attikamagen Lake, and another at such a camp near the north end of Ashuanipi Lake. In September Richard Geren reported an Otter at or near Guy's River. Lance Widnall saw an otter family playing in Mary Jo Lake, and said that another place for the species was between the Star Lakes. At Dodette Lake, in 1952, two men saw what they took to be two young Otters, playing with a disabled duck and seizing it as it would make for shore (Robert Slipp). (If perhaps not Otters, they were probably Mink.)

Brian M. Meikle told of a young Otter, 18–20 inches long, that was caught by surprise in the brush on a small island in Dyke Lake in July, 1952. Meanwhile the mother, which had been with it, escaped into the water. At first the youngster snarled and tried to bite, but within a week it became exceedingly tame, allowing itself to be handled without biting. It was allowed more or less liberty, and so made its escape after a week. Allen Thompson saw two Otters north of Mackenzie Lake in 1949. In 1951 James Murdoch obtained a view of one sticking its head out of the Hamilton River in the vicinity of Sandgirt Lake.

Robert Slipp spoke of seeing a group of four or five, including an adult and one or more young ones, about September 1 in a small pond west of Gabbro Lake and north of Ossokmanuan Lake. He added that when a person comes upon an old and a young one, the former will keep "porpoising" between the person and the young one, to give the latter a chance to escape. He also said that one may capture youngsters by chasing them in a small body of water, where they stay submerged as long as they can, and tire quickly.

Otter slides were reported along the Ashuanipi River north of Molson Lake (Captain Kai Mansa). Garth D. Jackson observed trails leading from lake to lake in the vicinity of Neal Lake. In January, 1953, an Otter was running about on the ice of Deception Lake or a neighboring lake at Mile 150 of the Q. N. S. and L. Railway, where it was overtaken and killed by a Newfoundland laborer with an axe handle; the hide fetched about $60 in Seven Islands (John C. V. Bishop). Georges Michel remarked that he himself had once succeeded in doing likewise (*cf.* Merrick, 1933:119). Ten Otters were taken during the winter of 1952–53 at Eric Lake (Willé Pinette). The species is also reported at Lac de Morhiban (Philip Loth). From January to March, 1955, J. L. Véronneau (*in litt.*, June 26, 1955) noted a number of otter tracks on lakes about the headwaters of the Nemiscau River; he also reported (*in litt.*, January 26, 1956) that the species seemed abundant about Lac Ochiltrie.

It may be appropriate to insert here a bit of Naskapi-Montagnais mythology concerning one or two kinds of otterlike animals in the Kaniapiskau River. Strong (1930:9–10) has given an account of similar animals with which the Naskapi people Seal Lake and Little Seal Lake, in the Naskaupi River drainage. It was from Sebastien McKenzie that I first heard about a furred animal, perhaps three? feet in length, that lives in a lake on the upper Kaniapiskau. It was seen beneath ice two inches in thickness, and it made a noise like a squirrel scolding. A figure he drew of it has a tadpolelike appearance, the tail being approximately equal in length to the body, but of less than the normal relative height for a tadpole's appendage. According to Jérôme St. Onge, the animal occurs at some rapids in the Kaniapiskau at about latitude 55°. This Otter is 8–9 feet long, and the Hudson's Bay Company is said to have offered $1,000 for its skin. But the Indians can not pursue it because the river at that point runs through an impassable canyon. The animals are said to be dark gray, with one or two white stripes on each side of the face. Jérôme was careful to add that he had not seen the species himself, but had merely heard of it! (There is a possibility that stray seals may have provided the basis for some of these reports.)

The wild fur production in Quebec, 1950–51, included 3,221 otter skins (Cowan, 1955:169); and in 1954–55, 3,127 skins (Canada Year Book 1956:606).

The records in the following summation are considered, at least provisionally, as applicable to the subspecies *chimo*. St. Lawrence drainage: headwaters of Peribonca River (Low, 1890:17); Matamek River (Eidmann, 1935:45); Otish Mountains (Pomerleau, 1950:14). Atlantic drainage: St. Peter Bay to Sandwich Bay (Cartwright, 1792: *passim*); north to Okak (Bell, 1884:50); upper Hamilton River (Low, 1896:316); lower Naskaupi River (Mrs. Hubbard, 1906:537); Ptarmigan Lake (Wallace, 1906:116); Black Bay and Okak (Bangs, 1912: 466); inland from Davis Inlet (Strong, 1930:7); Flour Lake and near Ossokmanuan Lake (Merrick, 1933:75,114,118,161). Ungava Bay drainage: hunted and traded by Naskapi of Fort Chimo (Low, 1896: 51,122, and 1898:22); head of George River (Wallace, 1907:131); The Forks (Bangs, 1912:466); Fort Chimo (Anderson, 1945:59); Payne Bay area and Lac Faribault (Eklund, 1957:75). Hudson and James bays drainage: north to Little Whale River (Bell, 1884:50); Lake Mistassini (Low, 1896:70; Cameron and Morris, 1951:125); Lower Seal Lake (Doutt, 1942:65); head of Povungnituk River (Doutt, 1954:238). See also Hall and Kelson (1959, 2:945, map 477).

"It is not certain that *chimo* is distinguishable from typical *canadensis*. On geographical grounds the specimens from Attikamagen and Ashuanipi Lakes may be referred to *chimo*" (C. O. H., Jr.).

Lynx canadensis canadensis Kerr

Canada Lynx; Loup-cervier (Fr.); Pisho (M.). (Map 41.)

The name Loup-cervier (commonly corrupted to Lucivee) means Deer-wolf (*cf.* Ord, 1815:296; Stephens, 1872:253).

There are a few Lynx in the Lac Aulneau area, according to Sebastien McKenzie. In the summer of 1953 Brian M. Meikle saw "cat" (presumably lynx) tracks, about 3 inches in diameter, near Syncline Lake. Ben McKenzie reported tracks of the "Loup-cervier" about Menihek Lake; in this general area, he indicated, there had been none of the animals during a recent period, but there were some in 1953. He also mentioned a case of one attacking a young Caribou (probably the Woodland species). In October John Rodriguez spoke of some one having seen a Lynx recently in the vicinity of Menihek Lake. William Bazuk gave a report of one seen in the headlights of a car near midnight on September 19 near Molson Lake. R. Gordon Racey said tracks had been common during the winter of 1952–53 about midway of the east side of Ashuanipi Lake. These reports indicate that in 1953 the species had become moderately common in the Ashuanipi and Menihek lakes area.

James Murdoch spoke of seeing tracks at Panchia Lake in June, 1951; they were identified by his canoeman, a trapper. There were formerly some Lynx on mountains 50 miles up the Moisie River (Ben McKenzie). One of the animals was seen at Gad Lake in 1953 (A. E. Boerner). One was reported as eating Muskrats out of traps on the Romaine River 75 miles above its mouth (Gilbert Simard). Alphonse Bourgeois said the species was present, but not common, in the Seven Islands area. In the Harrington Harbour area (where Woodland Caribou are commoner than farther west), there are "lots" of Lynx (Wallace Mansbridge). In January and February, 1955, tracks were found on a number of lakes about the headwaters of the Nemiscau River, and the following winter the species was considered abundant about Lac Ochiltrie (J. L. Véronneau, *in litt.*, June 26, 1955, and January 26, 1956).

Lynx skins to the number of 811 were taken in Quebec, 1950–51 (Cowan, 1955:169); and 1,714 in 1954–55 (Canada Year Book 1956: 606).

Records from the Ungava Peninsula (at least those from specific localities) are not very numerous. The dearth of recent information from the eastern coastal areas is particularly marked (*cf.* map 41). St. Lawrence drainage: between Lake St. John and Lake Mistassini in 1792 (Michaux, 1889:83); hunted along (south) coast (Stearns, 1883:112); 57 secured by two men in one winter, inland from Trinity Bay (Comeau, 1923:69); very rare, Matamek River (Eidmann, 1935: 46); not uncommon, Lake St. John area (Cameron and Orkin, 1950: 101). Atlantic drainage: Charles River and Sandwich Bay (Cartwright, 1792:212,304); many along Hamilton River in 1893, their numbers varying with those of the Snowshoe Rabbit (Low,1896:315). Ungava Bay drainage: trapped by Indians in Ungava district (Turner, 1888*b*:83; Low, 1896:51; Wallace, 1907:236). Hudson and James bays drainage: a few skins obtained at Fort George (Bell, 1884:49); eaten for Christmas dinner at Lake Mistassini (Low, 1890: 20); Lower Seal Lake (Doutt, 1942:65, but contradicted by Doutt, 1954:239); increasing in Mistassini area (Cameron and Morris, 1951:

125); vicinity of Fort George (Doutt, 1954:239). Anderson (1947: 75) and Miller and Kellogg (1955:777) are somewhat indefinite as to the distribution of the species in the Ungava Peninsula. Hall and Kelson (1959, 2:967, map 484) provide no specific locality records for this region, but their map indicates the range of the species as covering the entire peninsula.

Phoca vitulina concolor De Kay
Atlantic Harbor Seal; Loup marin (Fr.); Atshok (M.). (Map 42.)

One was seen in the harbor at Rimouski on May 21. In early summer (June and July) the Seals follow the Salmon up the Moisie River to a point about 30 miles above its mouth, where falls occur (Charles Grace). Jérôme St. Onge said that when he was young, these animals occurred by "millions" on the Gulf, where now there are only a "hundred."

Some of the Montagnais of the Seven Islands area wear sealskin moccasins. I saw two entire skins in the possession of a family on the Ashuanipi River, who had brought them from the coast.

The Harbor Seal occurs on all coasts of the peninsula, including the lower courses of the rivers: southern—10 miles up Esquimaux (=St. Paul) River (Packard, 1866:270); 10 miles up Natashquan River (Couper, 1868:8,11); "moaning or howling" off Mingan Islands (Merriam, 1882:104); 15–20 miles up rivers in spring (Stearns, 1883: 113); Mingan (Lucas, 1891:722); about 35 miles up Eskimo (=St. Paul) River (Cabot, 1920:321); 50 miles up Bersimis and Moisie rivers (Comeau, 1923:136–142); Moisie Bay (Eidmann, 1935:46); Moisie River and harbors to eastward (C. F. Jackson, 1938:432); near Havre St. Pierre (Weaver, 1940:421); Godbout and La Tabatière (Doutt, 1942:119); eastern—Black Bay (Lucas, 1891:722); hunted along east coast and used for clothing and dog food (Low, 1896:43); Okak (Bangs, 1912:464); less frequent than in Gulf (Anderson, 1940:70); Battle Harbour, 25 miles up Paradise River, Hamilton Inlet, Muskrat Falls on Hamilton River, and Hopedale (Doutt, 1942:73,119); more common than in Ungava Bay (Dunbar, 1949:9); northern—Hudson Strait (Bell, 1884:52); Killinek (Hantzsch, 1932: 34); above seven waterfalls at Fort Chimo (Freuchen, 1935:232); rare, Hudson Strait (Anderson, 1940:70); rivers entering Ungava Bay and Leaf Bay (Dunbar, 1949:9); western—rivers around Hudson Bay (Bell, 1884:52); south to Great Whale River and Belcher Islands (Doutt, 1942:85).

Phoca vitulina mellonae Doutt
Ungava Fresh-water Seal. (Map 42.)

There have been a fair number of reports of seals in interior waters (usually lakes) of the Ungava Peninsula, well above the lower reaches of the rivers. These seem to represent non-migratory, land-locked populations of some form of *Phoca vitulina*. The best-known case is that of the Ungava Fresh-water Seal, described by Doutt in several excellent papers (1939:233; 1942; 1954:239) as inhabiting Lower Seal Lake and Upper Seal Lake, on the upper waters of the Nastapoka and Little Whale Rivers. Here, in former years, the Indians killed annually more than 30 (Low, 1898:13).

Occurrence of seals also in Lake Minto, at the head of Leaf River, is reported by Flaherty (1918:119) and by Manning (1947:83–84), but questioned by Doutt (1942:66). Another locality specified by Manning (1947:84) is Beneta Lake, situated a few miles north of Larch River in longitude 72°17'; here a seal was seen by L. O. R. Dozois in 1944. In the area north and west of Nain, Wheeler (1953:254) reports seals in Tessersoahk Lake and in the lake at the head of Webb Brook. Prichard (1911:44) writes of *Phoca vitulina* in the upper Fraser River, which flows into Tessersoahk Lake. (It is not certain that these reports by Wheeler and Prichard pertain to land-locked populations.) Freuchen (1935:232) reports the species more than 60 miles up a river, and above four waterfalls, a little north of Davis Inlet; this is probably the Notakwanon. From Seal Lake and neighboring waters on the Naskaupi River there are reports by Low (1896:316), Mrs. Hubbard (1906:537), Wallace (1906:49), and Strong (1930:10); and from Lake Mistassini by Neilson (1948:154), Dunbar (1949:9), and Cameron and Morris (1951:125). The Seal Lake just mentioned is the only one known to Jérôme St. Onge where a land-locked population occurs in the peninsula.

The allegorical "large trout" of Lake Mistassini (Low, 1890:24) may have had its basis in the occurrence of a seal; likewise the "Great Grampus" of "Ungava Pond," which "raised tremendous seas and hauled boats under" (Cabot, 1912a:157). Apparently no scientific specimens of seals have been preserved from the above-mentioned interior localities, other than Lower Seal Lake. It may be expected that their morphological characters will prove to closely resemble, but not necessarily be identical with, those of *P. v. mellonae*.

Alces alces americana (Clinton)
Eastern Moose; Orignal (Fr.); Moose (M.). (Map 43.)

Dr. F. D. Foster reported moose tracks and fresh dung at Molson Lake in July, 1949. This is apparently the northeasternmost locality to which the species is known to have advanced to date. Peter Almond and Paul Dorion saw a hornless Moose at Julienne Lake on June 11, 1953, as it stood on a skyline at a distance of about 400 feet. Its shoulders were noticed to be higher than its hind quarters. Later in the season a good many tracks (more pointed than a Caribou's) were noticed by members of their party about Carol Lake. Lloyd Hogan reported tracks of Moose on September 24 near the north end of Ashuanipi Lake. The species is found about 100 miles north of Seven Islands (Sebastien McKenzie). Francis McKenzie reported its range as extending from the Moisie River west to the Bersimis, and north to latitude 52°. On October 13 I noticed a set of fresh antlers, a hide, and apparently a wrapped hind quarter being put aboard a steamer at Godbout. A Moose was killed at the south end of Wabush Lake in November, 1955 (H. E. Neal). Dr. D. A. Déry wrote on December 14, 1956, that Dr. G. Cyr had recently had a successful moose hunt near "Grand Lac Caribou," 75 miles north of Seven Islands.

"Moose now occur as far up as Oreway (Mile 186 on the Quebec North Shore and Labrador), *fide* Jos. Potvin, an engineer on that railway. . . . Civil engineer Henry L. Coiteux . . . first saw a young male near Mile 45 in July, 1953; Moose have wintered at Mile 28 since 1955." (Roland C. Clement, *in litt.*, August 8, 1957.)

The species is abundant about Lac Boisvert, in the Mistassibi River area. In January and February, 1955, a number of tracks were found about the headwaters of the Nemiscau River; here some Indian families were living in part upon moose meat. The following winter the tracks of two Moose were noted about Lac Ochiltrie. (J. L. Vérronneau, *in litt.*, April 30, 1954, June 26, 1955, and January 26, 1956.)

According to Stearns (1883:114), the Moose in his time was very rare and occasional in the western portion of the North Shore, north of Anticosti. Low (1896:70) reported it as almost extinct about Lake Mistassini; but there has been a notable recent increase in that area (Neilson, 1948:152–155; Cameron and Morris, 1951:129). It is also reported as nearly "everywhere" in the Lake St. John area (Cameron and Orkin, 1950:107); here it was common in 1634 (Tanner, 1947, 1: 425). An early report of an eastward spread comes from Speck (1935: 78): "South and west of the Saguenay River and in the Lake St. John

PLATE 1

FIG. 1.—A view northeastward across Mollie T. Lake, Quebec. Black spruce in foreground. The treeless condition of most of the opposite ridge (at approximate altitudes of 1,650 to 1,750 feet) possibly resulted from fire. Feeding-ground of Eastern Black Bear and Ungava Canada Goose. August 11, 1953.

FIG. 2.—A view eastward over a boggy pond at Mile 224 Airstrip, north of Ashuanipi Lake, Labrador. Young white spruce on upland in foreground; remaining trees mostly black spruce. Habitat of Labrador Redbacked Mouse and Labrador Spruce Mouse on the pond's boggy border. September 6, 1953.

PLATE 2

FIG. 1—A mossy "closed forest" on the Ashuanipi River 2 miles north of Ashuanipi Lake, Labrador. Black spruce, baked-apple berry, mosses (*Sphagnum* and *Pleurozium schreberi*), and a tree lichen (*Usnea*). Two Montagnais boys, Bastien and Michel Pinette. September 4, 1953.

FIG. 2.—Trail of Ungava Red Squirrel crossing a bed of *Cladonia alpestris* between clumps of black spruce 15 feet apart. Other plants: Labrador tea and crowberry. Lac Aulneau, Quebec. July 26, 1953.

PLATE 3

FIG. 1.—Juvenal Snowshoe Rabbit, in its keeper's hand. North end of Ashuanipi Lake, Labrador. August 25, 1953.

FIG. 2.—Subadult Labrador Varying Lemming, captured on Geren's Mountain, Quebec. Photographed at Leroy Lake, Quebec. August 20, 1953.

PLATE 4

Fig. 1.—Labrador Red-backed Mouse, black phase. Leroy Lake, Quebec. August 20, 1953.

Fig. 2.—Labrador Spruce Mouse. Leroy Lake, Quebec. August 20, 1953.

PLATE 5

FIG. 1.—Eastern Timber Wolf. Shelter Bay, Quebec. May 22, 1953. At left, Warden Alphonse Bourgeois; at right, Antonio Carby, who had trapped the animal about four months previously.

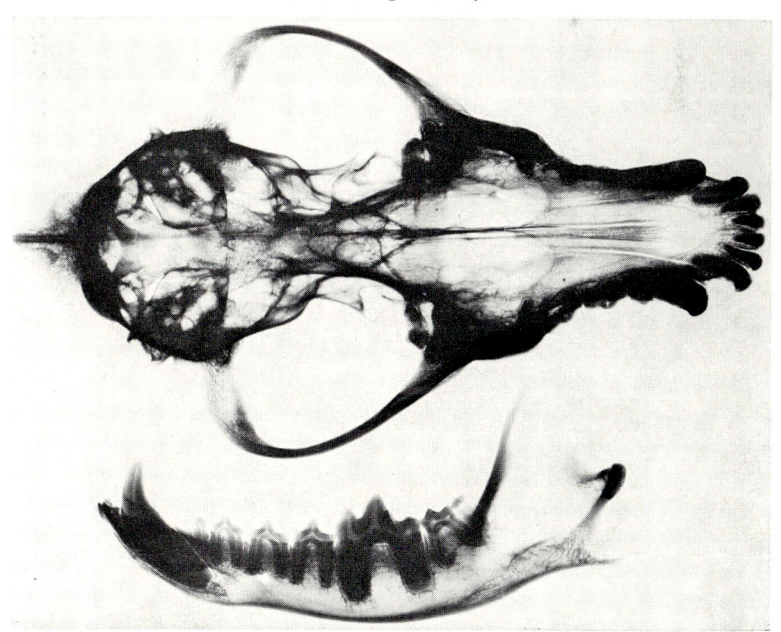

FIG. 2.—Skull and mandible of Eastern Timber Wolf, captured between Bagotville and St. Urbain, Charlevoix County, Quebec, March 24, 1956. X-ray by Dr. Viger Plamondon.

PLATE 6

FIG. 1.—American Black Bear. Near Greenbush Lake, Labrador. About July, 1953. Photographed by Pierre Côté.

FIG. 2.—Polar Bear, killed by Henri Gauthier near Peribonca, Lake St. John, Quebec, on October 20, 1938. Photographed by Chabot, Roberval.

PLATE 7

Cabot's Caribou, adult male. Near Dillon Lake on Rivière de Pas, Quebec, July 18, 1949. Trees probably chiefly black spruce; and shrubs, dwarf birch. Photographed by J. M. Harrison. (Courtesy of Geological Survey of Canada.)

PLATE 8

FIG. 1.—Cabot's Caribou, probably a yearling doe. Geren's Mountain, Quebec. June 27, 1957. Photographed by Roland C. Clement.

FIG. 2.—Eastern Woodland Caribou, fawn, with its keeper, Robert Darveau. Headwaters of Toulnoustouc River, Quebec. Probably August, 1948. (Courtesy of Robert Darveau.)

area the moose is found, and economic culture [among the Indians] centers largely around that animal. Of late years it has been observed that this animal is pressing gradually farther to the east than it has hitherto been seen." Pomerleau (1950:14) mentions tracks near the Otish Mountains. Distributional maps by Seton (1929, 3:161) and by Peterson (1952:fig. 1) restrict the Moose's northeastward range to a line extending from the southeastern part of James Bay past Lake Mistassini to a point on the North Shore of the Gulf midway between Godbout and Clarke City. Subsequently Peterson (1955:36) extends the range "eastward to Seven Islands." Peterson also (1955:46, fig. 8) shows a very significant advance of the Moose northward in Ontario between 1895 and 1950. The range suggested on the map in Hall and Kelson (1959, 2:1015) extends too far to the north and the east in the Ungava Peninsula.

Some of the more recent records, from points nearly 300 miles northeast of the former limit at Lake Mistassini, furnish perhaps the most striking example, among the mammals of the Ungava Peninsula, of an extension of range resulting from the amelioration of the climate during the past twoscore years (*cf.* Harper, MS). If the Moose still does not approach the borders of the Barren Grounds in this region, as it does in parts of northwestern Canada (*cf.* Preble, 1908:131, fig. 11; Peterson, 1952:fig. 1; Palmer, 1954:300, map; Harper, 1956:75), it may be deterred by the far greater mean annual snowfall—100 to 120 or more inches over the greater part of the Ungava Peninsula versus 40 to 60 inches in the Athabaska-Mackenzie region (*cf.* Thomas, 1953:109, chart 4–3).

Rangifer caboti G. M. Allen
Labrador Barren Ground Caribou; Cabot's Caribou;
Renne d'Ungava (Fr.). (Map 44.)

Naturalists now living have had so little contact with the scant remaining numbers of this Caribou that it seems well worth while to set down what little information may be gleaned about it here and there. One difficulty in securing more precise information in the central interior is that some of the Montagnais themselves do not seem to have too clear a conception of the distinction between this species and the Woodland Caribou.

Sebastien McKenzie, who was in charge of the Hudson's Bay Company's post at Fort McKenzie from 1916 to 1936, spoke of the last great migration passing that way, in January, 1916 (or very shortly before). This was apparently at some little distance south of Fort

McKenzie. He saw their tracks by "thousands, thousands," where they had passed westward. These animals, he said, had not been seen by the Indians living about the headwaters of rivers emptying into James Bay; and they never returned in appreciable numbers. Evidently something happened to them after they had passed to the northwestward of Fort McKenzie; and yet their bones were never found. Sebastien mentioned the supposition that they may have ventured out on to the ice of Hudson Bay and perished there; or that they may have migrated to the Mackenzie River region! In 1918 some of the animals were apparently sighted by Eskimos on Ungava Bay.

When Sebastien was 25 years old (about 1910), an aged Naskapi at George River, who was then perhaps 98–100 years old, said that when he was 15 years old (say 1825–30), there were plenty of "Deer." Then there ensued a period of 20 years, when there were "no more." Meanwhile no bones of the vanished animals were found. But after that period the Caribou became plentiful again. About 1891 (or 1892–93, according to Low, 1896:122), when the customary herds failed to materialize, 30 families between Whale River and the Kaniapiskau starved to death, after eating up their skin tents. In former times the abundance of Caribou enabled the Naskapi to keep teams of dogs more or less permanently, whereas the Montagnais, who have only the comparatively small numbers of the Woodland Caribou to depend upon, have perhaps only one dog per family—and sometimes none—to help in hauling their winter loads.

In years gone by, according to Sebastien, the Naskapi at Indian House Lake would intercept the Caribou in the fall as they crossed the middle or lower portion of the lake on their eastward migration, and in the spring, at a point toward the head of the lake as the animals passed westward. Apparently their migratory course was somewhat in the shape of an ellipse. At Mistunkoni Lake ("Big Ice Lake"), somewhere east of Las Aulneau, the Caribou would pass about the first of June, with their young fawns. The latter were presumably born on the Barrens east of the George River. There seem to be no reports of Caribou in the Fort McKenzie–Lac Aulneau area in recent years. Just where the animals passed the summer, after crossing the George River on their westward migration in the spring, is something of an unsolved mystery. If their destination were the Barren Grounds northwest of the Koksoak, they would still have more than 200 miles of largely forested country to negotiate. This would indicate quite a distinct migration pattern from that of *R. a. arcticus* in Keewatin and Mackenzie. The large numbers that seem to still migrate along the

Rivière de Pas in the fall can scarcely have come from northwest of the Koksoak.

On July 18, 1949, J. M. Harrison, of the Geological Survey of Canada, observed a buck Caribou about 2 miles northeast of Dillon Lake on the Rivière de Pas and secured a photograph of it (pl. 7) at a distance of about 75 feet, after it had been attracted to such close range by the waving of a cloth. This is quite possibly the first photograph ever taken of the species in the wild. The spread of the antlers, about two months before attaining their full development with the shedding of the velvet, is most impressive. The occurrence of the animal in mid-summer close to its southernmost known limits in this longitude, and well within the Hudsonian Life-zone, is also of great interest.

The foregoing record tempts me to refer to the same species, rather than to the Woodland Caribou, the following observation contributed by Gilbert Simard, although the locality is likewise surprising. In late June or early July, 1953, four Caribou passed within 100 feet of him in a wide depression in the Barrens southwest of Wakuach Lake (about lat. 55°25′ N., long. 67°38′ W.). Three of them were antlered, and one of these, that was killed, had "the most enormous horns" that Mr. Simard had ever seen on a Caribou. Apparently the antlers were deeply bowed, too.

In 1952 some Caribou were sighted from a plane along the Larch River, whereupon some Eskimos were brought in by air, and they secured quite a number of the animals (Arthur C. Newton). Allen Thompson saw 15 Caribou (presumably of the present species) in the latter part of September, 1949, on the northeast side of Michikamau Lake.

By questioning Francis McKenzie and some of his fellow Montagnais on June 22, with Jean P. Labrecque, of the RCAF, acting as interpreter, I gathered that they had secured Barren Ground Caribou in winter at "Kapikitiapiskao" Mountain, some 40 miles to the east of Knob Lake (and thus on or near the Labrador-Quebec boundary). According to Ben McKeKnzie, there is a treeless mountain about 10 miles east of Mollie T. Lake, where perhaps 100 long-horned Caribou used to be found in winter; but their numbers have become fewer since the prospecting activities commenced in this area.

About September 20, 1952, Lloyd Hogan, an air pilot, and Mathieu André, chief of the Seven Islands Montagnais, noticed "thousands" of tracks of Caribou in "moss" on the east side of the Rivière de Pas between latitudes 55°20′ and 55°40′ N. The line of march was NW–

SE, but the direction of the movement was not determined. Apparently the Rivière de Pas (river of tracks) is well named. At the Montagnais village east of Seven Islands I saw a photograph taken somewhere on the George River and showing four or five of the local men together with the antlers and skulls of perhaps 25 or 30 Barren Ground Caribou; these may have represented ancient kills by the Naskapi, before they abandoned that part of the country (*cf.* Wallace, 1907:129,153). On this subject Speck writes (1935:92): "The Ungava, Michikamau, and Barren Ground bands of Naskapi seem to have the custom of gathering together into heaps the antlers of slain animals after a caribou drive, as a propitiatory rite. This is not done toward the southwestern area."

Roland C. Clement had the good fortune to take Kodachrome photographs of two Caribou together, and of one of them separately (pl. 8, fig. 1), on the open summit of Geren's Mountain, some 25 miles northwest of Knob Lake, Quebec, on June 27, 1957; and he has most generously permitted the present utilization of them. They evidently represent yearling does of the Barren Ground species, with perhaps the merest knobs for horns. The animals still retain the winter pelage, generally cream-colored, with a wash of buffy on the head, back, and sides. On the snout there is a very small terminal patch of whitish in front of the nostrils. The remaining anterior portion of the snout, from behind the nostrils forward, and including the adjacent part of the lower jaw, is very dark. The area about the eye also is dark. The gangling limbs expand notably to their extremities. This is perhaps the first description to be published of the winter pelage of *R. caboti*, at any age or of either sex. It is considerably lighter in color than the corresponding pelage of *R. a. arcticus*, and is in distinct contrast to the Light Brownish Olive on the dorsum of the female *R. c. caribou* in winter pelage.

At dusk on a day in July, 1957, at Lac Montagni, 20 miles northeast of Attikamagen Lake, David B. Harper "saw a big horselike animal" (doubtless a Caribou, but species undetermined) on a bouldery ridge and "chased it half a mile right toward camp. . . . It was whitish with black splotches on the back and sides, and no antlers" (thus doubtless a doe, molting from winter to summer pelage). One of his companions, Alfred M. Ziegler, saw two Caribou in late August, 1957, at Retty Lake, a few miles northwest of Lac Montagni. One was an adult buck, with an antler spread of 4–5 feet and with a deep bow to the beams (thus probably *caboti*); the other, with much smaller antlers, was presumably a doe or a young buck. These two localities are only a few miles from Dillon Lake, where J. M. Harrison photographed an adult male *caboti* in 1949, as mentioned above. On the other hand, Woodland Caribou are known to occur, in winter as well as summer, on the treeless ridges extending from Knob Lake to Geren's Mountain.

In July, David Harper also sent word that "about 10,000" Caribou had been reported at Lac Le Fer during the previous winter. This number was doubtless grossly exaggerated. However, the unusual congregation attracted a number of Montagnais Indians, who were transported by plane to the scene and killed about 87 of the animals (Roland C. Clement, *in litt.*, August 21, 1957). The species was presumably *caboti*. Clement also wrote concerning the general status in Ungava: a pilot who has been flying a helicopter "for two years, mostly along . . . latitude 55° [which crosses Attikamagen Lake], told me that though they frequently saw caribou, since they fly low, the total population of the region was to be measured in hundreds rather than thousands."

J. D. Ives, of the McGill Sub-arctic Research Laboratory near Knob Lake, writes (April 8, 1959) concerning Caribou of that area, which were probably at least in part the Barren Ground species:

1955, Schefferville area. Caribou frequently seen in groups of 2 to 6 throughout summer, principally in higher hills 20 to 40 miles north of the town. On one occasion—end of July—we surprised a group of four adults and 3 or 4 young. Six or 7 reported to have run through town in July, 1957. . . .

1958, Helluva Lake, 50 miles north[west] of Schefferville. Groups of 3 to 7 seen on about 5 occasions during end of August and most of September.

In addition I hear that two local [Knob Lake] Indians shot 20 to 25 caribou during a three-week hunt in the 1957–58 winter. No reports of similar activities this winter.

He also writes concerning the Indian House Lake area in 1958:

From mid-June until end of July we frequently disturbed groups of 4 to 10. On almost every day. Sometimes we surprised them in mid-lake whilst in the canoe. In August the groups were smaller and less frequently seen but I would say that this general area carries quite a large number. [The Indian House Lake animals are unquestionably *caboti*. The numbers reported there indicate a very gratifying improvement over the status of several previous decades.]

From the same source there is also information concerning the present species in the Torngat Mountains. In 1956 there were no signs of Caribou about Kangalaksiorvik and Abloviak fiords. In 1957, from Saglek Fiord to Koroksoak, single Caribou were "seen in main valleys running down to Saglek Fiord on several occasions. Always followed by wolves. On one occasion two wolves virtually occupied our camp and refused to leave despite my firing five rounds over their heads! In the head streams of the Koroksoak we frequently surprised groups of 4 to 7 caribou. On about 6 occasions in three weeks."

In October, 1953, J. D. Cleghorn, curator of the Redpath Museum at McGill University, very kindly gave me an opportunity to inspect a mounted specimen that was then being installed in the exhibition halls. It had been secured in September, 1948, by Duncan M. Hodgson somewhere along the George River north of Indian House Lake. The descriptions of *caboti* that have so far appeared are so incomplete that the following rough notes on the specimen may be useful: great horns; pretty white neck; throat fringe about 8 inches long; drab brown on dorsum; a slightly darker ventrolateral stripe; lighter area above that stripe not very distinct or conspicuous; a light patch on the foreleg at the height of the elbow and extending a few inches posteriorly; legs dark; a narrow strip above the hoofs whitish; face all brown; snout whitish from anterior third of the nostrils forward; a light spot on the inner side of the heel.

A comparatively small number of sources in the published literature are utilized in presenting the following picture of the animal's history and distribution.

McLean (1932 (1849):205,208,224,230,253–255,261,262,274) writes of a herd seen between Fort Chimo and Erlandson Lake; a large herd between Whale and George rivers; a herd of 300 killed in a corral, after reappearing at Fort Chimo in early March; the Indian House Lake area abounding in Caribou, September 11; numbers, migrations, segregation of sexes, pelage, and antler shedding; persecution by the gad-fly; Caribou as the principal dependence of the Naskapi; their use as clothing and the tanning of their skins; also the utilization as clothing by the Eskimos.

Bell (1884:52) refers to their occurrence on the coasts of Hudson Bay and Hudson Strait; and later (1886:12) he mentions hunting by the Eskimos among the hills south of Cape Wolstenholme. Turner (1888a:99,100,105,110) tells of hunting and utilization by Eskimos along the Koksoak River; and he states that the Caribou are the principal food of the Naskapi, who pursue them with snares, bows, spears, and guns. The Naskapi make their clothing entirely of deerskins; there was a great scarcity in the winter of 1890–91 (H. G. Bryant, 1894:15,16).

Payne (1887:73) wrote of the species in the Stupart Bay area as a summer visitor to the coast, from April to November.

According to Turner (1894:276–278), fawning takes place in the

Cape Chidley area in May and June; the adult males and females meet from opposite directions (in the fall?) at or near The Forks of the Koksoak; and the females and young bucks cross this river at or near Fort Chimo about May 5–10, at least in each alternate year.

Low (1896:48,49,51,53,122,162,318) gives the following account. The Caribou were plentiful 200 miles up the George River, but had been exterminated in many parts of the country, so that the Indians had become partly dependent on flour. The animals were speared in the rivers by the Indians, and many were killed by the Eskimos north of the Koksoak River. Few skins had been traded at Fort Chimo in recent years. In 1892–93 27 families starved to death in that region, through failure of the Caribou to appear. In September the Indians assembled on the upper George River to spear the animals on their annual migration from the high Barrens behind Nain to the wooded interior. There were immense herds on the Barrens and semi-Barrens, ranging south to the Mealy Mountains. They were abundant about Davis Inlet and Nain. On the Hudson Bay coast they were formerly abundant south to Cape Jones, but then only north of Great Whale River. They spent the summer on barren highlands near the coast; they migrated in the autumn inland and southward into the semi-Barrens, and returned to the true Barrens in April and May. Three herds were recognized in the north. The first ranged between Nachvak and Nain. The second crossed the lower Koksoak to summer on the west side of Ungava Bay and Hudson Strait. The third passed north from Richmond Gulf and Clearwater Lake to summer on the northeastern side of Hudson Bay; but this herd had lately become greatly diminished. A fall hunt took place on the George River 100 miles north of Michikamau Lake, and also on the Koksoak River. There were paths on the Ashuanipi River and tracks of small herds below Grand Falls on the Hamilton River. (Thus the Ashuanipi and Hamilton rivers might appear to have constituted the former southern limits of *caboti*. But it now seems quite likely that the records from this area pertained, at least in large part, to the Eastern Woodland Caribou. And there is still no substantial evidence that Cabot's Caribou ever occurred in the Mealy Mountains or elsewhere south of Hamilton Inlet.)

Low reports later (1898:11,13,15,17) that the species was not abundant in summer between Richmond Gulf and Clearwater Lake, but plentiful at Seal Lake, along the upper Larch River, and at Natuakami Lake, where they were hunted by Indians; also that herds crossed the Larch River in the vicinity of Kenogamistuk (or Gué) River.

In 1905 Mrs. Hubbard (1906:537; 1908:112,123–139,144,152,153, 160,166,173,183) found thousands at Michikamats Lake, and reported others along the upper George River to a point just below the mouth of the Rivière de Pas; also at Indian House Lake and near the mouths of George and Whale rivers. Wallace (1907:123,129,135,137,139,140, 153,154,169,196,197,210,211,277) gives much the same information from the same areas. He reports the tracks between Michikamau and Michikamats lakes as passing eastward in late summer, and mentions great piles of antlers (left by the Naskapi) on the upper and middle courses of the George River.

Prichard (1911) provides an extensive account, with particular reference to the country between the Atlantic Coast and the George River. He encountered the animals—or signs of them—on the lower and upper Fraser River (pp. 39,41,44,54) and at Indian House Lake or in the country to the eastward (pp. 71–109). Some of them were traveling southeastward in August. In former times they crossed Indian House Lake in immense herds, and in Prichard's time they were still plentiful in the higher latitudes (p. 204). One herd, hunted by Eskimos inland from Nain and Okak, migrated northwestward in spring and southeastward in autumn; they had formerly appeared in great numbers in November on the coast south of Nain, but only one such mass had appeared there between 1903 and 1910 (pp. 205–207). The factor at Fort Chimo had once seen the Caribou pass for three days in "hundreds of thousands" (p. 214). Prichard discusses the useful role of Wolves (p. 214), the persecution by nostril flies and warble flies (p. 216), and the supposed intergradation between the Barren Ground and the Woodland Caribou near Hopedale and Makkovik (p. 219).

Cabot (1912a) gives an illuminating picture of the caribou situation in the largely treeless country between Davis Inlet and Indian House Lake on the George River during the first years of the present century. On a number of trips between these points, by way of the Assiwaban River, he found the animals well distributed, but most numerous toward the George River (pp. 86,232,276,285). Their numbers fluctuated considerably from year to year. In 1906 a few families of Naskapi Indians speared 1,200–1,500 at Mistinipi Lake (pp. 239, 290). In July and August movements were northward (pp. 60,264, 265, 288); in September, southward and westward (p. 245). Since that period the caribou population has so far declined that the Naskapi have been obliged to retreat from the interior to the coast.

Flaherty (1918:117,124,129) saw only five animals on a trip from Hudson Bay to Fort Chimo via Payne Lake and Leaf River, but he found evidence of former "hundreds of thousands" about that lake, which was once "the most famous deer-hunting ground of the northern interior." Strong (1930:2–5) discusses the role of the Caribou in the life of the Davis Inlet band of the Naskapi; they killed about 40 between January and April, 1928. Wheeler (1930:454–466) writes of the Caribou wintering on the high treeless plateau in the vicinity of Nain; there were many about Tessialuk Lake and the Fraser and Kingurutik rivers. "The caribou . . . herds, if they ever roamed the mountain valleys of the Torngat country, have now deserted them" (Odell, 1933:205). Anderson (1940:94) mentions untimely thaws and fires as causes of depletion; he states (1948:10) that no complete specimen was then known in Canada, and he predicted extinction within a few years.

At the beginning of the twentieth century, according to Tanner (1947, 2:501), the animals were hunted by Eskimos near Nachvak, Saglek, Nain, and Davis Inlet; they were in small herds of up to 70 individuals. He reports (1947, 1:422; 2:618) trails seen from the air between Petitsikapau and Michikamats lakes, indicating a tremendous migration; and he mentions snares set by the Montagnais about Michikamau Lake and the sources of the George and Kaipokok rivers. Of bygone conditions he writes (1947, 1:425): "The raven and the wolf announce the arrival of the migrating herd and soon it begins to live in the woods, wandering slowly from place to place. This special biological scene . . . is certainly past in Labrador."

Manning (1947:82) includes Lake Minto in the winter range; he saw one old track there. He summarizes (1948:20–21) past and present conditions as follows. There has been a gradual decrease over the region as a whole, and a comparatively rapid decrease in certain areas. In 1898 the animals were very numerous along Hudson Bay for 50 miles south from Cape Wolstenholme, and also plentiful in the interior as far south as the Nastapoka River (Low). In 1916 there were few in the country back of Cape Dufferin (Flaherty and Flaherty). On the Koksoak River no diminution was apparent in 1882–1884 (Turner, 1894), but the herds were decreasing by 1900 (Wallace); yet in 1912 there was a big kill (Flaherty and Flaherty). Prior to 1944 there had been a slight increase after a disappearance for some years in that area (Wright). At Indian House Lake 1,000 were killed in 1911 (Cabot), but the big bands diminished from that time to 1927 (Strong). There were still scattered herds about the heads of east-coast rivers (Wheeler). Four specimens were collected by Doutt in 1945 in the Povungnituk area. On an accompanying map (based on studies by R. M. Anderson) the southern limit is indicated by a curved line extending from the vicinity of Fort George on James Bay past Bienville, Knob, and Michikamau lakes and Goose Bay to the northern end of the Strait of Belle Isle (thus including the Mealy Mountains in the range of *caboti*).

There is no very plausible explanation for the sudden disappearance of the Caribou from the vicinity of Fort Chimo about 1919 (or a little earlier). There has been a great general reduction in the Ungava Bay region, but Eskimos traveling from the Labrador coast inland toward the George River make a considerable slaughter (Dunbar, 1948:18). Banfield's map (1949:fig. 1) indicates a southern limit similar to that of the above-mentioned map of 1948, from Richmond Gulf to Michikamau Lake; but thence the boundary extends eastward and northward to Hebron and Nachvak Fiord and nearly to Port Burwell; and also through the interior of the northwestern part of the peninsula nearly to Sugluk and Cape Wolstenholme. Unlike some previous authors, Banfield does not include the Mealy Mountains in the range. In the 1940's the animals no longer came to Indian House Lake (Clement, 1949:372). In 1948 the trails along the Kogaluk River had long since been abandoned, but three Caribou were seen on Payne River (Rousseau, 1949:126). In 1949–50, 29 were killed by Naskapi from Nutak, and 12 by one Eskimo from Nain (Frazer, 1950). Gabrielson and Wright (1951:128) report a single track near Fort Chimo. Bateman (1953:7) found old antlers south of Leaf Bay and reported some animals still remaining on the upper Payne, Leaf, and Koksoak rivers. Martin (1955:491) found skeletal remains and antlers common in the Chubb Crater area.

The fact that the very striking reduction in numbers in the Koksoak River area within the 1916–19 period coincided more or less with a similar reduction in the numbers crossing the George River, suggests that the same aggregation of animals migrated back and forth between these two areas, across a largely forested country about 200 miles in width.

Doutt (1954:245) reports small numbers about Lake Minto, Lower and Upper Seal lakes, and Clearwater Lake. In 1944–45 about 200 were killed by Eskimos inland from Povungnituk, and about the same number in the vicinity of Port Harrison. Tracks were found at

(Lower) Seal Lake in 1953. Doutt gives very cogent reasons for not attempting to replace the Caribou with domesticated Reindeer. Hantzsch (1932:8) reports the species as occurring occasionally in small numbers on Killinek Island, but more plentifully to the south, in the interior. He then adds: "To carry out the repeatedly agitated proposal of introducing reindeer into these districts, and to get rid of the dogs for this purpose, I consider a very hazardous interference with old habits and customs in the life of the [Eskimo] population." (On this point, see also Harper, 1955:74-78.)

At the time (1914) when Glover M. Allen described *caboti* on the basis of a single antler from 30 miles north of Nachvak, there were something like a dozen skulls and sets of antlers, besides one or two skins, in the United States National Museum. These had been brought from the Fort Chimo area in the 1880's by the able and indefatigable Lucien M. Turner. The tracks that Dr. Allen reported seeing at the Strait of Belle Isle in July, 1906, were almost certainly those of the Eastern Woodland Caribou.

Rangifer caribou caribou (Gmelin)
Eastern Woodland Caribou; Renne des bois (Fr.); Atok (M.).
(Map 45.)

According to Warden Alphonse Bourgeois, Woodland Caribou come within a few miles of Seven Islands. Two were reported killed during the winter of 1952-53 on the islands off that port. During the same winter some of these animals were sighted from the air, in numbers up to 15 in a band, on small frozen lakes between Lac de Morhiban and Magpie Lake; two came, rather trustfully, to a garbage pile at the former lake (Philip Loth). Presumably they assemble on the frozen lakes as a comparatively safe place for a noonday rest, just as the Barren Ground Caribou in western Canada do (*cf.* Harper, 1955: 10,13,14,38,41,80; Pruitt, 1959:169-170). They are present in the vicinity of Harrington Harbour (Wallace Mansbridge). Père Marcel Champagne, O. M. I., imparted the surprising information that the Indians in the Blanc Sablon area had killed 500 Caribou during the winter of 1952-53. Such news indicates that the population of this fine animal has not declined so far as generally supposed. Lloyd Hogan supplied corroborative information to the effect that it is numerous on the St. Augustin and St. Paul's rivers, although very scarce between that area and Seven Islands. During the winter of 1952-53 Willé Pinette secured three in the vicinity of Eric Lake. A doe and a fawn were seen several times in the summer of 1953 at Gad Lake (A. E. Boerner).

Through the kindness of J. L. Véronneau I have received the following account, by Robert Darveau, of a Woodland Caribou fawn (pl. 8, fig. 2). In the third week of July, 1948, its mother was killed near a lake on the headwaters of the Toulnustouc River (a tributary of the Manicouagan). The fawn was captured and brought to camp on a plane. It was tethered by a leg and was fed with canned milk and fresh potatoes. It also grazed of its own accord on caribou lichen (*Cladonia*). After two weeks it became very tame, and it would approach the nearest person as closely as its tether would permit. It always seemed hungry. It was not heard to utter a sound. Toward the end of August it was frightened by a Black Bear seeking the camp garbage, and it broke a leg in its efforts to escape. It was thereupon put out of misery. Photographs of this individual reveal only the very faintest trace of a dark ventrolateral stripe, such as is characteristic of fawns of *R. a. arcticus*.

Mr. Véronneau reported that in 1948 there were a good many Caribou about Lacs Ray, Dentelle, and Cassé on the headwaters of the Betsiamites River, close to the western border of Saguenay County. In January, 1954, he found tracks on Lac Boisvert (near the Mistassibi River), about 80 miles north of Lake St. John.

On September 11, 1949, Dr. F. D. Foster saw six Caribou at Astray Lake. During the same season he also noted tracks at Menihek and Evening lakes.

At Ashuanipi Lake I saw some antlers that had been picked up at an Indian camp about 10 miles from the north end of the lake; also some caribou fur at another camp on the lake. Some Montagnais children here were wearing caribou-skin moccasins (*pishakanesin*). A geologist spoke of seeing several Caribou during the summer in that general area—for the most part as they were swimming lakes. Lloyd Hogan stated that the animals were in the habit of congregating at Ashuanipi Lake up to about 1948–49. He had noticed them resting on the ice of this lake and of various little lakes along the right of way of the railroad. There were usually 10 to 15 in a band, but once he had seen about 50. In the spring, he said, they moved down toward the coast.

In the vicinity of Carol Lake members of a geological party noticed tracks quite frequently in September, 1953. An odd antler picked up there was presented by Frank Tuffy. On the neighboring Lorraine Mountain I found tracks about a little pond on the upper slopes, above timber-line. Another geological party saw one of the animals in August at Reid Lake. In that general area, near timber-line on the east side of Jackson Lake, Marek Mlojewski reported five Caribou seen in late August.

In July, 1951, at Ossokmanuan Lake, James Murdoch saw a doe with short horns, a doe with a fawn, and a buck; also a big buck with long antlers on the Hamilton River, east of Sandgirt Lake, about the middle of August. Robert McAulay, of the RCAF, reported sighting five Caribou in three different groups (one of which was a doe with a fawn) on a flight of June 23, 1953, between Goose Bay and Michikamau Lake.

H. E. Neal gave a report of a Caribou being seen near the north end of Ashuanipi Lake on June 3; also of some one seeing 50 of the animals swimming across Menihek Lake near Mile 290 about June 13. Cyrille Dufresne spoke of noticing a "caribou watch" near the Fleming Line, northwest of Burnt Creek; this was a circle of stones, presumably set up by Indians to hide within while awaiting the approach of Caribou. J. L. Véronneau saw tracks on August 24, 1953, on the shores of a small lake northwest of Leroy Lake.

At a Montagnais camp on the Iron Arm of Attikamagen Lake there was a set of antlers of a young buck, placed on the roof of a cabin (perhaps as some sort of fetish), and a rotting skin on the ground. On Sunny Mountain, above timber-line, I found an ancient fragment of an antler. Remi Kelly spoke of seeing a buck, with antlers 20–24 inches long, 2 miles north of Wye Lake in late July.

On September 17 two Montagnais in a surveying party at Harris Lake secured a buck whose age was estimated at three years. It had been with a doe and a fawn. A sketch of the antlers, made on the spot by J. L. Véronneau, indicates that they were still in the velvet, with a length of about 15 inches and with a spread of 12 inches between the tips. These dimensions are a fairly definite indication that the animal belonged to the Woodland species. After it was skinned and dismembered, one of the Montagnais danced several times, with a caribou bone in each hand, beating them together; but his fellows were too abashed to join him in the presence of other members of the party. All but one of the several Montagnais ate the marrow raw. When the skin (minus the lower part of the legs) was brought to Knob Lake a few days later, I made the following rough notes on its colors: mid-dorsum, from sides of face and nape backward, sort of light hair brown; becoming darker on rump; light drab on sides of neck and body, back to hind quarters; a slightly darker ventrolateral area; thighs and upper foreleg much darker, almost fuscous; rump whitish;

entire venter pretty white; outer side of ears drab like sides of neck; inside of ears lighter; chin and upper throat white. Length of skin, nose to tail, about 72 inches. No warbles were detected on the inside of the skin.

By way of comparison, I include the following notes on an adult male from Table Top Mountain on the Gaspé Peninsula, on exhibition in the Provincial Museum in Quebec City: hard horns; tip of snout white, back to middle of nostrils; tip of chin white; a slightly dark area on top of snout, but not sharply defined; a light area above eye and about lacrimal gland; ears more or less grayish on both surfaces; dorsum and sides almost uniform brownish, with slightly lighter hairs before and on hip joint; sides of neck and throat-fringe buffy white, the latter 7–8 inches in length; a light area on the shoulder joint, in the shape of an ellipse, about 8 inches in horizontal length and 6 inches in height; scarcely a suggestion of a dark ventrolateral stripe; whitish rump-patch apparently more restricted than in *R. a. arcticus*; venter brownish white anteriorly, whitish posteriorly; legs dark brown; whitish area above hoofs not extending higher up the legs than in *arcticus*, and thus differing from the pattern indicated by Seton (1929, 3:pl. 10).

Roland C. Clement has made available to me a Kodachrome of an adult buck that was killed in October, 1956, somewhere along the more or less treeless ridges extending from Burnt Creek to Geren's Mountain. The well-developed antlers are of a pale or light brownish color; the throat, the whole neck (as far as visible in the photograph), the chest, and the belly are very white; the head and the limbs appear for the most part very dark, but the latter become lighter at their upper extremities; the immediate border of the eye is conspicuously light-colored; and there is a conspicuous white ring above each hoof.

The Woodland Caribou is a type of animal that recedes steadily before the advance of civilization. Couper (1877:299) states that it replaces the Moose north of the St. Lawrence. T. J. O. (1878) tells of hunting this species in the vicinity of Valcartier, within 30 miles of Quebec City. Chambers (1896:237,293,296) considered it common in the entire St. John and Saguenay country, where a favorite feeding-ground was the valley of Belle Rivière. Mr. Charles Frémont informed me that it was common within his memory in the territory between Quebec City and the Saguenay River (presumably in the Laurentides National Park). Manning (1948:20) writes of it as surprisingly plentiful in the Laurentides Park until 1912. Anderson states (1948:10) that it disappeared from southwestern Quebec within the previous quarter of a century. By 1950 it had gone from the Lake St. John area, not remaining closer than 50-75 miles to the northward (Cameron and Orkin, 1950:108). Its retreat northward in this part of Quebec may be due in part to the warming of the climate since 1915 (cf. Harper, MS), as well as to the advance of settlement.

In the 1770's and 1780's Cartwright (1792:*passim*) found Caribou in considerable numbers along the east coast from Sandwich Bay to Niger Sound; they were present during every month of the year. In 1792 Michaux (1889:81) saw one a little southeast of Lake Mistassini. J. J. Audubon (in M. R. Audubon, 1897:409) mentioned that Caribou resorted in winter to offshore islands on the eastern part of the North Shore, and that there were not many inland from Natashquan. Cayley (1863:86) reported many tracks 50 miles up the Moisie River. By 1885 the species was believed to occur no longer in the Lake Mistassini area (Low, 1886:17). Later Low gave (1896:70,86,100,128,318) the following account. The last herd (of seven individuals) had been killed near Lake Mistassini; a few were left about the headwaters of the East Main and Hamilton rivers and about Nichicun Lake (where about a dozen were killed annually); though plentiful up to about 1870 on the southern watershed, the species was then practically exterminated there, except that small numbers remained about the heads of rivers entering the eastern part of the Gulf of St. Lawrence; the Naskapi and Montagnais at Northwest River were dependent upon Caribou.

Cameron and Morris remark (1951:129) that "the main herds are concentrated in the region of the Eastmain Mountains east to the north shore of the Gulf"; five were killed at Lake Mistassini in 1947. According to Pomerleau (1950:14), the Indians at Nichicun Lake could no longer count upon Caribou for food. Manning (1947:82) reports tracks at Mushalagan Lake. Comeau (1923:43,151ff.), referring to conditions in the latter part of the past century, records the species at the head of the Trinity River and describes a drive by Montagnais near the head of the Toulnustouc River in which 76 animals out of a herd of 160 were killed. In 1930 a small herd was observed at Trout Lake (Eidmann, 1935:58). C. F. Jackson (1938:434) found evidence about the Pigou and Moisie rivers. H. G. Bryant (1913:11) reports one killed on the St. Augustin River.

In the Atlantic drainage Caribou have been reported at Black Bay, though considered very rare (Bangs, 1898*b*:498; 1899:16; 1912:460); on the lower and upper Naskaupi River (Mrs. Hubbard, 1906:537; 1908:56,81); in the Susan River area (Wallace, 1906:70,75,87,89,103,

252,287); in the Naskaupi River area, including several lakes to the north and one (Kasheshibaw) to the west (Wallace, 1907:34,36,40, 70,74–78,85,108); and on Kenamu River (Leslie, 1931:210). Prichard (1911:219) maintained that many animals at Makkovik and Hopedale had features of both Barren Ground and Woodland Caribou. However, both this area and the Naskaupi River area are beyond the northern limit of the range of the latter species as indicated by Anderson (map following his paper of 1948). There is a little overlapping of the ranges of *caboti* and *caribou* in the central interior, but with no evidence of intergradation. Merrick (1933:147,153,322,337) found signs between Flour and Ossokmanuan lakes and north of Winokapau Lake, and reported a bad winter for Indians about Northwest River on account of the scarcity of Caribou. Tanner (1947, 1:422) considered the Woodland Caribou as probably completely exterminated in Newfoundland Labrador, with the result that the Naskapi had abandoned certain districts or died out. Addy *et al.* (1950?:80) sighted Caribou north and south of the Mealy Mountains, but leave their specific identity in doubt. According to Banfield (1949:486), the range comprises the Cartwright, Chicoutimi, and Lake St. John areas; the country bordering the North Shore of the Gulf; the Mealy Mountains; the upper Hamilton River; Lakes Kaniapiskau and Mistassini; and Rupert River.

There seems to be a particular dearth of definite, specifically identified summer records of Caribou in the Hudson and James bays drainage between East Main River in the south, Nichicun Lake in the east, and Clearwater Lake in the north.

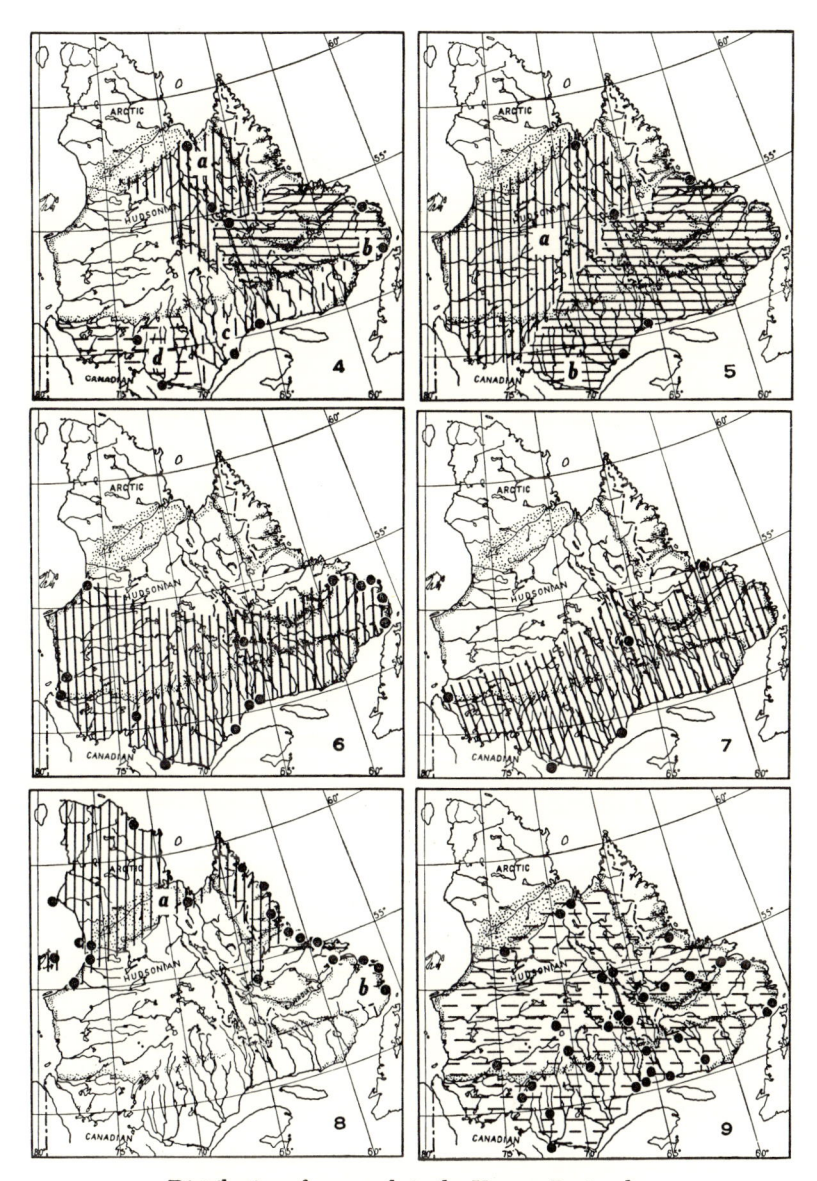

Distribution of mammals in the Ungava Peninsula:

MAP 4.—a, *Sorex palustris turneri*; b, *S. p. labradorius*; c, *S. p. gloveralleni*; d, *S. p. albibarbis*.
MAP 5.—a, *Microsorex hoyi alnorum*; b, *M. h. intervectus*.
MAP 6.—*Condylura cristata cristata*.
MAP 7.—*Myotis lucifugus lucifugus*.
MAP 8.—a, *Lepus arcticus labradorius*; b, *L. a. bangsii*.
MAP 9.—*Lepus americanus americanus*.

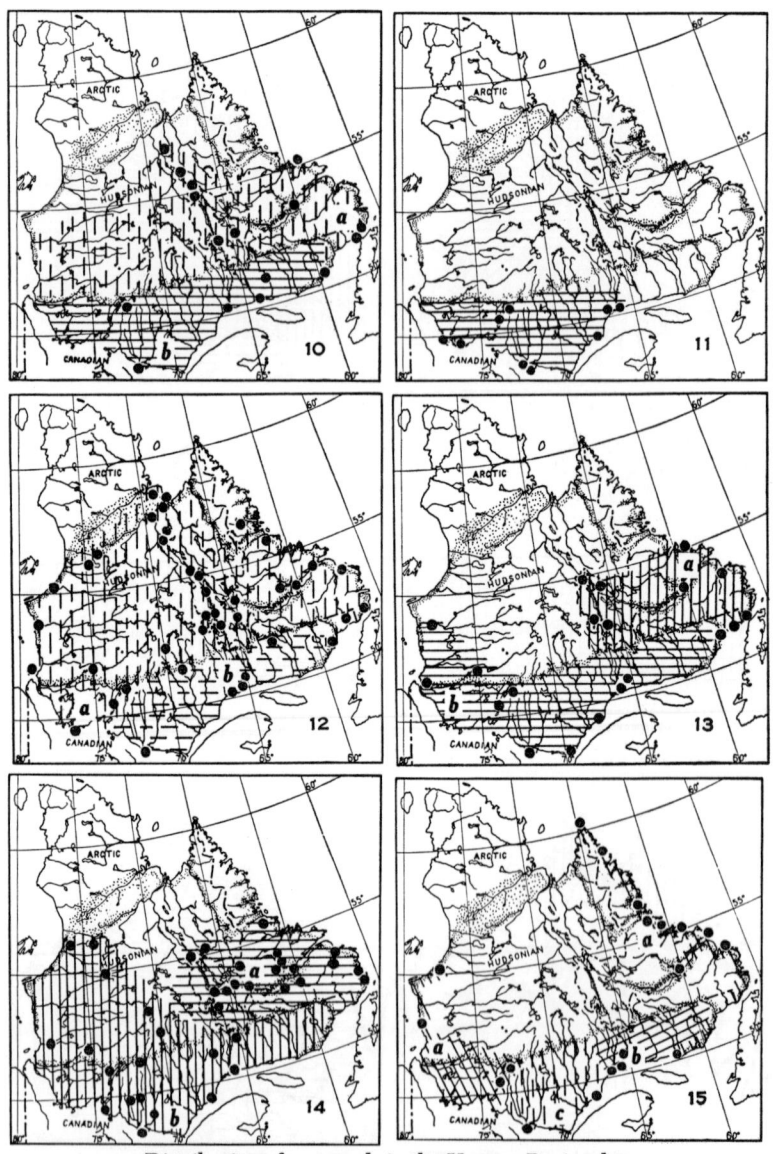

Distribution of mammals in the Ungava Peninsula:
MAP 10.—a, *Marmota monax ignava*; b, *M. m. canadensis*.
MAP 11.—*Tamias striatus quebecensis*.
MAP 12.—a, *Tamiasciurus hudsonicus ungavensis*; b, *T. h. laurentianus*.
MAP 13.—a, *Glaucomys sabrinus makkovikensis*; b, *G. s. sabrinus*.
MAP 14.—a, *Castor canadensis labradorensis*; b, *C. c. acadicus*.
MAP 15.—a, *Peromyscus maniculatus maniculatus*; b, *P. m. plumbeus*; c, *P. m. gracilis*.

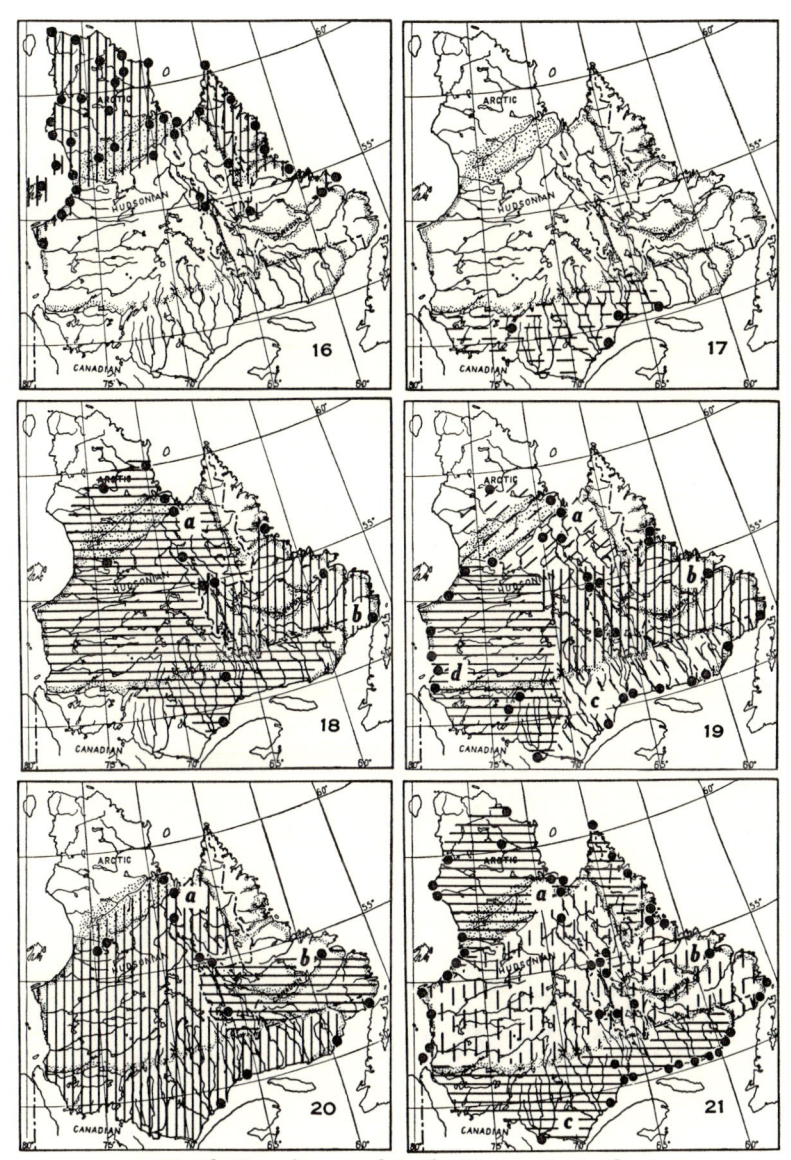

Distribution of mammals in the Ungava Peninsula:
MAP 16.—*Dicrostonyx hudsonius.*
MAP 17.—*Synaptomys cooperi cooperi.*
MAP 18.—a, *Synaptomys borealis innuitus;* b, *S. b. medioximus.*
MAP 19.—a, *Clethrionomys gapperi ungava;* b, *C. g. proteus;* c, *C. g. gapperi;* d, *C. g. hudsonius.*
MAP 20.—a, *Phenacomys ungava ungava;* b, *P. u. crassus.*
MAP 21.—a, *Microtus pennsylvanicus labradorius;* b, *M. p. enixus;* c, *M. p. pennsylvanicus.*

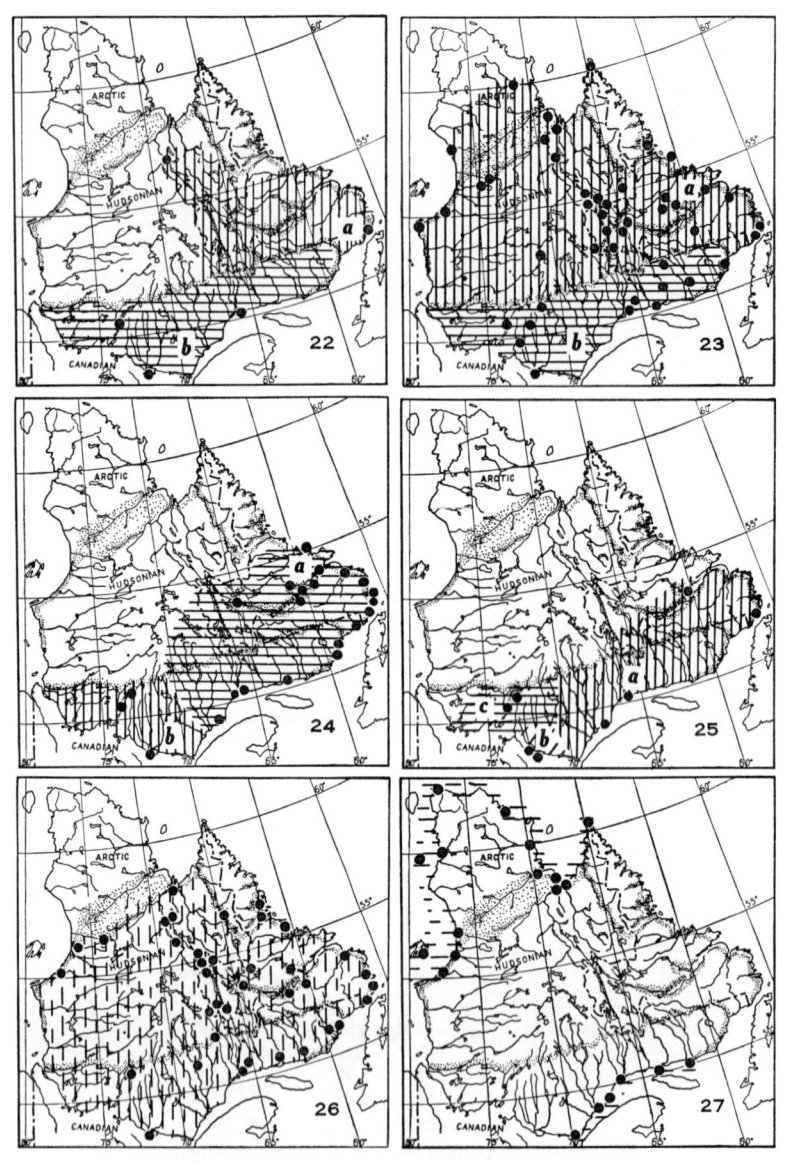

Distribution of mammals in the Ungava Peninsula:

Map 22.—a, *Microtus chrotorrhinus ravus*; b, *M. c. chrotorrhinus*.
Map 23.—a, *Ondatra zibethicus aquilonius*; b, *O. z. zibethicus*.
Map 24.—a, *Zapus hudsonius ladas*; b, *Z. h. canadensis*.
Map 25.—a, *Napaeozapus insignis saguenayensis*; b, *N. i. algonquinensis*; c, *N. i. abietorum*.
Map 26.—*Erethizon dorsatum dorsatum*.
Map 27.—*Delphinapterus leucas*.

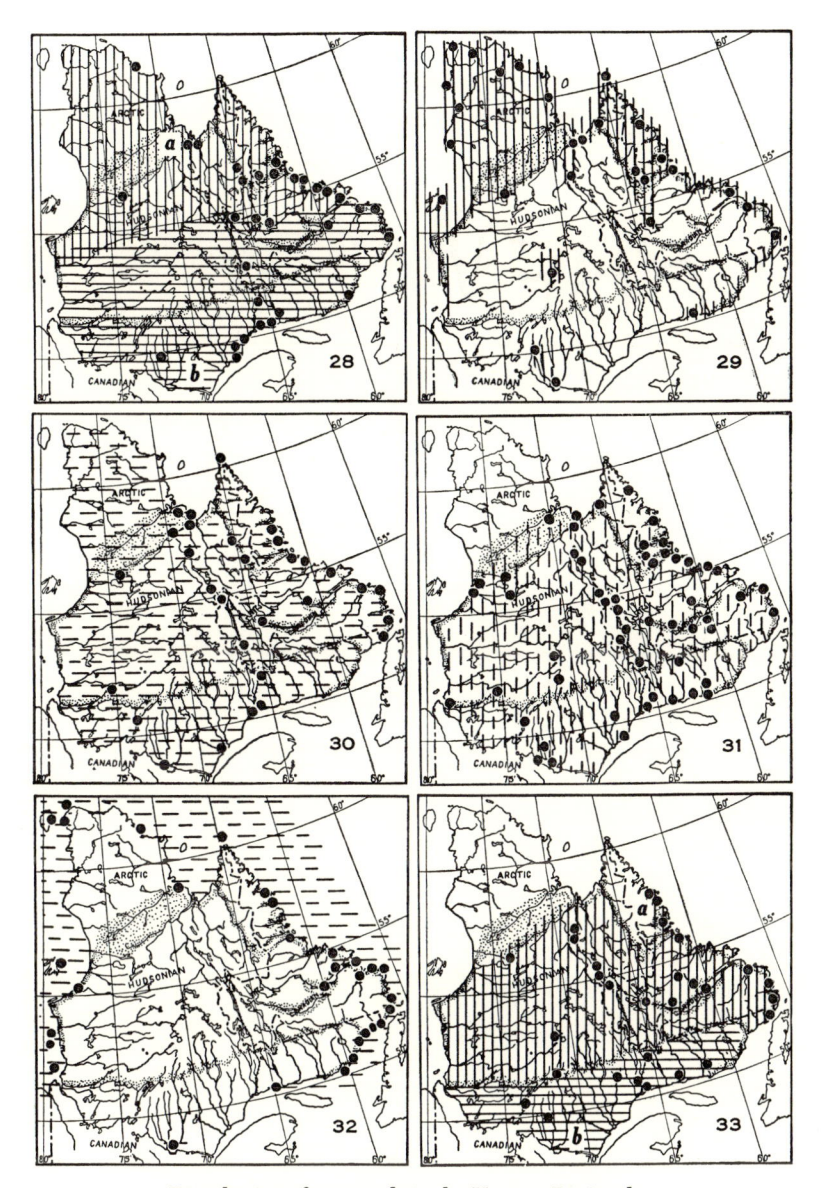

Distribution of mammals in the Ungava Peninsula:

Map 28.—a, *Canis lupis labradorius*; b, *C. l. lycaon*.
Map 29.—*Alopex lagopus ungava*.
Map 30.—*Vulpes fulva bangsi*.
Map 31.—*Euarctos americanus americanus*.
Map 32.—*Thalarctos maritimus*.
Map 33.—a, *Martes americana brumalis*; b, *M. a. americana*.

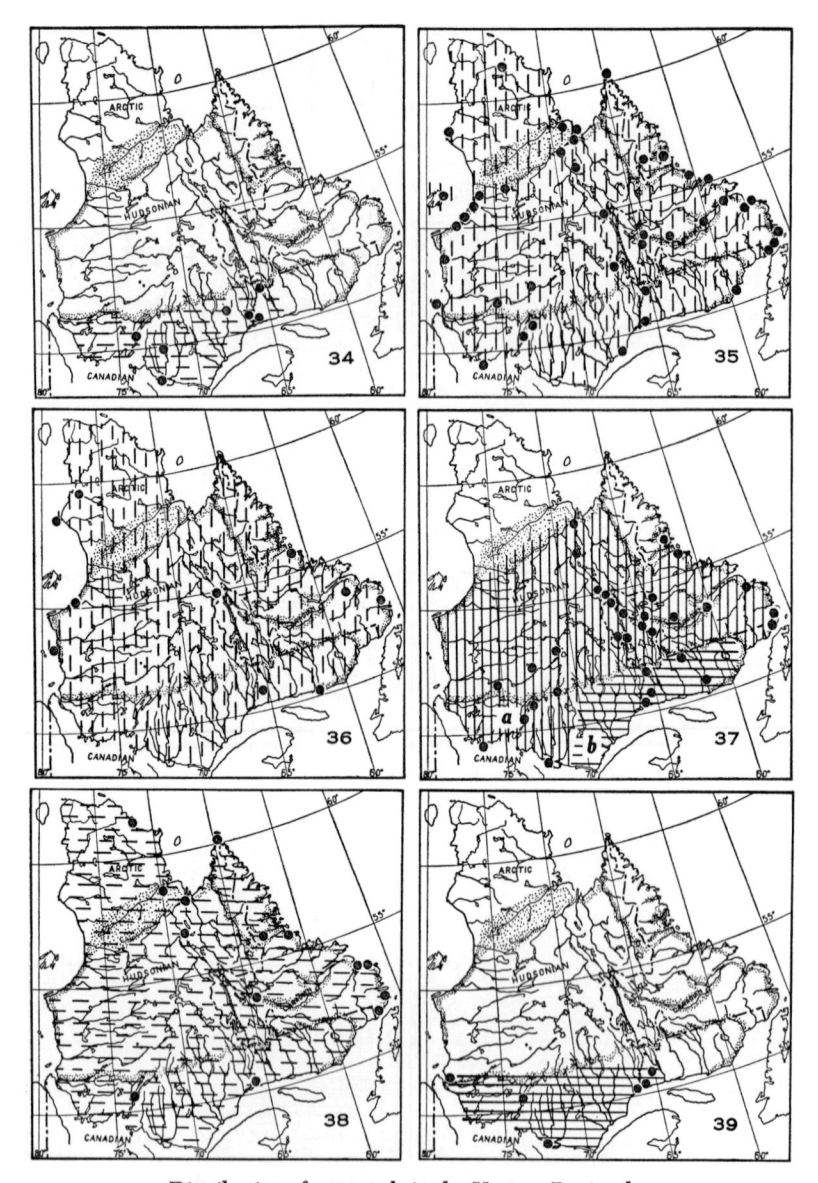

Distribution of mammals in the Ungava Peninsula:

MAP 34.—*Martes pennanti pennanti.*
MAP 35.—*Mustela erminea richardsonii.*
MAP 36.—*Mustela rixosa rixosa.*
MAP 37.—a, *Mustela vison lowii;* b, *M. v. vison.*
MAP 38.—*Gulo luscus luscus.*
MAP 39.—*Mephitis mephitis mephitis.*

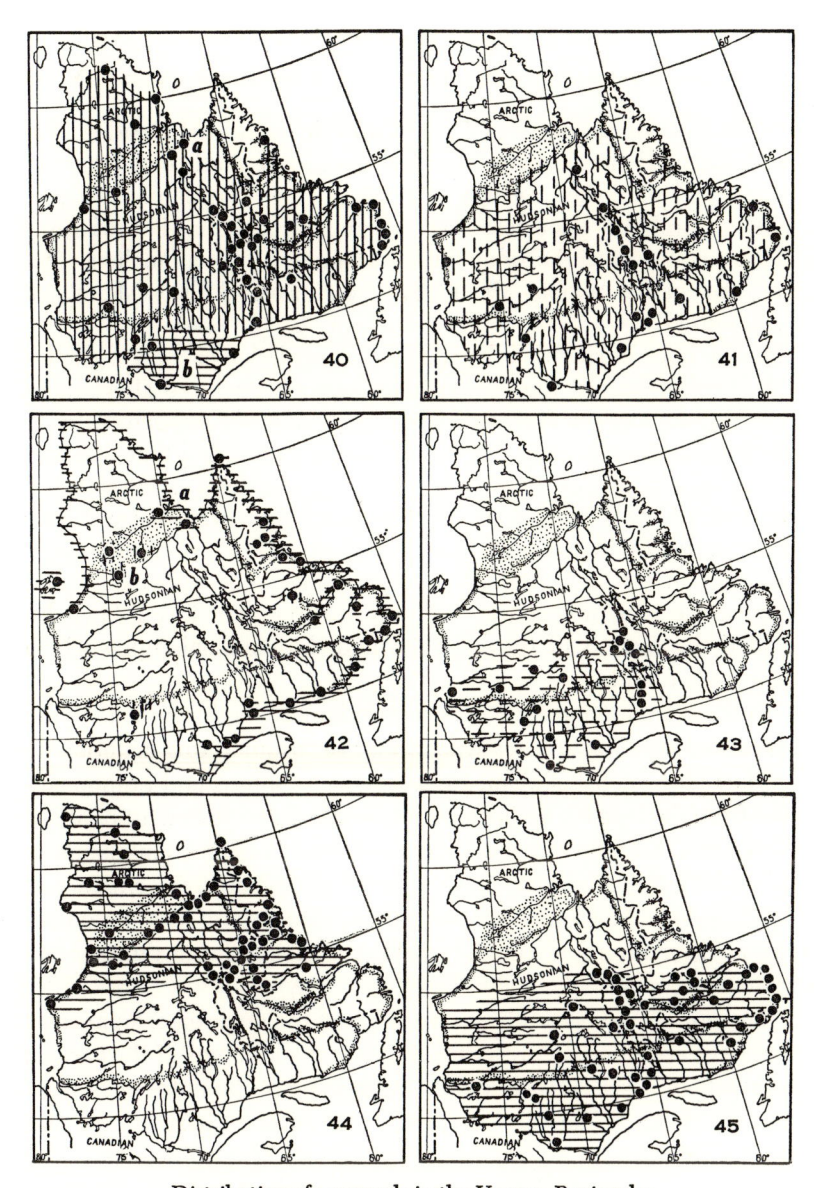

Distribution of mammals in the Ungava Peninsula:
MAP 40.—a, *Lutra canadensis chimo*; b, *L. c. canadensis*.
MAP 41.—*Lynx canadensis canadensis*.
MAP 42.—a, *Phoca vitulina concolor*; b, *P. v. mellonae* and other land-locked populations (status undetermined).
MAP 43.—*Alces alces americana*.
MAP 44.—*Rangifer caboti*.
MAP 45.—*Rangifer caribou caribou*.

A Systematic List of Mammalian Ectoparasites, with Host Records, from the Ungava Peninsula

"The eastern provinces of Canada and the coast of Labrador have been singularly neglected with reference to systematic collecting [of fleas], and published records of fleas are few" (Holland, 1949:5). There is probably good reason to complain of a similar lack of information concerning the other principal groups of mammalian ectoparasites of the region—the mites (Acarina) and the sucking lice (Anoplura).

In the hope of slightly advancing our knowledge of the geographical distribution and the host relationships of the three above-mentioned groups in the Ungava Peninsula, I carefully inspected almost every mammal specimen that came into my hands and that was preserved as a study skin. The search for ectoparasites was rewarded in the case of every species except the following: *Microsorex, Lepus americanus, Erethizon,* and *Euarctos.* Certain families of mites represented in the collection—the Phytoseiidae, Glycyphagidae, and Camisiidae—are not considered parasitic; nevertheless I have included the records of these species and the mammals upon which they were found.

In the Introduction (p. 30) acknowledgment has been made to the specialists on ectoparasites who kindly determined this material.

The following list of about 16 Acarina, 3 Anoplura, and 7 Siphonaptera from the Ungava Peninsula may be compared with a list of about 17 Acarina, 3 Anoplura, and 5 Siphonaptera obtained from mammals in southwestern Keewatin in a six-month period of 1947 (*cf.* Harper, 1956:80–84). At least ten species are common to both lists, but one or two of these are represented by different subspecies in the separate regions.

The present list is merely a summation of the notes on ectoparasites that have appeared on preceding pages in the accounts of the various mammalian hosts. It will be noted that some of the mites have been recorded from as many as four, five, or six different host species, and from a slightly larger number of different host subspecies. The earliest and latest dates of collection of the various mites, sucking lice, and fleas from each host species or subspecies are added to the record. Their seasonal incidence may be of some interest or possible significance.

The sequence of species in Acarina is that of Baker and Wharton

(1952); in Anoplura, that of Ferris (1951); and in Siphonaptera, that of Holland (1949).

Host records constituting additions to those supplied by Keegan (1951) for mites of the subfamily Haemogamasinae, by Ferris for the Anoplura, and by Holland (1949; 1958) for the Siphonaptera, are indicated as follows: for the subspecies, by one asterisk; for the species, by two asterisks; and for the genus, by three asterisks. No compendium of host records for the North American Acarina as a whole seems to be available.

Order ACARINA (mites)

Family Spinturnicidae

Spinturnix sp.:
   Myotis lucifugus lucifugus (September 3)

Family Haemogamasidae

Haemogamasus alaskensis Ewing:
   ***Sorex cinereus miscix* (May 29)
   ***Synaptomys borealis medioximus* (June 16)
   Clethrionomys gapperi proteus (July 4 to September 10)
   Clethrionomys gapperi ungava (July 27 and 28)
   Microtus pennsylvanicus enixus (July 16 and 18)

Haemogamasus ambulans (Thorell):
   Clethrionomys gapperi proteus (July 14 and August 17)
   Clethrionomys gapperi ungava (July 24)
   ***Phenacomys ungava crassus* (July 18)
   **Microtus pennsylvanicus enixus* (September 13)

Family Dermanyssidae

Hirstionyssus isabellinus (Oudemans):
   Dicrostonyx hudsonius (August 13)
   Clethrionomys gapperi proteus (August 17)
   Clethrionomys gapperi ungava (July 22 to 28)
   Phenacomys ungava ungava (July 24)
   Phenacomys ungava crassus (July 18)
   Microtus pennsylvanicus enixus (July 4)

Ichoronyssus britannicus Radford:
   Myotis lucifugus lucifugus (September 2 and 3)

Family Phytoseiidae (genus?) (non-parasitic)

   Clethrionomys gapperi proteus (July 3 and September 27)
   Clethrionomys gapperi ungava (July 27)

Family Laelaptidae

Laelaps alaskensis Grant:
   Myotis lucifugus lucifugus (September 2)
   Dicrostonyx hudsonius (August 13)
   Synaptomys borealis medioximus (June 16 and July 17)
   Clethrionomys gapperi proteus (July 21 to September 14)

Clethrionomys gapperi ungava (July 27)
Phenacomys ungava ungava (July 24)
Phenacomys ungava crassus (July 18)
Microtus pennsylvanicus enixus (June 15 to September 10)

Laelaps kochi Oudemans:
Dicrostonyx hudsonius (August 13)
Clethrionomys gapperi proteus (July 21 to September 17)
Microtus pennsylvanicus enixus (June 14 to September 13)
Ondatra zibethicus aquilonius (August 20)
Mustela vison lowii (September 21)

Laelaps multispinosus Banks:
Ondatra zibethicus aquilonius (August 20)

Laelaps sp.
Myotis lucifugus lucifugus (September 3)
Clethrionomys gapperi proteus (July 21)

Haemolaelaps glasgowi (Ewing):
***Synaptomys borealis medioximus* (June 16 and July 17)
**Clethrionomys gapperi proteus* (July 14 to September 17)
**Clethrionomys gapperi ungava* (July 22 and 24)
****Phenacomys ungava ungava* (July 24)
**Microtus pennsylvanicus enixus* (June 15 to July 18)

Family Glycyphagidae (non-parasitic)

Dermacarus sp.:
Clethrionomys gapperi proteus (August 19 to September 17)
Clethrionomys gapperi ungava (July 27 and 31)
Microtus pennsylvanicus enixus (July 28 and September 13)
Ondatra zibethicus aquilonius (August 20)

Suborder Sarcoptiformes

Superfamily Analgesoidea (not det.)

Clethrionomys gapperi proteus (September 27)—adventitious
Mustela vison lowii (September 21)—adventitious

Family Camisiidae (non-parasitic)

Camisia sp.:
Microtus pennsylvanicus enixus (June 27)

Nothrus sp.:
Clethrionomys gapperi proteus (September 13)

Heminothrus sp.:
Microtus pennsylvanicus enixus (July 27)

Order ANOPLURA (sucking lice)

Family Hoplopleuridae

Hoplopleura acanthopus (Burmeister):
**Clethrionomys gapperi gapperi* (May 24 and 25)
**Clethrionomys gapperi proteus* (June 20 to September 27)
**Clethrionomys gapperi ungava* (July 22 to 31)
**Microtus pennsylvanicus enixus* (June 14 to September 13)

Hoplopleura sciuricola Ferris:
  *Tamiasciurus hudsonicus ungavensis (September 30)
Polyplax borealis Ferris:
  ***Clethrionomys gapperi proteus* (July 3 to 18)
  ***Clethrionomys gapperi ungava* (July 27)

Order SIPHONAPTERA (fleas)

Family Hystrichopsyllidae

Corrodopsylla curvata curvata (Rothschild):
  *Sorex cinereus miscix (May 29 and June 1)

Family Ceratophyllidae

Opisodasys pseudarctomys (Baker):
  *Glaucomys sabrinus makkovikensis (September 7)
Orchopeas caedens durus (Jordan):
  *Tamiasciurus hudsonicus ungavensis (August 1 and September 30)
Malaraeus penicilliger athabascae Holland:
  Clethrionomys gapperi proteus (June 20 to August 17)
  Clethrionomys gapperi ungava (July 27 and 28)
Megabothris asio asio (Baker):
  ****Synaptomys borealis medioximus* (July 17)
  *Microtus pennsylvanicus enixus (September 10)
Megabothris quirini (Rothschild):
  Clethrionomys gapperi gapperi (May 24 and 25)
  *Clethrionomys gapperi proteus (July 9 and 14)
  *Clethrionomys gapperi ungava (July 24)

Family Ischnopsyllidae

Myodopsylla insignis (Rothschild):
  Myotis lucifugus lucifugus (September 2)

Literature Cited

Abbe, Ernst C.
  1955. Vascular plants of the Hamilton River area, Labrador. Contrib. Gray Herbarium Harvard Univ. 176:1–44, 2 figs., 2 maps.
Addy, C. E., L. D. Cool, G. F. Boyer, H. R. Webster, and R. Mosher.
  1950? Waterfowl breeding ground surveys in eastern Canada. U. S. Fish and Wildlife Service and Canadian Wildlife Service, Spl. Sci. Rept. Wildlife 8:80/84, 1 map.
Allen, Glover M.
  1914. The barren-ground caribou of Labrador. Proc. New England Zoöl. Club 4:103–107, 3 figs.
  1919. The American Collared Lemmings (Dicrostonyx). Bull. Mus. Comp. Zoöl. 62(13):509–540, 1 pl.
  1920. Hoy's shrew in Labrador. Jour. Mammalogy 1(3):139.
  1927. Dichromatism in a litter of red-backed mice. Jour. Mammalogy 8(3):248.
  1942. Extinct and vanishing mammals of the Western Hemisphere with the marine species of all the oceans. Am. Comm. Internat. Wild Life Protection Spl. Publ. 11:xv+620, 1 pl., 27 figs.
Allen, Glover M., and Manton Copeland.
  1924. Mammals from the MacMillan Expedition to Baffin Land. Jour. Mammalogy 5(1):7–12.
Allen, J. A.
  1910. The Black Bear of Labrador. Bull. Am. Mus. Nat. Hist. 28(1):1–6.
Anderson, Rudolph Martin.
  1934. Mammals of the Eastern Arctic and Hudson Bay. Canada's Eastern Arctic, Dept. Interior:67–108, 8 figs., 2 maps.
  1939. Mammals of the Province of Quebec. Provancher Soc. Nat. Hist. Canada Ann. Rept. 1938:50–114, 1 map.
  1940. Mammifères de la province de Québec. Soc. Provancher Hist. Nat. Canada Rapport Annuel 1939:37–111, 1 map.
  1942a. Canadian voles of the genus *Phenacomys* with description of two new Canadian subspecies. Canadian Field-Naturalist 56(4):56–61, 1 fig.
  1942b. Six additions to the list of Quebec mammals, with descriptions of four new forms. Provancher Soc. Nat. Hist. Canada Ann. Rept. 1941:31–43.
  1943. Summary of the large wolves of Canada, with description of three new arctic races. Jour. Mammalogy 24(3):386–393, 1 map.
  1945. Three mammals of the weasel family (Mustelidae) added to the Quebec list with descriptions of two new forms. Provancher Soc. Nat. Hist. Canada Ann. Rept. 1944:56–61.
  1947. Catalogue of Canadian recent mammals. Nat. Mus. Canada Bull. 102:v+238, 1 map, "1946."
  1948. A survey of Canadian mammals of the north. Prov. Quebec Assoc. Protection Fish and Game Ann. Rept.:9–17, 1 map.
Anderson, R. M., and A. L. Rand.
  1943a. Variation in the porcupine (genus *Erethizon*) in Canada. Canadian Jour. Research 21:292–309, 4 figs., 1 map.

1943b. A new lemming mouse (*Synaptomys*) from Manitoba with notes on some other forms. Canadian Field-Naturalist 57(6):101–103.

1945. The varying lemming (genus *Dicrostonyx*) in Canada. Jour. Mammalogy 26(3):301–306.

ANDERSON, WILLIAM ASHLEY.

1959. The angel of Hudson Bay. The true story of Maude Watt and her courageous husband, who saved a people from extinction. Saturday Evening Post 231:24,80–82, 3 figs., January 24.

ANONYMOUS.

1948. Lemming. Prov. Quebec Assoc. Protection Fish and Game Ann. Rept.:35.

AUDUBON, JOHN JAMES, AND JOHN BACHMAN.

1846. The viviparous quadrupeds of North America. Vol. 1. New York: xv+389.

AUDUBON, MARIA R.

1897. Audubon and his journals. Vol. 1. New York:xiv+532, 21 pls., 1 fig.

AUSTIN, OLIVER L., JR.

1932. The birds of Newfoundland Labrador. Mem. Nuttall Ornith. Club 7:[1]+229, 2 maps.

BAILEY, VERNON.

1897. Revision of the American voles of the genus *Evotomys*. Proc. Biol. Soc. Washington 11:113–138, 1 pl.

1898. Descriptions of eleven new species and subspecies of voles. Proc. Biol. Soc. Washington 12:85–90.

1900. Revision of American voles of the genus *Microtus*. U. S. Dept. Agric., N. Am. Fauna 17:1–88, 5 pls., 17 figs.

BAILEY, VERNON, AND J. KENNETH DOUTT.

1942. Two new beavers from Labrador and New Brunswick. Jour. Mammalogy 23(1):86–88.

BAKER, EDWARD W., AND G. W. WHARTON.

1952. An introduction to acarology. New York:xiii+465, 1 pl., 377 figs.

BANFIELD, A. W. F.

1949. The present status of North American caribou. Trans. Fourteenth N. Am. Wildlife Conf.:477–491, 2 maps.

1957. Records of two microtine rodents from the Quebec tundra. Canadian Field-Naturalist 70(2):99, "1956."

1960a. The distribution of the barren-ground grizzly bear in northern Canada. Nat. Mus. Canada Bull. 166:47–59, 3 maps.

1960b. Some noteworthy accessions to the National Museum mammal collection. Nat. Mus. Canada Nat. Hist. Papers 6:1–2.

BANFIELD, A. W. F., AND J. S. TENER.

1958. A preliminary study of the Ungava caribou. Jour. Mammalogy 39(4):560–573.

BANGS, OUTRAM.

1896a. On a small collection of mammals from Lake Edward, Quebec. Proc. Biol. Soc. Washington 10:45–52.

1896b. Preliminary description of a new vole from Labrador. Am. Naturalist 30:1051.

1897. On a small collection of mammals from Hamilton Inlet, Labrador. Proc. Biol. Soc. Washington 11:235–240, 1 pl., 1 fig.
1898a. The eastern races of the American Varying Hare, with description of a new subspecies from Nova Scotia. Proc. Biol. Soc. Washington 12:77–82.
1898b. A list of the mammals of Labrador. Am. Naturalist 32:489–507, 1 fig.
1898c. A new rock vole from Labrador. Proc. Biol. Soc. Washington 12:187–188.
1899. Notes on some mammals from Black Bay, Labrador. Proc. New England Zoöl. Club 1:9–18.
1900. Three new rodents from southern Labrador. Proc. New England Zoöl. Club 2:35–41.
1912. List of the mammals of Labrador. In: Wilfred T. Grenfell and others, Labrador, the country and the people, appendix 4:458–468. New York.

BARTRAM, EDWIN B.
1954. Mosses of the Ungava Peninsula, northeastern Canada. Bryologist 57(4):273–278.

BATEMAN, BOB.
1953. Observations on the natural history of the Leaf Bay–Fort Chimo region, Ungava, Quebec. Intermediate Naturalist 8:1–7, 1 pl.

BELL, ROBERT.
1879. Report on exploration of the east coast of Hudson's Bay 1877. Geol. Survey Canada Rept. Progress 1877–78:[1], 1C–37C, 6 pls., 3 figs., 1 map.
1884. Observations on the geology, mineralogy, zoology and botany of the Labrador coast, Hudson's Strait and Bay [made in 1884]. Geol. and Nat. Hist. Survey Canada Rept. Progress 1882–83–84:1DD–62DD, 2 pls.
1886. Observations on the geology, zoology and botany of Hudson's Strait and Bay, made in 1885. Geol. and Nat. Hist. Survey Canada Ann. Rept. 1 (n. s.):1DD–27DD, 2 pls., 3 figs., 1 map.
1895. The Labrador Peninsula. Scottish Geog. Mag. 11(7):335–361, 7 pls., 1 map.

BINNEY, GEORGE.
1929. Hudson Bay in 1928. Geog. Jour. 74(1):1–27, 4 pls., 1 map.

BLAIR, W. FRANK.
1939. A swimming and diving meadow vole. Jour. Mammalogy 20(3):375.

BOURQUE, FIRMIN.
1958. Flying squads and poachers. (Abstract.) Northeastern Wildlife Conf., Montreal, January, 1958:93–94.

BRYANT, HENRY G.
1894. A journey to the Grand Falls of Labrador. Geog. Club Philadelphia Bull. 1(2):37–86, 8 pls., 2 maps.
1913. An exploration in southeastern Labrador. Geog. Soc. Philadelphia Bull. 11(1):1–15, 10 figs., 1 map.

BURT, WILLIAM HENRY.
1938. A new water-shrew (*Sorex palustris*) from Labrador. Occas. Papers Mus. Zool. Univ. Michigan 383:1–2.
1946. The mammals of Michigan. Ann Arbor:xv+288, 13 pls., 107 figs., 67 maps.
1958. Some distribution records of mammals from Hudson Bay. Jour. Mammalogy, 39(2):291.

CABOT, WILLIAM B.
1912a. In northern Labrador. Boston:xii+292, 48 pls., 2 maps.
1912b. The Indians. In: Wilfred T. Grenfell and others, Labrador, the country and the people:184–225, 5 pls. New York.
1920. Labrador. London:xiii+354, 48 pls., 2 maps.

CAMERON, AUSTIN W.
1950. A new chipmunk (*Tamias*) from Ontario and Quebec. Jour. Mammalogy 31(3):347–348.

CAMERON, AUSTIN W., AND WILLIAM A. MORRIS.
1951. The mammals of the Lake Mistassini and Lake Albanel regions, Quebec. Nat. Mus. Canada Bull. 123:120–130.

CAMERON, AUSTIN W., AND PHILIP A. ORKIN.
1950. Mammals of the Lake St. John region, Quebec. Nat. Mus. Canada Bull. 118:95–108.

CARTWRIGHT, GEORGE.
1792. A journal of transactions and events, during a residence of sixteen years on the coast of Labrador .... Newark [England]: 1:xvi+[6]+287, 1 pl., 2 maps; 2:x+505; 3:x+248+15.

CAYLEY, EDWARD.
1863. Up the River Moisie. Trans. Liter. and Hist. Soc. Quebec, n. s., 1, pt. 1:75–92.

CHAMBERS, E. T. D.
1896. The Ouananiche and its Canadian environment. New York:xxii+357, illus.

CLEMENT, ROLAND C.
1949. Labrador notes on gyrfalcons. Bull. Massachusetts Audubon Soc. 33(1):371–374, 1 fig.

COMEAU, NAPOLEON A.
1923. Life and sport on the North Shore of the lower St. Lawrence and Gulf. Ed. 2. Quebec:1–440, 16 pls., 3 figs., 1 map. (Original edition in 1909; third in 1954.)

COMEAU, NÖEL M.
1940. Notes préliminaires sur la présence du *Canis tundrarum ungavanensis*, n. ssp. dans la province de Québec. Annales Assoc. Canadienne-Française Avancement Sciences 6:121–122.

COUPER, WILLIAM.
1868. Investigations [in 1867] of a naturalist between Mingan and Watchicouti, Labrador. Quebec:1–14.
1877. Notes on mammals of Canada. Forest and Stream 8(19):299–300.

Cowan, Ian McTaggart.
  1955. Wildlife conservation in Canada. Jour. Wildlife Management 19(2): 161–176.
Crisler, Lois.
  1958. Arctic wild. New York:xv+301, 32 pls.
Cross, E. C.
  1938. *Synaptomys borealis* from Godbout, Quebec. Jour. Mammalogy 19(3):378.
Davis, David E.
  1936. Status of *Microtus enixus* and *Microtus terraenovae*. Jour. Mammalogy 17(3):290–291.
Dix, W. L.
  1956. Lichens and hepatics of the Ungava Peninsula. Bryologist 59(1): 43–50.
Doan, K. H., and C. W. Douglas.
  1953. Beluga of the Churchill region of Hudson Bay. Fisheries Research Board Canada Bull. 98:[4]+27, 7 figs., 1 map.
Doutt, J. Kenneth.
  1939. The expedition to Hudson Bay. Carnegie Mag. 12(8):227–236, 6 figs., 2 maps.
  1942. A review of the genus *Phoca*. Annals Carnegie Mus. 29(4):61–125, 12 pls., 8 figs., 5 maps.
  1954. Observations on mammals along the east coast of Hudson Bay and the interior of Ungava. Annals Carnegie Mus. 33(14):235–249.
Dunbar, M. J.
  1948. Caribou in the Ungava. Prov. Quebec Assoc. Protection Fish and Game Ann. Rept.:18–19, 1 map.
  1949. The Pinnipedia of the Arctic and Subarctic. Fisheries Research Board Canada Bull. 85:1–22.
  1952. The Ungava Bay problem. Arctic 5(1):4–14, 5 figs., 1 map.
Dunbar, M. J., and H. H. Hildebrand.
  1952. Contribution to the study of the fishes of Ungava Bay. Jour. Fisheries Research Board Canada 9(2):83–128, 1 fig.
Durgin, George Francis.
  1908. Letters from Labrador. Concord, N. H.:1–117, 8 pls.
Eidmann, H.
  1935. Zur Kenntnis der Säugetierfauna von Südlabrador. Zeitschr. f. Säugetierkunde 10:39–61, 1 fig., 8 maps.
Ekblaw, W. Elmer.
  1926. Ungava and Labrador. In: Victor E. Shelford (editor), Naturalist's guide to the Americas:102–111. Baltimore.
Eklund, Carl R.
  1957. Bird and mammal notes from the interior Ungava Peninsula. Canadian Field-Naturalist 70(2):69–76, 1 map, "1956."
Eklund, Carl R., and Leon D. Cool.
  1949. Waterfowl breeding ground survey in the Ungava Peninsula, Quebec, 1949. U. S. Fish and Wildlife Service and Dominion Wildlife Service, Spl. Sci. Rept. Wildlife 2:19–23, 1 map.

ELTON, CHARLES S.
    1942. Voles, mice and lemmings. Oxford:[iii]+496, 1 pl., 14 figs., 8 maps.
    1954. Further evidence about the barren-ground grizzly bear in northeast Labrador and Quebec. Jour. Mammalogy 35(3):345–357, 1 map.

FERRIS, G. F. (with the collaboration of CHESTER J. STOVANOVICH).
    1951. The sucking lice. Mem. Pacific Coast Entom. Soc. 1:iii–ix, 1–320, 124 figs.

FETHERSTON, K.
    1947. Geographic variation in the incidence of occurrence of the blue phase of the Arctic fox in Canada. Canadian Field-Naturalist 61(1):15–18, 1 map.

FLAHERTY, ROBERT J.
    1918. Two traverses across Ungava Peninsula, Labrador. Geog. Rev. 6(2): 116–132, 12 figs., 1 map.

FLAHERTY, ROBERT J., in collaboration with FRANCES HUBBARD FLAHERTY.
    1924. My Eskimo friends. "Nanook of the North." Garden City, N. Y.: [11]+170, 18 pls., 6 maps.

FOSTER, J. B.
    1956. The Phenacomys vole in eastern Canada. Ontario Field Biologist 10: 18–22.

FRAZER, JOHN E.
    1950. Labrador winter notes, 1950. Arctic 3(2):126.

FREUCHEN, PETER.
    1935. Mammals. Part 2. Field notes and biological observations. Rept. Fifth Thule Exped. 1921–24, 2 (4/5):68–278, 1 map.

FULLER, W. A.
    1951. Natural history and economic importance of the muskrat in the Athabasca-Peace Delta, Wood Buffalo Park. Canadian Wildlife Service, Wildlife Management Bull. ser. 1, 2:[1], 1–82, 40 figs., 2 maps.

GABRIELSON, IRA N., AND BRUCE S. WRIGHT.
    1951. Notes on the birds of the Fort Chimo, Ungava district. Canadian Field-Naturalist 65(4):127–140, 3 figs.

GOLDMAN, EDWARD A.
    1944. Classification of wolves. Part 2 in: Stanley P. Young and Edward A. Goldman, The wolves of North America:387–636, 44 pls., 1 map. Washington.

GRENFELL, WILFRED T.
    1930. A Labrador doctor. The autobiography of Wilfred Thomason Grenfell. 13th impression. Boston and New York:[5]+441, 24 pls.

GRENFELL, WILFRED T., AND OTHERS.
    1922. Labrador, the country and the people. New ed. New York:xxvi+529, 47 pls., 19 figs., 6 maps.

GRINNELL, JOSEPH, JOSEPH S. DIXON, AND JEAN M. LINSDALE.
    1937. Fur-bearing mammals of California: their natural history, systematic status, and relations to man. Vol. 1. Berkeley:xii+375, 7 pls., 125 figs., 13 maps.

HAGMEIER, EDWIN M.
    1958. Inapplicability of the subspecies concept to North American marten. Systematic Zool. 7(1):1–7, 8 maps.

HALL, E. RAYMOND.
  1951a. A synopsis of the North American Lagomorpha. Univ. Kansas Publ., Mus. Nat. Hist., 5(10):119–202, 53 figs., 15 maps.
  1951b. American weasels. Univ. Kansas Publ., Mus. Nat. Hist., 4:1–466, 41 pls., 22 figs., 9 maps.
HALL, E. RAYMOND, AND E. LENDELL COCKRUM.
  1953. A synopsis of the North American microtine rodents. Univ. Kansas Publ., Mus. Nat. Hist., 5(27):373–498, 120 figs., 29 maps.
HALL, E. RAYMOND, AND KEITH R. KELSON.
  1959. The mammals of North America. New York: 1:xxx+546+79, 380 figs., 320 maps; 2:i–viii, 547–1083+79, 362 figs., 179 maps.
HAMILTON, WILLIAM J., JR.
  1937. Growth and life span of the field mouse. Am. Naturalist 71:500–507, 4 figs.
  1940. Life and habits of field mice. Sci. Monthly 50:425–434, 10 figs.
HANTZSCH, BERNHARD.
  1932. Contributions to the knowledge of extreme north-eastern Labrador. (Translated by M. B. A. Anderson.) [Two installments.] Canadian Field-Naturalist 46(1):7–12; (2):34–36.
HARE, F. KENNETH.
  1950. Climate and zonal divisions of the boreal forest formation in eastern Canada. Geog. Rev. 40(4):615–635, 6 figs., 6 maps.
  1952. The Labrador frontier. Geog. Rev. 42(3):405–424, 7 figs., 4 maps.
  1959. A photo-reconnaissance survey of Labrador-Ungava. [Canada] Dept. Mines and Technical Surveys, Geog. Branch Mem. 6. Ottawa: 1–83, 14 pls., 11 maps.
HARE, F. KENNETH, AND REGINALD G. TAYLOR.
  1956. The position of certain forest boundaries in southern Labrador-Ungava. Geog. Bull. 8:51–73, 6 figs., 7 maps.
HARPER, FRANCIS.
  1928. Miller and Allen's "American bats of the genera *Myotis* and *Pizonyx*": a review. Bull. Boston Soc. Nat. Hist. 49:13–15, 1 fig.
  1929. Notes on mammals of the Adirondacks. New York State Mus. Handbook 8:51–118, 17 figs.
  1932. Mammals of the Athabaska and Great Slave Lakes region. Jour. Mammalogy 13(1):19–36, 3 pls.
  1955. The Barren Ground Caribou of Keewatin. Univ. Kansas Mus. Nat. Hist. Misc. Publ. 6:1–163, 28 figs., 1 map.
  1956. The mammals of Keewatin. Univ. Kansas Mus. Nat. Hist. Misc. Publ. 12:1–94, 6 pls., 8 figs., 1 map.
  1958. Birds of the Ungava Peninsula. Univ. Kansas Mus. Nat. Hist. Misc. Publ. 17:3–171, 6 pls., 26 maps.
  MS. Changes in climate, faunal distribution, and life zones in the Ungava Peninsula.
HAWKES, E. W.
  1916. The Labrador Eskimo. Canada Dept. Mines, Geol. Survey Mem. 91:x+165, 35 pls., 32 figs., 1 map.
HILDEBRAND, HENRY.
  1949. Notes on an abundance of shrews (*Sorex cinereus cinereus*) and

other small mammals in the Ungava Bay region of far northern Quebec. Jour. Mammalogy 30(3):309–311.

HINTON, MARTIN A. C.
 1926. Monograph of the voles and lemmings (Microtinae)—living and extinct. Vol. 1. London:xvi+488+[xv], 15 pls., 110 figs.

HOLLAND, GEORGE P.
 1949. The Siphonaptera of Canada. Canada Dept. Agric. Tech. Bull. 70: 1–306, 42 pls., 44 maps.
 1958. Distribution patterns of northern fleas (Siphonaptera). Proc. Tenth Internat. Congress Entomology 1 (1956):645–658, 6 maps.

HOLLISTER, N.
 1911. A systematic synopsis of the muskrats. U. S. Dept. Agric., N. Am. Fauna 32:1–47, 5 pls., 1 map.
 1913. A synopsis of the American minks. Proc. U. S. Nat. Mus. 44:471–480.

HOPKINS, G. H.
 1949. Host-associations of lice of mammals. Proc. Zool. Soc. London 119, pt. 2:387–604.

HOWELL, A. BRAZIER.
 1926. Voles of the genus *Phenacomys*. U. S. Dept. Agric., N. Am. Fauna 48:iv+66, 7 pls., 6 figs., 5 maps.
 1927. Revision of the American lemming mice (genus *Synaptomys*). U. S. Dept. Agric., N. Am. Fauna 50:ii+38, 2 pls., 6 figs., 5 maps.
 1935. Observations on the white whale. Jour. Mammalogy 16(2):155–156.

HOWELL, ARTHUR H.
 1915. Revision of the American marmots. U. S. Dept. Agric., N. Am. Fauna 37:1–80, 15 pls., 3 maps.
 1918. Revision of the American flying squirrels. U. S. Dept. Agric., N. Am. Fauna 44:1–64, 7 pls., 4 maps.
 1929. Revision of the American chipmunks (genera *Tamias* and *Eutamias*). U. S. Dept. Agric., N. Am. Fauna 52:1–157, 10 pls., 9 maps.
 1936. A revision of the American Arctic hares. Jour. Mammalogy 17(4): 315–337, 3 figs., 1 map.

HUBBARD, MINA BENSON.
 1906. Labrador from Lake Melville to Ungava Bay. Am. Geog. Soc. Bull. 38(9):529–539, 6 pls., 1 map.
 1908. A woman's way through unknown Labrador. London:xvi+338, 50 pls., 1 map.

HUSTICH, ILMARI.
 1949. Phytogeographic regions of Labrador. Arctic 2(1):36–42, 4 maps.
 1951a. The lichen woodlands in Labrador and their importance as winter pastures for domesticated reindeer. Acta Geographica 12(1):1–48, 19 figs., 4 maps.
 1951b. Forest-botanical notes from Knob Lake area in the interior of Labrador Peninsula. (With catalogue of the vascular plants, by A. E. Porsild, pp. 201–216.) Nat. Mus. Canada Bull. 123:166–217, 13 figs., 2 maps.

Jackson, C. F.
　　1938. Notes on the mammals of southern Labrador. Jour. Mammalogy 19(4):429–434.
　　1939. A new subspecies of *Peromyscus* from the north shore of the Gulf of St. Lawrence. Proc. Biol. Soc. Washington 52:101–104.
Jackson, Hartley H. T.
　　1915. A review of the American moles. U. S. Dept. Agric., N. Am. Fauna 38:1–100, 6 pls., 21 figs., 6 maps.
　　1928. A taxonomic review of the American long-tailed shrews (genera *Sorex* and *Microsorex*). U. S. Dept. Agric., N. Am. Fauna 51:vi+238, 13 pls., 5 figs., 19 maps.
　　1939. Polar bear in Lake St. John district, Quebec. Jour. Mammalogy 20(2):253.
Jenness, John L.
　　1949. Permafrost in Canada. Arctic 2(1):13–27, 5 figs., 2 maps.
Johnson, David H.
　　1951. The water shrews of the Labrador Peninsula. Proc. Biol. Soc. Washington 64:109–113.
Keegan, Hugh L.
　　1951. The mites of the subfamily Haemogamasinae (Acari: Laelaptidae). Proc. U. S. Nat. Mus. 101:203–268, 15 figs.
Kohlmeister, Benjamin [G.], and George Kmoch.
　　1814. Journal of a voyage from Okkak, on the coast of Labrador, to Ungava Bay, west of Cape Chudleigh; undertaken to explore the coast, and visit the Esquimaux in that unknown region. London: 1–83, 1 map.
Krutzsch, Philip H.
　　1954. North American jumping mice (genus *Zapus*). Univ. Kansas Publ., Mus. Nat. Hist., 7(4):349–472, 43 figs., 4 maps.
Leslie, Lionel A. D.
　　1931. Wilderness trails in three continents. London: xvi+223, 27 pls. (This reference should have appeared in "Birds of the Ungava Peninsula," Univ. Kansas Mus. Nat. Hist. Misc. Publ. 17:158, 1958, as well as here.)
Lewis, Harrison F.
　　1923. Additional notes on birds of the Labrador Peninsula. Auk 40(1):135–137.
Lewis, Harrison F., and J. Kenneth Doutt.
　　1942. Records of the Atlantic walrus and the polar bear in or near the northern part of the Gulf of St. Lawrence. Jour. Mammalogy 23(4):365–375, 1 map.
Linsdale, Jean.
　　1927. Notes on the life history of *Synaptomys*. Jour. Mammalogy 8(1):51–54.
Löve, Doris, James Kucyniak, and Gordon Johnston.
　　1958. A plant collection from interior Quebec. Naturaliste Canadien 85 (2/3):25–69, 1 fig., 3 maps.
Low, A. P.
　　1886. Report of the Mistassini Expedition, 1884–5. Geol. and Nat. Hist. Survey Canada Ann. Rept. (n. s.) 1:1D–55D.

1890. The Mistassini region. Ottawa Naturalist 4:11–28.
1896. Report on explorations in the Labrador Peninsula along the East Main, Koksoak, Hamilton, Manicuagan and portions of other rivers, in 1892–93–94–95. Geol. Survey Canada Ann. Rept., n. s., 8, 1895: 1L–387L, 4 pls.
1897. The Labrador Peninsula. In: Trail and camp-fire, the book of the Boone and Crockett Club:15–50.
1898. Report on a traverse of the northern part of the Labrador Peninsula from Richmond Gulf to Ungava Bay. Geol. Survey Canada Ann. Rept. (n. s.) 9:1L–43L, 4 pls.

LUCAS, FREDERIC A.
1891. Explorations in Newfoundland and Labrador in 1887, made in connection with the cruise of the U. S. Fish Commission schooner *Grampus*. Rept. U. S. Nat. Mus. 1888–'89:709–728, 1 map.

McLEAN, JOHN.
1849. Notes of a twenty-five years' service in the Hudson's Bay territory. London: 1:xii+308; 2:vii+328.
1932. John McLean's notes of a twenty-five year's service in the Hudson's Bay territory. (Edited by W. S. Wallace.) Publ. Champlain Soc. 19. Toronto:xxxvi+402, 1 map. (Originally published in 1849.)

MACOUN, JAS. M.
1886. List of plants collected at Lake Mistassini, Rupert River and Rupert House, by Jas. M. Macoun, 1885. Geol. and Nat. Hist. Survey Canada Ann. Rept. (n. s.) 1, 1885:36D–44D.

MANNING, T. H.
1947. Bird and mammal notes from the east side of Hudson Bay. Canadian Field-Naturalist 60(4):71–85, 4 figs., 1 map, "1946."
1948. Preliminary report on a background study of the caribou, *Rangifer caribou caribou* (Gmelin) and *Rangifer arcticus caboti* Allen of the Labrador Peninsula and the Province of Quebec north of the St. Lawrence. Prov. Quebec Assoc. Protection Fish and Game Ann. Rept.:20–21, 1 map.

MANNING, T. H., AND A. H. MACPHERSON.
1952. Birds of the east James Bay coast between Long Point and Cape Jones. Canadian Field-Naturalist 66(1):1–35, 4 pls., 1 map.

MARTIN, N. V.
1955. Limnological and biological observations in the region of the Ungava or Chubb Crater. Jour. Fisheries Research Board Canada 12(4): 487–496, 2 figs., 2 maps.

MERRIAM, C. HART.
1882. The vertebrates of the Adirondack region, northeastern New York. [First instalment.] Trans. Linnaean Soc. New York 1:5–106.
1889. Description of fourteen new species and one new genus of North American mammals. U. S. Dept. Agric., N. Am. Fauna 2:v+52, 8 pls., 7 figs.
1898. Life zones and crop zones of the United States. U. S. Dept. Agric., Div. Biol. Survey, Bull. 10:1–79, 1 map.
1900. Preliminary revision of the North American red foxes. Proc. Washington Acad. Sci. 2:661–676, 2 pls.

MERRIAM, C. HART, VERNON BAILEY, E. W. NELSON, AND E. A. PREBLE.
    1910. Fourth provisional zone map of North America. In: Check-list of North American birds, prepared by a committee of the American Ornithologists' Union, ed. 3:frontispiece. New York.

MERRICK, ELLIOTT.
    1933. True north. New York:[5]+353, 8 pls., 1 map.

MICHAUX, ANDRÉ.
    1889. Portions of the journal of André Michaux . . . 1785 to 1796. (Edited by C. S. Sargent.) Proc. Am. Philos. Soc. 26:1–145.

MILLAIS, J. G.
    1915. The grizzly & the black bear. In: The gun at home & abroad. The big game of Asia and North America:360–383, 4 pls. London.

MILLER, GERRIT S., JR.
    1897a. Synopsis of voles of the genus *Phenacomys*. Proc. Biol. Soc. Washington 11:77–87.
    1897b. Revision of the North American bats of the family Vespertilionidae. U. S. Dept. Agric., N. Am. Fauna 13:1–140, 3 pls., 40 figs.
    1899. A new Polar Hare from Labrador. Proc. Biol. Soc. Washington 13:39–40.

MILLER, GERRIT S., JR., AND GLOVER M. ALLEN.
    1928. The American bats of the genera *Myotis* and *Pizonyx*. U. S. Nat. Mus. Bull. 144:viii+218, 1 pl.

MILLER, GERRIT S., JR., AND REMINGTON KELLOGG.
    1955. List of North American Recent mammals. U. S. Nat. Mus. Bull. 205:xii+954.

MURIE, OLAUS J.
    1926. The porcupine in northern Alaska. Jour. Mammalogy 7(2):109–112, 1 fig.
    1954. A field guide to animal tracks. Boston:xxiii+375, illus.
    1957. Wolf. Audubon Mag. 59(5):218–221, 3 figs.

NEILSON, JAMES M.
    1948. The Mistassini territory of northern Quebec. Canadian Geog. Jour. 37(4):144–157, 23 figs., 1 map.

NELSON, E. W.
    1909. The rabbits of North America. U. S. Dept. Agric., N. Am. Fauna 29:1–314, 13 pls., 3 figs., 16 maps.

O., T. J.
    1878. Caribou hunting. Forest and Stream 11(7):129–130.

ODELL, N. E.
    1933. The mountains of northern Labrador. Geog. Jour. 82(3):193–210; (4):315–325, 6 pls., 1 map.

ORD, GEORGE.
    1894. A reprint of the North American zoology, by George Ord. Being an exact reproduction of the part originally compiled by Mr. Ord for Johnson & Warner, and first published by them in their second American edition of Guthrie's geography, in 1815. . . . To which is added an appendix on the more important scientific and historic questions involved. By Samuel N. Rhoads. Haddonfield, N. J.:v–x, [1], 290–361, 1–90, 1 pl.

Osgood, Wilfred H.
    1909. Revision of the mice of the American genus *Peromyscus*. U. S. Dept. Agric., N. Am. Fauna 28:1–285, 7 pls., 13 maps.

Packard, Alpheus Spring, Jr.
    1866. List of vertebrates observed at Okak, Labrador, by Rev. Samuel Weiz, with annotations by A. S. Packard, Jr., M. D. Proc. Boston Soc. Nat. Hist. 10:264–277.
    1891. The Labrador coast. . . . New York:1–513, 4 pls., 33 figs., 13 maps.

Palmer, Ralph S.
    1954. The mammal guide: mammals of North America north of Mexico. Garden City:1–384, illus.

Payne, F. F.
    1887. Flora and fauna of Prince of Wales Sound, Hudson Straits. In: Report of the Hudson's Bay Expedition of 1886 under the command of Lieut. A. R. Gordon, R. N.:70–83. Sessional Papers Parliament of Canada 14(15).

Peterson, Randolph L.
    1947. Further observations on swimming and diving of meadow voles. Jour. Mammalogy 28(3):297–298.
    1952. A review of the living representatives of the genus *Alces*. Contrib. Royal Ontario Mus. Zool. and Palaeont. 34:[1]+30, 6 figs., 2 maps.
    1955. North American moose. Toronto:xi+280, 58 figs., 8 maps.

Polunin, Nicholas.
    1949. Arctic unfolding. London:1–348, 33 pls., 3 maps.

Pomerleau, René.
    1950. Au sommet de l'Ungava. Revue Université Laval 4(9):1–16, 2 maps.

Porsild, A. E.
    1945. Mammals of the Mackenzie delta. Canadian Field-Naturalist 59(1): 4–22.

Preble, Edward A.
    1899. Revision of the Jumping Mice of the genus *Zapus*. U. S. Dept. Agric., N. Am. Fauna 15:1–42, 1 pl., 4 figs.
    1902. A biological investigation of the Hudson Bay region. U. S. Dept. Agric., N. Am. Fauna 22:1–140, 13 pls., 1 map.
    1908. A biological investigation of the Athabaska-Mackenzie region. U. S. Dept. Agric., N. Am. Fauna 27:1–574, 21 pls., 12 figs., 8 maps.

Prichard, H. Hesketh.
    1911. Through trackless Labrador. London:xv+254, 54 pls., 1 map.

Pruitt, William O., Jr.
    1959. Snow as a factor in the winter ecology of the Barren Ground caribou (*Rangifer arcticus*). Arctic 12(3):158–179, 4 figs., 3 maps.

Quick, E. R., and A. W. Butler.
    1885. The habits of some Arvicolinae. Am. Naturalist 19:113–118, 1 pl.

Rand, A. L.
    1944a. Canadian forms of the Meadow Mouse (*Microtus pennsylvanicus*). Canadian Field-Naturalist 57 (7/8):115–123.
    1944b. The status of the fisher, *Martes pennanti* (Erxleben), in Canada. Canadian Field-Naturalist 58(3):77–81.

Ridgway, Robert.
    1912. Color standards and color nomenclature. Washington:iv+44, 53 pls.
Ross, W. Gillies.
    1957. Knob Lake on Canada's new frontier. Canadian Geog. Jour. 54(6): 238–245, 9 figs., 2 maps.
Rousseau, Jacques.
    1949. À travers l'Ungava. Mém. Jardin Botanique Montréal 4:83–131, 1 map.
Rowe, J. S.
    1959. Forest regions of Canada. Canada Dept. Northern Affairs and National Resources Bull. 123:1–71, 1 map.
Schad, G. A.
    1954. Helminth parasites of mice in northeastern Quebec and the coast of Labrador. Canadian Jour. Zoology 32(3):215–224, 8 figs., 1 map.
Scheffer, Victor B.
    1955. Body size with relation to population density in mammals. Jour. Mammalogy 36(4):493–515.
Schubert, [Gotthilf Heinrich].
    1844. Correspondenz-Nachrichten aus Labrador. b) Verzeichniss der in Labrador befindlichen Landsäugthiere. Gelehrte Anzeigen K. Bayer. Akad. Wissen. München 18(52):columns 418–421.
Sergeant, D. E., and H. D. Fisher.
    1957. The smaller Cetacea of eastern Canadian waters. Jour. Fisheries Research Board Canada 14(1):83–115, 7 figs., 1 map.
Seton, Ernest Thompson.
    1929. Lives of game animals. Garden City: 1:xxxix+[1]+640, 118 pls., 16 figs., 12 maps; 2:xvii+[1]+746, 98 pls., 27 figs., 13 maps; 3:xix+[1]+780, 96 pls., 23 figs., 10 maps; 4:xxii+[1]+949, 112 pls., 62 figs., 20 maps.
Snyder, Dana P.
    1954. Skull variation in the meadow vole (*Microtus p. pennsylvanicus*) in Pennsylvania. Annals Carnegie Mus. 33(13):201–234, 6 figs., 2 maps.
Soper, J. Dewey.
    1944. On the winter trapping of small mammals. Jour. Mammalogy 25(4): 344–353, 5 figs.
Speck, Frank G.
    1931. Montagnais-Naskapi bands and early Eskimo distribution in the Labrador peninsula. Am. Anthropologist, n. s., 33(4):557–600, 2 maps.
    1935. Naskapi: the savage hunters of the Labrador Peninsula. Norman, Okla.:3–248, 20 pls., 28 figs., 1 map.
Spencer, Miles.
    1889. Notes on the breeding habits of certain mammals, from personal observations and enquiries from Indians. In: A. P. Low, Report on explorations in James' Bay and country east of Hudson Bay . . . , appendix 3:76J–79J. Geol. and Nat. Hist. Survey Canada Ann. Rept., n. s., 3, pt. 2. (Not altogether accurate; no specific localities given.)

STAINER, JOHN.
  1938. A canoe journey in Canadian Labrador. Geog. Jour. 92(2):153–158, 2 pls., 1 map. (This reference should have appeared in "Birds of the Ungava Peninsula," Univ. Kansas Mus. Nat. Hist. Misc. publ. 17: 162, 1958, as well as here.)

STEARNS, W. A.
  1883. Notes on the natural history of Labrador. Proc. U. S. Nat. Mus. 6: 111–137.

STEPHENS, C. A.
  1872. Lynx-hunting. Philadelphia:1–3, 7–283, 8 pls.

STIRLING, E.
  1884. The grizzly bear in Labrador. Forest and Stream 22:324.

STRONG, WILLIAM DUNCAN.
  1930. Notes on mammals of the Labrador interior. Jour. Mammalogy 11(1):1–10.

TANNER, VÄINÖ.
  1947. Outlines of the geography, life & customs of Newfoundland-Labrador. Cambridge: 1:1–436, 186 figs., 23 maps; 2:437–906, 130 figs., 3 maps.

THOMAS, MORLEY K.
  1953. Climatological atlas of Canada. Ottawa:3–253, 74 charts.

THOREAU, HENRY D.
  1877. The Maine woods. Ed. 9. Boston:[3]+328.

TOWNSEND, CHARLES W.
  1913. A short trip into the Labrador Peninsula by way of the Natashquan River. Bull. Geog. Soc. Philadelphia 11(3):170–182, 4 pls.

TOWNSEND, CHARLES W., AND GLOVER M. ALLEN.
  1907. Birds of Labrador. Proc. Boston Soc. Nat. Hist. 33(7):277–428, 1 map.

TRUE, FREDERICK W.
  1894. Diagnoses of new North American mammals. Proc. U. S. Nat. Mus. 17:241–243.

TURNER, LUCIEN M.
  1885. List of the birds of Labrador, including Ungava, East Main, Moose, and Gulf districts of the Hudson Bay Company, together with the island of Anticosti. Proc. U. S. Nat. Mus. 8:233–254.
  1888a. On the Indians and Eskimos of the Ungava district, Labrador. Trans. Royal Soc. Canada 1887, 5, sect. 2:99–119.
  1888b. Physical and zoological character of the Ungava district, Labrador. Trans. Royal Soc. Canada 1887, 5, sect. 4:79–83.
  1894. Ethnology of the Ungava district, Hudson Bay Territory. Ann. Rept. Bur. Ethnology Smithsonian Institution 1889–'90:159–350, 8 pls., 135 figs.

VLADYKOV, VADIM D.
  1944. Chasse, biologie et valeur économique du Marsouin blanc ou Béluga (*Delphinapterus leucas*) du fleuve et du golfe Saint-Laurent. Département des Pêcheries Québec:1–194, 1 pl., 52 figs., 5 maps.

1946. Nourriture du Marsouin blanc ou Béluga (*Delphinapterus leucas*) du fleuve Saint-Laurent. Contrib. Département des Pêcheries Québec 17:5–155, 1 pl., 39 figs., 3 maps.

WALLACE, DILLON.
    1906. The lure of the Labrador wild. Ed. 6. New York:1–339, 16 pls., 3 maps.
    1907. The long Labrador trail. New York:xii+315, 27 pls., 2 maps.

WEAVER, RICHARD LEE.
    1940. Notes on a collection of mammals from the southern coast of the Labrador Peninsula. Jour. Mammalogy 21(4):417–422.

WETZEL, RALPH M.
    1955. Speciation and dispersal of the southern bog lemming, *Synaptomys cooperi* (Baird). Jour. Mammalogy 36(1):1–20, 4 figs., 1 map.

WHEELER, E. P., 2ND.
    1930. Journeys about Nain. Winter hunting with the Labrador Eskimo. Geog. Rev. 20(3):454–468, 8 figs., 1 map.
    1953. Notes on Pinnipedia. Jour. Mammalogy 34(2):253–255.

WRIGHT, GEORGE M., AND BEN H. THOMPSON.
    1935. Fauna of the national parks of the United States. U. S. Dept. Interior, Nat. Park Service, Fauna Series 2:viii+142, 61 figs.

YOUNG, STANLEY P.
    1944. The wolves of North America. Part 1. Their history, life habits, economic status, and control. In: Stanley P. Young and Edward A. Goldman, The wolves of North America:1–385, 74 pls., 4 figs., 8 maps. Washington.

Index

Abies balsamea, 24
Academy of Natural Sciences of Philadelphia, 30
Acarina, 30, 65, 70, 72, 74, 79, 152, 153
Agathon, Oshin, 108
Alces alces americana, 18, 20, 23, 128–129; map 43
Alder(s), 31, 33, 39, 43, 49, 58, 60, 62, 69, 85
  mountain, 24
Alectoria
  implexa, 24, 63
  ochroleuca, 24, 71
Almond, Peter, 30, 90, 128
Alnus, 69
  crispa, 24
Alopex, 109
  lagopus, 20
  lagopus ungava, 18, 21, 97–98; map 29
American Philosophical Society, 30
Analgesoidea, 117, 154
Anderson, Rudolph M., 11, 138
André, Mathieu, 95, 131
Anoplura, 30, 65, 70, 79, 152–154
Arctic Institute of North America, 5, 29
Arctostaphylos uva-ursi, 25

Baker, E. W., 30
Balsam (fir), 24, 31, 39, 41, 45, 60, 62, 89
Bangs, Outram, 11
Barrett, Ron, 90
Bat,
  Acadian, 20, 36
  Little Brown, 22, 35; map 7
Bazuk, William, 125
Bear(s),
  American Black, 20, 22, 30, 42, 93, 99–104, 107, 140; map 31; pl. 6, fig. 1
  barren ground, 105–107, 109
  (Black), 10, 105, 108
  Brown, 106–108
  cinnamon, 106
  Polar, 20, 30, 110–112; map 32; pl. 6, fig. 2
  Ungava Grizzly, 104–110
  white, 106, 111
Bearberry, common, 25, 60
Beaudet, Père J. E., 23
Beaver, 22, 112
  Labrador, 48–50; map 14
  New Brunswick, 50–51; map 14
Bell, Robert, 109
Beluga, 92; map 27
Berry, baked-apple, 24; pl. 2, fig. 1
Betula
  glandulosa, 24, 62, 71, 73, 76; pl. 7
  papyrifera, 24
Bilberry, bog, 25
Birch, 33
  canoe, 24
  dwarf, 24, 34, 37, 58, 62, 73; pl. 7
Birdseye, Clarence, 96
Bishop, John C. V., 123
Bistort, alpine, 24
Blackfish, 92
Blarina brevicauda talpoides, 18, 20, 26, 35
Blueberry, 54, 60
  low sweet, 25
Boerner, A. E., 30, 36, 38, 42, 46, 53, 82, 90, 95, 102, 116, 125, 140
Bourgeois, Alphonse, 94, 98, 125, 139; pl. 5, fig. 1
Brivoisac, Jean, 101
Buckbean, 25, 78
Bunchberry, 24, 60
Burke, M. T., 35
Burnet, Canadian, 24

Cabot, William B., 10
Calamagrostis canadensis, 24, 62
Cameron, Austin W., 11
Camisia, 79, 154
Camisiidae, 152, 154
Canis, 109
  lupus, 18, 20, 23; map 28
  lupus labradorius, 93–94; map 28
  lupus lycaon, 93, 94–97; map 28; pl. 5, figs 1–2
  tundrarum ungavanensis, 97
Carby, Antonio, 94; pl. 5, fig. 1
Carcajou, 118, 119
Carex, 24, 54, 71, 76
Caribou,
  Barren Ground, 139
  Cabot's or Labrador Barren Ground, 10, 23, 27, 30, 93, 95, 110, 118, 129–139, 144; map 44; pl. 7 and pl. 8, fig. 1
  (Eastern) Woodland, 20, 23, 29, 30, 51, 93, 95, 96, 118, 119, 124, 125, 129–131, 133, 135, 136, 139–144; map 45; pl. 8, fig. 2
Carter, T. Donald, 108
Cartwright, George, 122
Castor
  canadensis, 18, 22; map 14
  canadensis acadicus, 49, 50–51; map 14
  canadensis labradorensis, 48–50; map 14
Cat, Domestic, 64, 78
Ceratophyllidae, 155

Cestode, 89
Chamaedaphne calyculata, 25, 74
Champagne, Père Marcel, 139
Chipmunk, Quebec, 20, 41; map 11
Cinquefoil, shrubby, 24
Cladonia, 31, 54, 140
   alpestris, 24, 37, 41, 44, 60, 62, 69, 71, 73; pl. 2, fig. 2
   gracilis, 24, 73
   rangiferina, 24, 62, 73
Cleghorn, J. D., 134
Clement, Roland C., 30, 39, 85, 120, 128, 132, 133, 142; pl. 8, fig. 1
Clethrionomys, 31, 71, 78, 79, 114
   gapperi, 18–20, 22; map 19
   gapperi athabascae, 67
   gapperi gapperi, 20, 21, 60–61, 154, 155; map 19
   gapperi hudsonius, 61, 71; map 19
   gapperi proteus, 21, 56, 58, 60, 61–68, 70, 73, 76, 77, 153–155; map 19; pl. 4, fig 1
   gapperi ungava, 62, 68–71, 72, 153–155; map 19
Clintonia, yellow, 24
Clintonia borealis, 24, 31
Club-moss, 88
Coiteux, Henry L., 128
Coltsfoot, sweet, 25
Comeau, Napoleon A., 10
Condylura cristata cristata, 18, 20, 35; map 6
Coptis groenlandica, 24, 58, 64, 73
Cornus canadensis, 24, 31, 33, 58, 62, 73, 76
Corrodopsylla curvata curvata, 32, 155
Côté, Adrien, 102
Côté, Pierre, 30, 102
Craig, Jack, 36
Cranberry, mountain, 25, 31, 54, 60
Cree, 106, 110
Cristivomer namaycush, 78
Crowberry (black), 24, 54; pl. 2, fig 2
Currant, skunk, 24
Cyr, G., 128

Dandelion, 25, 54
Darveau, Robert, 30, 140; pl. 8, fig. 2
Deer-wolf, 124
Delmage, Norman, 40
Delphinapterus leucas, 9, 92–93; map 27
Dermacarus, 65, 70, 79, 83, 154
Dermanyssidae, 153
Déry,
   Alphonse, 96
   D. A., 30, 96, 110, 128
Deschampsia flexuosa, 24, 77
Desgagné, J. B., 96
Dewey, James A., 89
Dicrostonyx, 109, 110

hudsonius, 18, 21, 22, 53–57, 73, 153, 154; map 16; pl. 3, fig. 2
Dogribs (Indians), 110
Dogs, 130, 139
Dorion, Paul, 117, 128
Doutt, J. Kenneth, 11, 138
Dryas integrifolia, 24, 54
Dufresne, Cyrille, 40, 83, 141
Dwyer, Jack, 101

Eklund, Carl R., 11
Emond, Wilfrid, 78
Empetrum nigrum, 24, 62, 69, 71, 73, 74, 76
Epilobium angustifolium, 24, 62, 78
Equisetum, 34, 76
   sylvaticum, 24, 62, 74
Erethizon
   dorsatum dorsatum, 18, 20, 22, 87–92, 152; map 26; fig. 3
   dorsatum picinum, 88–91
Ermine, Richardson's, 114–115; map 35
Eskimo(s), 84, 106–108, 130, 131, 134–139
Esox lucius, 117
Euarctos
   americanus, 20, 106, 107
   americanus americanus, 18, 22, 99–104, 152; map 31; pl. 6, fig. 1
Événement-Journal, 103

Farah, Fred, 28, 30, 35, 47, 53, 101, 115
Ferguson, Roger, 85
Finlayson, Nicol, 9
Fireweed, 24, 78
Fisher(s), Eastern, 20, 92, 113–114; map 34
Flea(s), 30, 32, 36, 45, 47, 59, 60, 65, 70, 79, 152, 155
Flies,
   nostril, 136
   warble, 136
Foster, F. D., 30, 45, 49, 83, 90, 102, 128, 140
Fox,
   Blue, 97
   Cross, 99
   Labrador Red, 21, 22, 98–99; map 30
   Red, 20, 96
   Silver, 99
   Ungava Arctic, 19–21, 97–98; map 29
   White, 97
Free Library of Philadelphia, 30
Frémont, Charles, 30, 142

Gad-fly, 134
Gale, sweet, 24, 34, 85
Gallant, Rudy, 101
Gaultheria hispidula, 25

Gauthier, Henri, 111; pl. 6, fig. 2
Gelinas, Leopold, 38, 48, 90, 102
Geological Survey of Canada, 10, 17, 30, 86, 131; pl. 7
Geren, Richard, 29, 40, 122
Girardin, Robert, 29
Glaucomys
  sabrinus, 18, 20, 22; map 13
  sabrinus makkovikensis, 47–48, 155; map 13
  sabrinus sabrinus, 46–47, 48; map 13
Globicephala scammonii, 92
Glycyphagidae, 152, 154
Goldberg, Aaron, 30
Goldenrod, 25
Goldthread, 24
Grace, Charles, 35, 126
"Grampus, Great," 127
Grass,
  blue-joint, 24
  sweet, 24
Grizzly (Bear), 104–106, 108, 110
  Barren Ground, 106–108
  Labrador, 26, 106
  true (or western), 106, 107, 109, 110
  Ungava, 108–110
Gulo luscus, 20
  luscus luscus, 18, 118–119; map 38

Habenaria dilatata, 24, 34
Haemogamasidae, 153
Haemogamasinae, 153
Haemogamasus
  alaskensis, 32, 59, 65, 70, 79, 153
  ambulans, 65, 70, 74, 79, 153
Haemolaelaps glasgowi, 59, 65, 70, 72, 79, 85, 154
Hairgrass, common, 24, 77
Hall, E. Raymond, 30
Hallendy, Norman, 101
Handley, Charles O., Jr., 30, 32, 34, 38, 46, 48, 54, 55, 60–62, 69, 71, 73, 75, 81, 83, 85, 89, 118, 124
Hare,
  American Varying, 22, 37; map 9
  Arctic, 21; map 8
  Labrador Arctic, 36; map 8
  Newfoundland Arctic, 19, 37; map 8
Hare Indians, 110
Harper,
  Bertram H., 90
  David B., 76, 102, 132, 133
Harrison, J. M., 30, 130, 133; pl. 7
Heminothrus, 79, 154
Hierochloë odorata, 24, 31
Hirstionyssus, 30
  isabellinus, 55, 65, 70, 72, 74, 79, 153
Historical Society of Pennsylvania, 30
Hodgson, Duncan M., 134

Hogan, Lloyd, 36, 95, 128, 131, 139, 140
Hogg, Glenn, 90
Hood, William C., Jr., 90, 122
Hoplopleura
  acanthopus, 60, 65, 70, 79, 154
  sciuricola, 45, 155
Hoplopleuridae, 154
Horsetail, wood, 24
Huard, Leo, 100
Hubbard,
  Leonidas, Jr., 10
  Mrs. Leonidas, Jr., 10
Hudson's Bay Company, 9, 123
Hylocomium pyrenaicum, 24, 58
Hypnum crista-castrensis, 24, 60, 88
Hystrichopsyllidae, 155

Ichoronyssus, 30
  britannicus, 36, 153
Indians, 84
  (Eastern Cree), 38, 50, 51, 102, 127, 128, 130, 143
  (Montagnais), 43, 50, 105, 139–141, 144
  (Naskapi), 105–107, 125, 135
Ischnopsyllidae, 155
Ives, J. D., 133

Jackson, Garth D., 38, 45, 90, 115, 123
Jackson, Howard, 48, 98
Jays, Labrador, 44
Johnson,
  David H., 68, 80
  Phyllis T., 30

Kalmia angustifolia, 25
Kelly, Remi, 45, 49, 90, 141
Kennedy, William, 105, 109
Knotterus-Meyer, Th., 110
Koopman, Karl F., 81

Labrecque, Jean P., 23, 131
Laelaps, 36, 65, 154
  alaskensis, 36, 55, 59, 65, 70, 72, 74, 79, 153
  kochi, 55, 65, 79, 83, 117, 154
  multispinosus, 83, 154
Laelaptidae, 153
Lanius excubitor borealis, 78
Laporte, Joe, 40
Larix laricina, 24, 62, 69, 76
Lark, Northern Horned, 19
Larouche, Henry, 33, 102
Laurel, sheep, 25, 60
Leather-leaf, 25
Ledum
  decumbens, 25, 71
  groenlandicum, 24, 62, 63, 69, 71, 73, 74, 76

Lemming, Labrador Varying, 19, 21, 22, 53–57, 73; map 16; pl. 3, fig. 2
Lepus
  americanus americanus, 18, 22, 37–39, 152; map 9
  arcticus, 18, 20, 21; map 8
  arcticus bangsi, 37; map 8
  arcticus labradorius, 36, 37; map 8.
Leslie, Robert, 119
Library of Parliament, Ottawa, 30
Lice (or louse), sucking, 30, 45, 60, 65, 70, 79, 152, 154
Lichen, caribou, 24, 33, 140
Linnaea borealis var. *americana*, 25, 31, 76
Liverwort, 58
Loth, Philip, 38, 41, 82, 102, 116, 123, 139
Loucheux (Indians), 110
Loup-cervier, 124
Low, A. P., 10, 109
Lucivee, 124
Lutra, 27, 109
  canadensis, 18, 20; map 40
  canadensis canadensis, 120–121, 124; map 40
  canadensis chimo, 22, 121–124; map 40
Lycopodium annotinum, 88
Lynx, Canada, 22, 82, 124–126; map 41
Lynx canadensis canadensis, 18, 22, 124–126; map 41

Macdonald,
  D. O., 30
  R. D., 29
Macko, John, 35, 47
Malaraeus penicilliger athabascae, 65, 70, 155
Malkin, J., 99, 117
Manning, T. H., 11, 55
Mansa, Kai, 123
Mansbridge, Wallace, 95, 114, 119, 125, 139
Marmota
  monax, 18–20, 22, 41; map 10
  monax canadensis, 39–40; map 10
  monax ignava, 21, 40–41; map 10
Marten(s), 29, 32
  Eastern American, 22, 112–113, 116; map 33
  Labrador, 113; map 33
Martes
  americana, 18; map 33
  americana americana, 22, 112–113; map 33
  americana brumalis, 112, 113; map 33

pennanti pennanti, 18, 20, 113–114; map 34
McAulay, Robert, 141
McFarland, Ross, 36
McGill University, 30
McKenzie,
  Ben, 30, 48, 54, 83, 95, 102, 113, 115, 116, 118, 121, 124, 125, 131
  Francis, 23, 30, 95, 128, 131
  Peter, 106
  Sebastien, 23, 30, 32, 36, 44, 48, 50, 52, 62, 83, 90, 95, 97, 101, 108, 113, 115, 117, 118, 121, 123, 124, 128–130
  W. A., 92
McLean, John, 9, 108
Megabothris
  asio asio, 59, 79, 155
  quirini, 60, 65, 70, 155
Meikle, Brian M., 102, 122, 124
Mendry, William, 9
Menyanthes trifoliata, 25, 76, 78
Mephitis mephitis mephitis, 18, 20, 119–120; map 39
Merriam, C. Hart, 10, 19
Mice, 10, 114, 117
  Meadow, 78, 114
  Red-backed, 114
Michaux, André, 9
Michel, Georges, 30, 48, 54, 73, 82, 121, 123
Microsorex, 27, 152
  hoyi, 18; map 5
  hoyi alnorum, 22, 34; map 5
  hoyi intervectus, 34–35; map 5
Microtus, 31, 56, 63, 71, 83, 109
  chrotorrhinus, 18; map 22
  chrotorrhinus chrotorrhinus, 81; map 22
  chrotorrhinus ravus, 21, 81; map 22
  pennsylvanicus, 18–20, 22, 62, 66, 70; map 21
  pennsylvanicus enixus, 21, 56, 58, 75–81, 153–155; map 21
  pennsylvanicus fontigenus, 75
  pennsylvanicus labradorius, 75, 80, 81; map 21
  pennsylvanicus pennsylvanicus, 20, 21, 74–75, 78, 80; map 21
Mictomys, 59
Mink, 22
  Northeastern, 116–117; map 37
  Ungava, 117–118; map 37
Mitella nuda, 24, 73, 76
Miterwort, 24
Mites, 30, 32, 36, 55, 59, 65, 70, 78, 83, 85, 117, 152, 153
Mittleberger, ——, 104, 105
Mlojewski, Marek, 141
Mole, Star-nosed, 35; map 6
Monoecocestus variabilis, 89

Montagnais, 28–30, 44, 48, 54, 82, 84, 99, 102, 107, 113, 117, 121, 123, 126, 129–131, 133, 137, 141, 143; pl. 2, fig. 1
Moose, Eastern, 15, 23, 128–129; map 43
Mooseberry, 25
Moss, A. E., 29, 117
Moss(es), 62
  caribou, 44
  feather, 24
  hair-cap, 24, 62
  sphagnum, 24, 58
Mouse,
  Algonquin Woodland Jumping, 87; map 25
  Cooper's Lemming, 20, 57; map 17
  Hamilton Inlet Meadow, 21, 75–81; map 21
  House, 20, 85
  Hudsonian Red-backed, 71; map 19
  Labrador Lemming, 21, 22, 57–60; map 18
  Labrador Meadow Jumping, 21, 85–86; map 24
  Labrador Red-backed, 21, 55, 61–68; map 19; pl. 4, fig. 1
  Labrador Spruce, 21, 55, 72–74; map 20; pl. 4, fig. 2
  Labrador White-footed, 51–52; map 15
  Le Conte's White-footed, 20, 53; map 15
  Lemming, 18; map 18
  Meadow, 19, 22; map 21
  North Shore White-footed, 20, 22, 52–53; map 15
  Northern Woodland Jumping, 87; map 25
  Ontario Red-backed, 20, 60–61; map 19
  Pennsylvania Meadow, 20, 74–75; map 21
  Quebec Meadow Jumping, 86–87; map 24
  Red-backed, 19, 22, 25, 77; map 19
  Saguenay Woodland Jumping, 87; map 25
  Spruce, 19, 22; map 20
  Ungava Lemming, 57; map 18
  Ungava Meadow, 81; map 21
  Ungava Red-backed, 68–71, 78; map 19
  Ungava Spruce, 71–72; map 20
  White-footed, 19; map 15
Muesebeck, C. F. W., 30
Murdoch, James, 29, 38, 40, 49, 83, 90, 99, 117, 122, 125, 141
Mus musculus domesticus, 18, 20, 26, 85
Muskrat, 19, 22, 115

Eastern, 81–82; map 23
Labrador, 21, 82–84; map 23
Mustela
  erminea, 20
  erminea richardsonii, 18, 22, 114–115; map 35
  rixosa, 20
  rixosa rixosa, 18, 23, 116; map 36
  vison, 18, 22; map 37
  vison lowii, 116–118, 154; map 37
  vison vison, 116–117; map 37
Myodopsylla insignis, 36, 155
Myotis
  keenii septentrionalis, 18, 20, 26, 36
  lucifugus lucifugus, 18, 20, 22, 35–36, 153–155; map 7
Myrica gale, 24, 31, 35, 69, 74, 76

Napaeozapus, 27, 86, 87
  insignis, 18, 20, 86; map 25
  insignis abietorum, 86, 87; map 25
  insignis algonquinensis, 87; map 25
  insignis saguenayensis, 86, 87; map 25
Naskapi, 10, 27, 28, 32, 106, 109, 123, 124, 130, 132, 134, 136–138, 143, 144
National Museum of Canada, 30
National Science Foundation, 5, 29
Neal, H. E., 29, 90, 128, 140
Nematodes, 89
Newton, Arthur C., 30, 38, 45, 90, 99, 121, 131
Norman, Peter, 44
Nothrus, 65, 154

Office of Naval Research, 5, 29
Office of The Surgeon General of the Army, 5, 29
Ondatra
  zibethicus, 18–20, 22; map 23
  zibethicus aquilonius, 21, 82–84, 154; map 23
  zibethicus zibethicus, 81–82; map 23
Opisodasys pseudarctomys, 47, 155
Orchis, leafy white, 24
Orchopeas caedens durus, 45, 155
Osborn, Dale J., 11
Ottawa Public Library, 30
Otter, 20
  Eastern Canada, 120–121; map 40
  Ungava, 22, 121–124; map 40
Oxyria digyna, 24, 54

Palmer, Ralph S., 30
Parmelia centrifuga, 24, 54, 71
Peromyscus
  maniculatus, 18–20, 51; map 15
  maniculatus gracilis, 20, 53; map 15
  maniculatus maniculatus, 51–52; map 15

maniculatus plumbeus, 20–22, 52–53; map 15
Petasites palmatus, 25, 62
Peterson, Richard S., 86
Phenacomys, 78
  intermedius, 74
  intermedius celatus, 72
  ungava, 18, 19, 22, 73; map 20
  ungava crassus, 21, 56, 58, 71–74, 153, 154; map 20
  ungava ungava, 69, 71–72, 74, 153, 154; map 20
Phoca
  vitulina concolor, 9, 126; map 42
  vitulina mellonae, 127; map 42
Phytoseiidae, 65, 70, 152, 153
Picea
  glauca, 24, 62, 76
  mariana, 24, 62, 69, 76
Pike, 117
Pine, jack, 24, 31, 60
Pinette,
  Bastien, pl 2, fig. 1
  Kom, 30, 40, 49, 83
  Michel, pl. 2, fig. 1
  Willé, 30, 38, 50, 90, 95, 99, 100, 112, 113, 115, 116, 119, 123, 139
Pinus banksiana, 24
Pipit, American, 19
Plamondon, Viger, 30, 96; pl. 5, fig. 2
Pleurozium schreberi, 24, 37, 62, 73, 74, 76; pl. 2, fig. 1
Polis, Joe, 84
Polygonum viviparum, 24, 77
Polyplax borealis, 65, 70, 155
Polytrichum, 24, 62, 77
Poole, Earl L., 121
Porcupine,
  Canada, 20
  Eastern Canada, 22, 87–92, 113, 114; map 26
Porsild, A. E., 25
Potentilla fruticosa, 24, 76
Potvin, Jos., 120, 128
Powell, Richard, 98
Prichard, H. Hesketh, 10
Pruitt, William O., Jr., 94
Ptarmigan, Willow, 19

Rabbit(s), American Snowshoe, 37, 41, 43, 114, 125; map 9; pl. 3, fig. 1
Racey, R. Gordon, 30, 35, 36, 99, 125
Rangifer, 109, 110
  arcticus arcticus, 130, 132, 140, 142
  caboti, 18, 20, 23, 93, 129–139, 144; map 44; pl. 7 and pl. 8, fig. 1
  caribou, 20
  caribou caribou, 18, 23, 93, 132, 139–144; map 45; pl. 8, fig. 2
Raspberry, 24, 31

Rat,
  Brown, 85
  Norway, 85
Rattus norvegicus, 18, 26, 85
Raven, 137
Reindeer (Caribou), 93
Reindeer, domesticated, 139
Ribes glandulosum, 24, 31
Rodriguez, John, 124
Rubus, 58, 73
  chamaemorus, 24, 62, 69, 74, 76
  idaeus var. *strigosus*, 24
  pubescens, 76

St. Onge,
  Joseph Georges, 30, 82, 113
  Jérôme, 30, 55, 83, 102, 111, 112, 118, 123, 124, 126, 127
Salix, 69, 71
  planifolia, 24, 62, 76
  vestita, 24, 62, 69, 76, 77
Salmon, 111, 126
Sanguisorba canadensis, 24, 62
Sarcoptiformes, 154
Schrøpfer, William, 38, 99
Seal(s), 124
  Atlantic Harbor, 126; map 42
  Ungava Fresh-water, 127; map 42
Shrew,
  Acadian Water-, 33; map 4
  Alder Pygmy, 22, 34; map 5
  Arctic Saddle-backed, 32
  Common Masked, 31; map 3
  Gapper's Short-tailed, 20, 35
  Labrador Masked, 21, 31; map 3; fig. 1
  Labrador Water-, 21, 33; map 4
  Masked, 19; map 3
  Northern Pygmy, 34; map 5
  Saddle-backed, 20
  Turner's Water-, 22, 33; map 4
  White-lipped Water-, 34; map 4
Shrike(s), Northern, 44, 78
Simard, Gilbert, 29, 33, 49, 65, 82, 90, 98, 102, 112, 113, 117, 119, 121, 125, 131
Siphonaptera, 30, 65, 70, 79, 152, 153, 155
Skunk, Northeastern Striped, 20, 119–120; map 39
Slipp, Robert, 30, 38, 40, 44, 83, 90, 98, 101, 120–123
Smilacina trifolia, 24, 74, 76
Smith, Hugh, 38
Snowberry (creeping), 25, 60
Solidago, 25, 64
Solomon's seal, three-leaved, 24
Sorex
  arcticus arcticus, 18, 20, 26, 32
  cinereus, 18, 19; map 3
  cinereus cinereus, 31, 32, 34; map 3

cinereus miscix, 21, 31–32, 34, 153, 155; map 3; fig. 1
  palustris, 18; map 4
  palustris albibarbis, 33, 34; map 4
  palustris gloveralleni, 33; map 4
  palustris labradorensis, 21, 33; map 4
  palustris turneri, 22, 33; map 4
Sorrel, mountain, 24
Spermophilus, 104
Sphagnum moss, 24, 58
Sphagnum, 24, 62, 69, 73, 74, 76; pl. 2, fig. 1
Spinturnicidae, 153
Spinturnix, 36, 153
Spruce,
  black, 24, 41, 43, 44, 48, 60, 62, 73, 74, 76, 89; pl. 1, figs. 1–2; pl. 2, figs. 1–2; pl. 7
  white, 24, 34, 37, 41, 43, 44, 57, 58, 62, 73, 88, 89; pl. 1, fig. 2
Squirrel(s),
  Flying, 22; map 13
  ground, 104
  Hudson Bay Flying, 46–47; map 13
  Labrador Flying, 47–48; map 13
  Laurentian Red, 41–42; map 12
  Red, 22, 115; map 12
  Ungava Red, 42–46, 48; map 12
Star-flower, 25
Stereocaulon fastigiatum, 73
Stewart, James, 98
Strandtmann, R. W., 30
Streptopus, 24, 73
Swan, Trumpeter, 122
Synaptomys, 74, 78
  borealis, 18, 19, 59; map 18
  borealis innuitus, 57, 60; map 18
  borealis medioximus, 21, 22, 57–60, 153–155; map 18; fig. 2
  cooperi, 59
  cooperi cooperi, 18, 20, 57; map 17
  cooperi gossii, 59

Tamarack, 24, 46, 58, 62, 71, 76, 89
Tamias striatus quebecensis, 18, 20, 41; map 11
Tamiasciurus, 27
  hudsonicus, 18, 22, 115; map 12
  hudsonicus laurentianus, 41–42; map 12
  hudsonicus ungavensis, 42–46, 155; map 12
Taraxacum, 25
Tea,
  common Labrador, 24, 31, 33, 37, 58, 60; pl. 2, fig. 2
  narrow-leaved Labrador, 25
Thalarctos, 110
  maritimus, 9, 18, 20, 110–112; map 32; pl. 6, fig. 2

Thompson, Allen, 49, 90, 117, 122, 131
Thomson, William, Jr., 37
Traub, Robert, 30
Trientalis borealis, 25, 58
Trout,
  Brook, 78
  Lake, 76, 78, 83
Tuffy, Frank, 140
Turner, Lucien M., 9, 83, 106, 108, 139
Tursiops, 92
Twinflower, 25
Twisted-stalk, 24

United States National Museum, 10, 30, 139
University of North Carolina, 30
Ursus, 104–110
  horribilis richardsoni, 106
  richardsoni, 107, 109
Usnea, 24, 58, 60; pl. 2, fig. 1

Vaccinium
  angustifolium, 25, 73
  uliginosum, 25, 37, 62, 71, 73
  vitis-idaea var. *minus*, 25, 71, 100
Véronneau, J. L., 30, 31, 33, 38, 40, 45, 46, 49, 50, 83, 95, 99, 102, 112, 114, 115, 118, 121, 123, 125, 128, 140, 141
Viburnum edule, 25, 58, 62, 73, 76
Viola, 24, 31, 58, 73, 76
Violet, 24
Vole,
  Heather, 72
  Labrador Rock, 21, 81; map 22
  New England Rock, 81; map 22
Vulpes, 109
  fulva, 20
  fulva bangsi, 18, 21, 22, 98–99; map 30
  fulva rubricosa, 99

Wallace, Dillon, 10
Weasel,
  Least, 20, 23, 116; map 36
  Richardson's Short-tailed, 22, 114–115; map 35
  Short-tailed, 20
Wellcomia evoluta, 89
Whale, White, 92–93; map 27
Widnall, Lance, 117, 122
Willow(s), 24, 49, 54, 58, 60, 62, 69, 73, 76, 77
Wolf (or Wolves), 20, 23, 118
  Eastern Timber, 30, 94–97, 103, 104; map 28; pl. 5, figs 1–2
  Labrador, 10, 93–94, 133, 136, 137; map 28

Wolverine, 20, 29, 118–119; map 38
Woodchuck, 19, 22
  Canadian, 39; map 10
  Labrador, 21, 40; map 10

Yeo, Mr. and Mrs., 48, 117
Yellowknives (Indians), 110

Zapus
  hudsonius, 18, 86, 87; map 24
  hudsonius canadensis, 85–87; map 24
  hudsonius hudsonius, 86
  hudsonius ladas, 21, 85–87; map 24
Ziegler, Alfred M., 132